P9-EDY-709

Contemporary Spanish-Speaking Writers and Illustrators for Children and Young Adults

Contemporary Spanish-Speaking Writers and Illustrators for Children and Young Adults

A Biographical Dictionary

Edited by
Isabel Schon

With the collaboration of
Lourdes Gavaldón de Barreto

*Translation from the Spanish
by Jason Douglas White*

Greenwood Press
Westport, Connecticut • London

Library of Congress Cataloging-in-Publication Data

Contemporary Spanish-speaking writers and illustrators for children
and young adults : a biographical dictionary / edited by Isabel
Schon with the collaboration of Lourdes Gavaldón de Barreto ;
translation from the Spanish by Jason Douglas White.
    p.   cm.
  ISBN 0-313-29027-X (alk. paper)
  1. Children's literature, Spanish American — Bio-bibliography —
Dictionaries. 2. Authors, Spanish American — 20th century —
Biography — Dictionaries. 3. Authors, American — 20th century —
Biography — Dictionaries. 4. Illustrators — Latin America —
Biography — Dictionaries. 5. Illustrators — United States —
Biography — Dictionaries.   I. Schon, Isabel.   II. Gavaldón de
Barreto, Lourdes.
PQ7082.C48C66 1994
860.9'9282'098 — dc20   93-11529
[B]

British Library Cataloguing in Publication Data is available.

Copyright © 1994 by Isabel Schon

All rights reserved. No portion of this book may be
reproduced, by any process or technique, without the
express written consent of the publisher.

Library of Congress Catalog Card Number: 93-11529
ISBN: 0-313-29027-X

First published in 1994

Greenwood Press, 88 Post Road West, Westport, CT 06881
An imprint of Greenwood Publishing Group, Inc.

Printed in the United States of America

The paper used in this book complies with the
Permanent Paper Standard issued by the National
Information Standards Organization (Z39.48-1984).

10 9 8 7 6 5 4 3 2

Contents

Preface

The purpose of this biographical dictionary is to provide accurate biographical and bibliographical information on more than 200 contemporary Spanish-speaking writers and illustrators for children and young adults. These authors and illustrators reside in Mexico, Spain, the United States, and the Spanish-speaking countries of Central and South America.

An attempt has been made to include in this dictionary all of the authors and illustrators for children and young adults who are currently publishing/illustrating in Spanish-speaking countries and the United States, making this book the only guide to contemporary Spanish-speaking authors and illustrators for young readers.

The editor of this guide, a Mexican author well known in the field of publishing, developed a questionnaire that was sent to all the Spanish-speaking authors included in Isabel Schon's *Books in Spanish for Children and Young Adults: An Annotated Guide*, Series I-VI, 1978-1993; *A Basic Collection of Children's Books in Spanish*, 1986; *A Hispanic Heritage: A Guide to Juvenile Books about Hispanic People and Cultures*, Series I-IV, 1980-1991. In addition, the presidents of various international boards on books for young people, ministries of education, and/or major foreign publishing houses for young readers in Spain, Cuba, Mexico, Argentina, Bolivia, Chile, Costa Rica, the Dominican Republic, El Salvador, Honduras, Nicaragua, Panama, Peru, Uruguay, and Venezuela were contacted requesting their assistance in forwarding an explanatory letter and questionnaire to authors and illustrators for young readers in their respective countries. The questionnaires, completed in Spanish by each author/illustrator, were returned to the editor.

Most entries include the following information:

- Personal Data: date and place of birth; name of parents, spouse, children; colleges attended and degrees earned.

- Address: complete home and office addresses and telephone numbers.

- Career: name of employer, position, and dates for each career post.

- Professional Organizations: memberships in professional and civic organizations.

- Awards, Honors: literary and professional awards received and dates.

- Writings/Illustrations: bibliography of books written/illustrated.

- Sidelights: revealing personal comments on special interests, aspirations and thoughts.

- Critical Sources: articles, books, and reviews in which the writer's/ illustrator's work has been discussed.

Authors/illustrators represented in *Contemporary Spanish-Speaking Writers and Illustrators for Children and Young Adults: A Biographical Dictionary* appear alphabetically in an appendix organized by country of birth and/or citizenship.

The editor wishes to thank Linda Amador, Shannon Boardman, Jacqueline M. Borin, Professor David W. Foster, Catherine S. Herlihy, Cathy Pullman and María Cecilia Silva-Díaz for their wonderful cooperation and assistance.

I hope that you find this biographical dictionary a useful reference tool and welcome your comments about this work. I regret sincerely the exclusion of those persons that time, geography, nonresponse, or unavailability at the time of compilation prevented us from including. Suggestions of authors to include in future editions of *Contemporary Spanish-Speaking Writers and Illustrators for Children and Young Adults: A Biographical Dictionary* also are welcome. Please send comments and suggestions to Dr. Isabel Schon, Center for the Study of Books in Spanish for Children and Adolescents, California State University San Marcos, San Marcos, California 92096-0001.

The Dictionary

ALCÁNTARA, Luis Ricardo (1946-)

PERSONAL DATA: Born November 24, 1946, in Montevideo, Uruguay; citizen of Spain; unmarried. Father, Bernardino; mother, María del Carmen. *Education:* licentiate in psychology.

ADDRESS: (Home) Compte Borrel 162-3:2 izda; 08015, Barcelona, Spain. Telephone: 4549222.

PROFESSIONAL ORGANIZATIONS: Asociación de Escritores.

AWARDS, HONORS: Honorable Mention, Governor's Prize in Children's Literature, Secretary of Culture, Sports, and Tourism, Sao Paulo, Brazil, 1973; Special Mention, Fernando Chinaglia Prize, Brazilian Writers' Union, Rio de Janeiro, Brazil, 1974; First Prize, State Prizes for Literature, Secretary of Culture, Sports, and Tourism, Guanabara, Brazil, 1974; Best Book of the Year for Children's Literature, *Serra d'Or* Magazine Prize, Barcelona, 1979; Honors List, Prizes for Spanish Children's Literature, Spanish Catholic Commission for Children (CCEI), Madrid, 1982, 1983, 1987, 1989, 1990; Ten Best Books for Children, from Banco del Libro Honors List, Caracas, Venezuela, 1983; Anthology of Spanish Stories, Society of Spanish-American Studies, University of Nebraska, Lincoln, Nebraska, 1985; Second Place, Apelles Mestres Prizes Ed. Destino, Barcelona, 1985; Third Prize, Barco de vapor Awards, Santa Maria Foundation, Madrid, 1985; Lazarillo Award for Literary Creations, Minister of Culture, Madrid, 1987; Austral Award for Children's Literature and Illustration, Ed. Espasa-Calpe, Madrid, 1987; Honors List, CLIJ Magazine, Barcelona, 1990, 1991.

WRITINGS:
Convertido en poesía. Sao Paulo: Ed. Unidas, 1974.

Guaracú. Barcelona: Ed. La Galera, 1978.

Pohopol. Barcelona: Ed. La Galera, 1980.

La bruja que quiso matar el sol. Barcelona: Ed. Hymsa, 1981.

Kinango. Barcelona: Ed. La Galera, 1982.

Guenkel. Barcelona: Ed. Argos-Vergara, 1982.

Kalyndi. Barcelona: Ed. Hymsa, 1983.

Kunka-ta. Barcelona: Ed. Argos-Vergara, 1983.

La jirafa y el mar. Barcelona: Ed. Argos-Vergara, 1984.

Hil-lady. Barcelona: Ed. Argos-Vergara, 1984.

Los personajes de Caetano. Barcelona: 1984.

¿Dónde has estado, Aldo? Barcelona: Ed. Juventud, 1986.

La estrella de Joanjos. Barcelona: Ed. Ultramar, 1986.

Aprendiz de cazador. Barcelona: Ed. La Galera, 1986.

La venganza de Karbiná. Barcelona: Ed. Teide, 1986.

El tren de los sueños. Barcelona: Ed. Edebé, 1986.

Al paso de las golondrinas. Barcelona: Ed. Edebé, 1986.

Tal para cual. Barcelona: Ed. Destino, 1986.

Betania. Barcelona: Ed. Juventud, 1986.

Cuenta estrellas. Barcelona: Ed. Juventud, 1986.

Salta No-Non. Barcelona: Ed. La Galera, 1987.

La madre del agua. Barcelona: Ed. Aliorna, 1987.

A través del periscopio. Barcelona: Ed. Edebé, 1987.

Natalia y la luna. Barcelona: Ed. Juventud, 1987.

Fulgencio el cazador. Barcelona: Ed. Juventud, 1987.

¡Vaya invento! Barcelona: Ed. La Galera, 1988.

Los deshollinadores. Barcelona: Ediciones B, 1988.

Un cuento grande como una casa. Madrid: Ed. Anaya, 1988.

Tomás y el lápiz mágico. Zaragoza: Ed. Edelvives, 1988.

El viaje de los pájaros. Barcelona: Ed. Juventud, 1988.

La segunda infancia de Don Honorato. Madrid: Ediciones SM, 1988.

El valle de los ecos. Gijon: Ediciones Júcar, 1988.

14 de febrero San Valentín. Barcelona: Ed. Aliorna, 1989.

Un cabello azul. Madrid: Ed. Espasa-Calpe, 1989.

El viejo chopo. Barcelona: Ediciones B, 1989.

El pirata valiente. Madrid: Ediciones SM, 1989.

La pintura mágica. Barcelona: Ediciones B, 1989.

El planeta Klee. Barcelona: Ediciones B, 1989.

¿Quién recoge las cacas del perro? Zaragoza: Ed. Edelvives, 1989.

Uña y carne. Barcelona: Ed. Destino, 1990.

Gustavo y los miedos. Madrid: Ediciones SM, 1990.

¿Quién ayuda en casa? Madrid: Ed. Edelvives, 1990.

No llores, Miguel. Madrid: Ediciones SM, 1991.

Un gato muy listo. Barcelona: Ed. Edebé, 1991.

El caballo acróbata. Barcelona: Ediciones B, 1991.
El misterio de las letras. Barcelona: Ed. Edebé, 1991.
Caray...¿dónde se habrá metido? Barcelona: Ed. Edebé, 1991.
El pequeño Morubay y su amiga Kita-Kita. Barcelona: Ed. Edebé, 1991.
¿Te acuerdas, Fernando? Barcelona: Ed. Edebé, 1991.
La pequeña Wu-Li. Madrid: Ediciones SM, 1991.
El aguijón del diablo. Madrid: Alfaguara, Ed. 1991.
¿Quién usa las papeleras? Zaragoza: Ed. Edelvives, 1991.
Orejas de conejo. Barcelona: Ed. La Galera, 1991.
Tulinet, las siete vidas del gato. Madrid: Ed. Edelvives, 1991.
¡Huy, qué miedo! Barcelona: Ed. Edebé, 1991.

SIDELIGHTS: "I write because I am attracted to the special form of the universe of children, to their imagination, and to their particular manner of seeing and living in their environment. I try to use life in each of its nuances as my source of inspiration. My favorite themes are how people live together, the surmounting of difficulties, friendship and anything that attracts my attention."

CRITICAL SOURCES:
Carlos Bárcena. *CLIJ.*
Pep Durán. *Robafabes.*
Teresa Durán. *El Periódico.*
Teresa Maña. *El País.*

ALFARO, Oscar (1921-1963)

PERSONAL DATA: Born September 5, 1921, in Tarija, Bolivia, and died December 25, 1963, in La Paz, Bolivia, he was the son of Darío González and Carmen Alfaro Baldiviezo. His wife was Fanny Mendizábal, and they had two children, Sandra and Oscar. *Education:* pursued studies at various universities.

ADDRESS: (Of his wife) Casilla Postal 3860, La Paz, Bolivia. Telephone: 795839.

CAREER: Teacher, journalist, poet, and short story writer.

PROFESSIONAL ORGANIZATIONS: Founded the Institución Gesta Bárbara.

AWARDS, HONORS: IBBY Honors List, Germany, 1992.

WRITINGS:
Cien poemas para niños. La Paz: Ed. Don Bosco, undated.
Colección Cuentos Alfaro. Perú: editados en España, undated.
Circo de papel (poesía). La Paz: Ed. Don Bosco, undated.
Escuela de fiesta. La Paz: Ed. Don Bosco, undated.
Sueño de azúcar. La Paz: Ed. Popular, undated.
El sapo que quería ser estrella. Buenos Aires: Ed. Plus Ultra, undated.
Don Quijote en el siglo XX (cuento). Spain: Ediciones Alfaro, 1985.

SIDELIGHTS: Oscar Alfaro was a born poet. His favorite themes were the environment, nature, his love for children, simple things, and his love for his homeland. He was also concerned with prevailing social injustices in our world.

CRITICAL SOURCES:
Armando Soriano Badani. "Páginas Literarias," in *Última Hora.*
Carlos Castañón Barrientos. *Presencia Literaria.* La Paz, Bolivia.
Monseñor Juan Quiroz. *Presencia Literaria.* La Paz, Bolivia.

ALFONSECA, Manuel (1946-)

PERSONAL DATA: Born April 24, 1946, in Madrid, Spain. His parents are Manuel Alfonseca and Carmen Moreno. He is married to María Angel Cubero; his children are María de los Angeles and Enrique. *Education:* holds a degree in data processing and doctorate in electrical engineering from the Universidad Politécnica de Madrid.

ADDRESS: (Home) Belianes 2, 28043 Madrid, Spain. Telephone: 3812013. (Office) IBM, Santa Hortensia 26-28, 28002 Madrid, Spain. Telephone: 8071216.

CAREER: He has worked for IBM since 1972. He is currently a senior technical staff member.

PROFESSIONAL ORGANIZATIONS: Member of the New York Academy of Sciences; Associate Member of the Association of Computer Machinery (ACM); Associate Member of the Institute of Electrical/Electronics Engineering (IEEE); Member of the Asociación Española de Periodismo Científico.

AWARDS, HONORS: Cross of Alfonso X the Wise (with honors from the Spanish government), 1970; National Graduation Award, 1970; Lazarillo Award for Literary Creations for Children and Adolescents, 1988; CCEI Honors List, 1990.

WRITINGS:
Crónicas del rompecabezas mágico (5 vols.). Madrid: Siglo Cultural, 1986.
El rubí del Ganges. Barcelona: Ed. Noguer, 1989.
Un rostro en el tiempo. Barcelona: Ed. Noguer, 1989.
La herencia del rey escorpión. Madrid: Ed. Aguilar, 1989.
La aventura de Sir Karel de Nortumbria. Madrid: Ed. Espasa-Calpe, 1990.
Mano escondida. Madrid: Ed. Alfaguara, 1991.
Ennia. Barcelona: Ed. Noguer, not yet released.

SIDELIGHTS: "I enjoy this type of literature, and since my books have little sex or violence, they are automatically classified as books for children. My favorite themes are the historical novel, the imagination, adventure, and science fiction, at times all combined in a single book (like, for instance, *Un rostro en el tiempo*). My sources of inspiration are principally the classics (especially Dante, whom I consider the greatest writer of our civilization), and, in general, anything that I read. C.S. Lewis is one of my favorite writers."

CRITICAL SOURCES:
Jesús Ballaz. *J.* June 20, 1989.
Carlos Murciano. *Escuela Española.* November 30, 1989.
Concha Palacios. *El País.* September 3, 1989.
Norma Sturniolo. *De Libros.* January, 1990.
Norma Sturniolo. *El Independiente.* July 5,1990.

ALIBÉS I RIERA, María Dolors (1941-)

PERSONAL DATA: Born January 2, 1941, in Vidra, Girona, Spain, she is the daughter of Pauli and Enriqueta. She is married to Joan López and has three children, Enriqueta, Joan, and Ester. *Education:* Licentiate in history from the Universidad de Barcelona.

ADDRESS: Telephone: 5552592.

CAREER: Teaches Catalan to adults and children; advisor to the Department of Teaching.

AWARDS, HONORS: Cavall Fort Award, 1983; Award from the National Library of Munich, 1983.

WRITINGS:

Buscando un nombre. Illust. by Irene Bordoy. Barcelona: Ed. La Galera, 1979.

Máquinas de empaquetar humo. Illust. by Pilarín Bayés. Barcelona: Ed. La Galera, 1980.

Tres embrollos y una vaca. Illust. by Rita Culla. Barcelona: Ed. La Galera, 1980.

Gran orquesta maravillas. Illust. by Pilarín Bayés. Barcelona: Ed. La Galera, 1981.

Peonza. Illust. by Llucià Navarro. Barcelona: Ed. Teide, 1982.

La estrella. Illust. by Mercé Aranega. Barcelona: Ed. Teide, 1983.

Invasores vegetarianos. Illust. by Montse Tobella. Barcelona: Ed. Teide, 1983.

Tasma, el fantasma. Illust. by Roser Capdevila. Barcelona: Ed. Teide, 1983.

El cultivo sorpresa. Illust. by Marta Balaguer. Barcelona: Ed. Teide, 1984.

Una peripecia de gigantes. Illust. by Lluisa Jover. Barcelona: Ed. Teide, 1984.

Una lluvia amarillenta. Barcelona: Ed. Teide, 1985.

Vamos a contar ratones. Illust. by Pau Estrada. Barcelona: Ed. La Galera, 1985.

Li, un libro que sabe leer. Illust. by María Rius. Ed. Aliorna, 1987.

Un botón llorón. Illust. by Isidre Monés. Barcelona: Ed. La Galera, 1987.

Cuentos para la hora de los postres. Illust. by Francisco Meléndez. Zaragoza: Ed. Edelvives, 1988.

El planeta Mo. Illust. by Montse Ginesta. Barcelona: Ed. Cruillá, 1988.

Niebla en los bolsillos. Illust. by Pau Estrada. Barcelona: Ed. La Galera, 1989.

Superfantasmas en el supermercado. Illust. by Joma. Madrid: Ed. Bruño, 1989.

Cuentos para enfriar la sopa. Illust. by Francisco García del Águila. Zaragoza: Ed. Edelvives, 1989.

Cuentos para la hora del baño. Illust. by Gerardo Amechazurra. Zaragoza: Ed. Edelvives, 1989.

Cómo se hace un cómic. Illust. by Jan. Ed. Onda, 1990.

Leo. Illust. by Pere Puig. Ed. Onda, 1990.

La luna quiere un hijo. Illust. by Luis Filella. Barcelona: Ed. Cruillá, 1992.

El mejor disfraz. Ed. Torray, 1992.

The work of Alibés Riera is originally written in Catalan.

ALMÁRCEGUI, José María (1961-)

PERSONAL DATA: Born in Zaragoza, Spain, in 1961. *Education:* Began the study of medicine but later abandoned it.

CAREER: He has worked a multitude of occupations but is at present principally involved in illustration and making posters, in addition to work in theatrical stage settings. He is a screenwriter and a writer of literature.

AWARDS, HONORS: Finalist for the Lazarillo Award, 1990; Barco de vapor Awards, (shared with Fernando Lalana), 1991.

WRITINGS:
Mi amigo Fernández, Co-written by Fernando Lalana. Madrid: Anaya, 1989.
La bomba, Co-written by Fernando Lalana. Madrid: Bruño, 1991.
Silvia y la máquina Qué, Co-written by Fernando Lalana. Madrid: Ediciones SM, 1992.

ALMENA, Fernando Santiago (1943-)

PERSONAL DATA: Born in Cordoba, Spain, on May 12, 1943, he is the son of Rufino and María Almena. His wife is María de las Mercedes, and he has two sons, Fernando and Jorge. *Education:* Technical architect.

ADDRESS: (Home) Vicente Aleixandre 4, 3° D, 28220 Majadahonda, Madrid, Spain. Telephone: 6383380.

CAREER: Since 1966 he has worked for a construction company. Additionally, in 1971 he became a professor at the University of Technical Architecture at Granada. He finds his professional career compatible with his career as a writer.

PROFESSIONAL ORGANIZATIONS: Asociación Colegial de Escritores; Asociación de Escritores y Artistas Españoles; Sociedad General de Autores Españoles; Membership in the Asociación Española de Amigos del Libro Infantil y Juvenil (OEPLI), IBBY Spanish branch; Vice-president of the AETIJ (the Spanish affiliate of the ASSITEJ).

AWARDS, HONORS: Barco de vapor Award, for *Un solo clarinete*; AETIJ Prize for Theater, for *La boda del comecocos*; Guerra Theater Prize, for *El cisne negro*. CCEI Honors List, 1985, 1988; List of the Best Books Published in the Spanish Language, from Banco del Libro, Caracas, Venezuela, 1988.

WRITINGS:
Drama:
Gran guardabosque gran. Barcelona: Ediciones Don Bosco, 1984. 2nd ed., 1987.
La boda del comecocos. Madrid: ASSITEJ, 1984. Also Madrid: Ed. Escuela

Española, 1987. 2nd ed., 1991.
El mandamás más más . . . y sus máquinas pitipitroncas. Madrid: Ed. Escuela
Española, 1985. 2nd ed., 1988.
Teatro para escolares. León: Ed. Everest, 1986. 2nd ed., 1986; 3rd ed., 1991.
Morito de Caracatucon. Valladolid: Caja de Ahorros Popular de Valladolid, 1987.
Los pieles rojas no quieren hacer el indio. Madrid: Bruño, 1988. 5th ed., 1992.
El llanto de un fideo. Madrid: Ed. Escuela Española, 1988.
El cisne negro. Madrid: Bruño, 1991. 2nd ed., 1991.

Novels:
Un solo de clarinete. Madrid: Ediciones. SM, 1984. 11th ed., 1991.
El pavo Facundo y Gustavo, el vagabundo. Madrid: Ed. Escuela Española, 1985.
El maestro Ciruela. Madrid: Susaeta Ediciones, 1987. Trans. into French as *Le
Professeur Ciboule.* Paris: Ed. Ronde du Tournesol, 1991. Trans. into Catalan
as *Un maestre genial.* Barcelona: Alimara Ediciones, 1992.
Tartesos. Madrid: Ed. Espasa-Calpe, 1988. 2nd ed., 1990.
Pocachicha. Madrid: Ed. Magisterio Español, 1988. 4th ed., 1989. Trans. into
Catalan as *En Carquinyoli.* Barcelona: Alimara Ediciones, 1992.
Marcelo Crecepelos. Madrid: Bruño, 1989. 5th ed., 1991.
El Cuchipando. Madrid: Susaeta Ediciones, 1989. 3rd ed., 1990. Also Medellin:
Edilux Ediciones, 1991.
El bandido carahigo. Madrid: Ed. Magisterio Español, 1989. 2nd ed., 1990.
Pan Gu. Madrid: Anaya, 1991.

Stories: "El muñeco de cuerda," *Compañero de sueños.* Madrid: Bruño, 1992.
"Los Gurilis," "Abencio," "Marinero," and "El boniato" have been published in
various magazines and journals, including *Ya* in Madrid, *Ideal* in Granada, and
Kanora in Colombia.

SIDELIGHTS: "I write for children because I am greatly interested in childhood and
because I enjoy writing for it. I work in the genres of narrative and theater. I consider
theater essential for childhood because children are the roots of the future theater.
Theater performed by children is especially important because it helps them to
develop their personalities: to overcome timidity, to relate to others, and to control
the expression of their minds and bodies. Humor figures prominently in my work
because children like to enjoy themselves, because humor is what provides them with
a lively approach to literature. My themes surround people who are unreal and, at
times, extravagant. However, I also write serious works in which there are, in
general, historical bases or which derive from legends or mythology. But I don't
write with the eagerness of a historian, without recreation; instead I carry history and
mythology to children in magic and fantastic forms."

CRITICAL SOURCES:
These works have been reviewed in the daily press and in magazines and journals,

including *Familia Cristiana*, *Ya*, and *ABC*. There has also been literary criticism in specialty publications, including *Educación y Biblioteca* and *CLIJ*. In addition, there have also been graduate studies that investigate the works of Fernando Almena.

ALONSO, Fernando (1941-)

PERSONAL DATA: Born in Burgos, Spain, in 1941. *Education:* Studied philology at the Universidad de Madrid. He holds a graduate degree in literature for children.

CAREER: In 1965 he began to work for the Ed. Santillana. In 1972 he moved to television as the advisor for programs for children. He has written radio plays and books of fiction and nonfiction.

WRITINGS:
Feral y las cigueñas. 1970.
El hombrecito de papel. 1978.
El hombrecito vestido de gris. 1978.
El duende y el robot. 1981.
El faro del viento. 1981.
Un castillo de arena. 1984.
Sopaboba. 1984.

ALONSO GÓMEZ, Manuel Luis (1948-)

PERSONAL DATA: Born March 14, 1948, in Zaragoza, Spain. His parents are Manuel and Victoria Alonso, and he has a son, Daniel. *Education:* He began but did not conclude studies in journalism.

ADDRESS: Bailen 49, 2° izda, 28005 Madrid, Spain. Telephone: 2656935.

CAREER: Executive; journalist; independent writer since 1979.

AWARDS, HONORS: Altea Prize, 1989; White Ravens (Internationale Jugenbibliothek), Munich, 1990; Finalist, International Europe Award, 1991.

WRITINGS:
El último hombre libre. Zaragoza: Ed. Edelvives, 1988.

Consuelo está sola en casa. Ed. Altea, 1989.
¡Sorpresa, sorpresa! Madrid: Ediciones. SM, 1989.
Jim. Madrid: Ed. Anaya, 1989.
El fantasma novato. Zaragoza: Ed. Edelvives, 1990.
Pilindrajos. Madrid: Ediciones SM, 1990.
Lejos de casa. Madrid: Ed. Didascalia, 1990.
El impostor. Madrid: Ed. Anaya, 1991.
Algodón. Ed. Rialp, 1991.
La tienda mágica. Madrid: Ediciones SM, 1991.
El fantasma novato y el enigma de los pasteles. Zaragoza: Ed. Edelvives, 1991.
La isla de las montañas azules. Madrid: Ed. Anaya, 1992.

SIDELIGHTS: "I write about liberty and dignity, about friendship, and about everyone's need for others in order to be fulfilled themselves. I am also profoundly interested—like one of the masters, Stevenson—in the boundary between good and evil. Another theme for which I have a special interest is love. I am the first Spanish author to write a history of love (*Jim*) for eleven-year-old readers."

CRITICAL SOURCES: A citation from one critic concerning *El impostor:* "A tense work, measured and skillfully structured, with a brilliant beginning and a narrative progression that moves *in crescendo*, leading toward a sharp surprise ending; very convincing." Victoria Fernández, *El País*, April 21, 1991.

AMAT Y LEÓN GUEVARA, Consuelo (1951-)

PERSONAL DATA: Born on April 7, 1951, in Lima, Peru. Her parents are Jorge Amat y León and Celina Guevara. She is married to Antum Curich and has three children, Gianina Mercedes, Jesús Alberto, and Antum Nicolás. *Education:* National School of Fine Arts of Peru.

ADDRESS: (Home) Bajada a los Baños 343, Barranco, Lima, Peru. Telephone: 772808. (Office) Bajada a los Baños 369, Barranco, Lima, Peru. Telephone: 671886.

CAREER: Artist in the plastic arts at Tejidos La Unión (Diseños) since 1976; CESPAC (Illustrations), 1980; Supplemental for Children of the Future, *Visión*, Daily, Illustration no. 82; FAO, Holland, 1989-90.

PROFESSIONAL ORGANIZATIONS: Asociación de Artistas Plásticos del Perú (ASPAP).

AWARDS, HONORS: Third Prize, National School of Fine Arts Promotion, 1984; Quipu Award for Illustration, 1985.

WRITINGS:
Relatos selectos. (design and illustration) Peru: Ediciones Quipu, undated.
Cuentos inolvidables. (design and illustration) Peru: Ediciones Quipu, undated.
Cuentos peruanos. (design and illustration) Peru: Ediciones Quipu, undated.
La guerra de los animales. Venezuela: Ediciones El Mácaro, undated.
Cuentos clásicos. Peru: Ediciones Quipu, undated.
La niña y su hermanito. Peru: CEDILIJ, undated.
En las punas. Peru: CEDILIJ, undated.
Huertos Caseros. Peru: CESPAC, undated.
Alpacas. Peru: CESPAC, undated.
Parques nacionales. Peru: CESPAC, undated.

Plus additional educational texts for first, second, third, and fourth graders published by: Editora Casa Nuestra, undated.

ANGLADA D'ABADAL, María Àngels (1930-)

PERSONAL DATA: Of Catalan origin, this writer was born in Barcelona on March 9, 1930. Her parents are Joan and María; she is married to Jordi Geli and has three daughters, María, Rosa, and Mariana. *Education:* She studied classical philology.

ADDRESS: (Home) C. Muralla, 10, 3° 17600 Figueres, Girona, Spain.

CAREER: Writer since 1988; professor.

PROFESSIONAL ORGANIZATIONS: Pen Club, Amnesty International, Insitut d'Estudis Catalans, Associació d'Escriptors en Llengua Catalana.

AWARDS, HONORS:
The Josep Pla Prize, Critics' Award; Lletra d'Or Prize.

WRITINGS:
Los cercados. Barcelona: Ed. Destino, 1986.
El bosque de vidrio. Barcelona: Ed. Destino, 1987.

She is also the author of children's stories written in Catalan that have not yet been translated into English or Spanish.

SIDELIGHTS: "I am attracted to the historical novel, especially of the nineteenth century (*Sandalies d'escuma*, Greece, s. III a. C.). I am fascinated with nature, the landscape of my country, Catalonia, and all of the Mediterranean; I am interested in all about our culture that relates to Greece, and everything related to music. I have written the lyrics for children's songs and two cantatas (narrative songs) for children's chorale groups. I am also passionately interested in the themes of liberty, ecology, and a cultural feminism that is not aggressive. My interest in the world of children comes from my three grandaughters and my grandson."

CRITICAL SOURCES:
Isidor Consul. *Serra d'Or.*
Joan Triadú. *Serra d'Or.*
Joan Triadú. *Avui.*
Ramón Pla. *El País.*
Robert Saladrigas. *La Vanguardia.*
Alex Susanna and Isabel-Clara Simó. *Institució de les lletres Cataland.* Trans. into English as *Catalan Writing.*

ARANDA VIZCAÍNO, Vicente (1948-)

PERSONAL DATA: Born December 10, 1948, in the Campo de Criptana, Ciudad Real, Spain, he is the son of Vicente Aranda Vidal and Alejandra Vizcaíno Redruello. *Education:* Bachelor's degree; graduate studies in music and dance. He studied at the Real Escuela Superior de Arte Dramático and expanded upon his studies in England and the United States.

ADDRESS: (Home) Paseo de los Artilleros 15, 2° A 28032 Madrid, Spain. Telephone: 7765576. (Office) Paseo de los Artilleros 15, 3°D, 28032 Madrid, Spain. Fax: 7762651.

PROFESSIONAL ORGANIZATIONS: ADE. (Asociación de Directores de Escena), ACE (Asociación Colegial de Escritores de España).

WRITINGS:
El deshollinador feliz. Madrid: Ed. Escuela Española, 1987. 2nd ed., 1989.
Una ciudad para soñar. Madrid: Ed. Escuela Española, 1988.
Un juguete y una canción. Ed. Gijon: Júcar, 1990.
Fantasía en Gordolandia. Madrid: Ed. Escuela Española, 1990.

Historias para teatro. Madrid: Ed. Escuela Española, 1992.

SIDELIGHTS: Vicente Aranda says: "Since I was an actor first and later a director, I observed that there was very little theater for the young. One day I decided that I would try to start a children's theater and so went about writing for children. I had many objectives, but the most important for me was to have fun and to entertain the children, using an infinity of themes. At first we made a sort of human puppet theater, in which the actors imitated puppets, who were themselves an imitation of flesh-and-blood actors. Then I became interested in the environment, stimulating children to nurture and to protect it while amusing them. Much later, there were the rights of children, the decline and glory of the theater . . . the circus . . . etc."

CRITICAL SOURCES:
El Correo de América. "El deshollinador feliz," fall 1988.
Nuevo Diario de Córdoba. "Una ciudad para soñar," May 14, 1989.
El Adelantado de Segovia. "Una ciudad para soñar," June 15, 1989.
Covadonga Molero. *Platero.* "Un juguete y una canción," 1991.

Alfredo Asensi discussed *Una ciudad para soñar* in his radio program (Antena-3, Cordoba).

ARMIJO NAVARRO-REVERTER, Consuelo (1940-)

PERSONAL DATA: Born in Madrid, Spain, on December 14, 1940, she is the daughter of José Armijo and Teresa Navarro-Reverter.

ADDRESS: Menéndez Valdés 54, 6° D, 28015 Madrid, Spain. Telephone: 5433111.

CAREER: Writer of stories, poetry, and children's theater.

AWARDS, HONORS: Lazarillo Award, 1974; CCEI Prize, 1976, 1982; Barco de vapor Award, 1978; Santa Maria Foundation Prize, 1978; ACCESIT AETIJ (Theater), 1984; CCEI Honors List for "Más batautos," "El pampinoplas," "El mono imitamonos" and "Los batautos en Butibato."

WRITINGS:
Los batautos. Illust. by Jordi Ciuró. Barcelona: Ed. Juventud, 1979. Also Illust. by Marta Balaguer. Valladolid: Ed. Miñón, 1983. Also Madrid: Ed. Susaeta, undated. Also Madrid: Ediciones SM, undated.

Más batautos. Illust. by Jordi Ciuró. Barcelona: Ed. Juventud, undated. Also
    Valladolid: Ed. Miñón, undated.
Los batautos hacen batautadas. Illust. by Alberto Urdiales. Barcelona: Ed.
    Espasa-Calpe, 1986. Also Valladolid: Ed. Miñón, undated.
Los batautos en Butibato. Valladolid: Ed. Miñón, undated.
Mercedes e Inés o cuando la tierra da vueltas al revés. Illust. by Carmen Noguer.
    Barcelona: Ed. Noguer, 1982.
Inés y Mercedes o cuando los domingos caían en jueves. Barcelona: Ed. Noguer,
    undated.
Bam bim bom arriba el telón (theater for children). Valladolid: Ed. Miñón, 1981.
    Also Ed. Susaeta, undated.
Guiñapo y pelaplátanos (theater for children). Valladolid: Ed. Miñón, 1985. Also
    Ed. Susaeta, undated.
El pampinoplas. Illust. by Antonio Tello. Madrid: Ediciones SM, 1983.
Aniceto el vencecangelos. Illust. by Margarita Puncel. Madrid: Ediciones SM, 1982.
El mono imitamonos. Illust. by Alfonso Ruano. Madrid: Ediciones SM, 1985.
PII. Madrid: Ediciones SM, undated.
Risas, poesía y chirigotas. Illust. by Marta Balaguer. Valladolid: Ed. Miñón, 1984.
Mone (poetry). Valladolid: Ed. Miñón, undated.
Macarrones con cuentos. Illust. by Clara Pérez Escrivá. Madrid: Ed. Emiliano
    Escolar, 1981.
Los machafatos. Madrid: Ed. Edelvives, 1987.
Los machafatos siguen andando. Illust. by Francisco Meléndez. Zaragoza: Ed.
    Edelvives, 1990.

SIDELIGHTS: Consuelo Armijo attempts through her stories "to amuse (children)
and to avoid the real world." Until now, she says, "I have not tried to inculcate anyone
through determined teaching in my works. I only try to awaken the imagination and
to foment the habit of reading, because childhood is the time when the development
of these things are most important."

CRITICAL SOURCES: The author of the "batautos" is considered one of the most
important writers of literature for children in Spain. There are more than 120 articles
and critical reviews that discuss her work; among them are the following:
Josefina Carabias. "Los batautos," *Ya*, December 23, 1975.
Felicidad Orquín. "Los pequeños seres verdes de fantasía," *El País*, March 30, 1980.
Rosana Torres. "El <nonsense> para los niños," *El País*, May 24, 1981.
Francisco Cubells Salas. "Bibliografía crítica para niños y adolescentes," *Comunidad*
    Educativa, June 10, 1981.
Cristina Gil. "Consuelo Armijo: La literatura infantil está en ebullición," *Ya*,
    December 9, 1982.
Mercedes Gómez del Manzano. "Nuevos caminos para la literatura infantil en
    España," *Critica*, September-October 1982.

Antonio García Teijeiro. "El humor y el disparate como vehículo literario," *Faro de Vigo*, February 23, 1986.

Aurora Díaz-Plaja. "Obras de teatro para lectores infantiles," *Leer*, June-Sept. 1986.

Rosa Lanoix. "Consuelo Armijo: cuando todo es posible en un libro," *Ya*, February 16, 1988.

Pedro de Juan Guyatt. "El pampinoplas," *CLIJ*, November 1990.

ARREDONDO, Inés (1928-)

PERSONAL DATA: On March 20, 1928, Inés Arredondo was born in Culiacan, Sinaloa, Mexico. She is the daughter of Mario Camelo y Vega y de Inés Arredondo de Camelo. Her husband is Ruíz Sanchez, and they have three children: Inés, Ana, and Francisco Segovia Camelo. *Education:* She has the following degrees: letters, philosophy, and theater; graduate degree in letters and graduate studies in library science.

ADDRESS: (Home) Atlixco 105, Depto. 402 Col. Condesa, 06140 Distrito Federal, Mexico. (Office) Telephone: 2860635.

CAREER: Writer.

AWARDS, HONORS: Villaurrutia Prize, 1979; Doctorate Honoris Causa from the Universidad Autónoma de Sinaloa, 1982; Fairfield Foundation Fellowship; CONACULTA Fellowship; Fellow of the Centro Mexicano de Escritores.

WRITINGS:
La señal. Mexico: Ed. Era, 1965.
Río subterráneo. Mexico: Ed. Joaquín Mortiz, 1979.
Historia verdadera de una princesa. Mexico: Ed. CIDCL, 1985.
Los espejos. Mexico: Ed. Joaquín Mortiz, 1988.

CRITICAL SOURCES: Her work has been the subject of critical commentary from writers and literary critics, including Huberto Batiz, Juan García Ponce, and Juan Vicente Melo.

ARRIETA, Yolanda (1963-)

PERSONAL DATA: Born in Etxebarria, Vizcaya, Spain, in 1963. *Education:* She holds a professor's diploma in EGB, specializing in Basque philology.

CAREER: Implemented programs for the education and franchise of Basque adults in various professional fields. A lover of the theater, she has also directed diverse theatrical productions and researched in related areas.

AWARDS, HONORS: Legazpi de Guión Award for Theater, 1990; El Candil Prize, 1990; Pedro Barrutia Award for Theater, 1991; Baporea Prize, 1992.

WRITINGS: Begigorritarren erlojua. Madrid: Ediciones SM, 1992.

SIDELIGHTS: The idea to write was born "after ten years of working in two activities that integrate, in my idea, as the way to live life: the theater and literature. Literature and the theater: These are two sister activities, parallels, that mutually enrich each other. The theater has convinced me to work with children and young people, and it has been much fun: They play at living, and they live in a game. Every day is, in potential, a celebration for them. They are open to fantasy, adventure; they have energy and they are logical, critical—at times they are realists. And they are the future."

ARTECHE, Miguel (1926-)

PERSONAL DATA: Born June 4, 1925, in Nueva Imperial, Chile, he is the son of Luis and Isabel Arteche; he is married to Ximena and has six children, Juan Miguel, Andrea, Isabel, Rafael, Amparo, Cristóbal, and Ignacio. *Education:* Three years of law study at the Universidad de Chile. He studied literature at the Universidad Central de Madrid.

ADDRESS: (Home) Martín Alonso Pinzón, 6676, Santiago de Chile, Chile. Telephone: 2200817.

CAREER: Principally a journalist, although he has also worked in various fields related to communications. Cultural specialist for the Chilean embassy in Spain, 1965-70; director of a poetry workshop at the Universidad de Chile, the Universidad Católica, and the Biblioteca Nacional; founder of the Taller Nueve, 1979-89, professor at the Escuela de Periodismo, Universidad Católica; he has also served as the subdirector for the Department of Libraries, Archives, and Museums of Chile.

PROFESSIONAL ORGANIZATIONS: Member of the Academia Chilena de la Lengua; corresponding member of the Real Academia Española; member of the Colegio de Periodistas of Chile; member of the Sociedad de Escritores of Chile.

AWARDS, HONORS: Award from the Federación de Estudiantes de la Universidad de Concepción, 1950; Municipal Poetry Award, 1950, 1964, 1977; Alerce Prize, 1960; Book of Gold Award for Poetry, 1977; Instituto Goethe de Santiago de Chile Award, 1979; Finalist, Biblioteca Breve, Ed. Seix-Barral, 1971; IBBY Honors List, 1986; Finalist, Andrés Bello Prize, 1984; Fellow of the Fundación Andes, 1992.

WRITINGS:
Llaves para la poesía. 1984.
Escribir como niño para niños. 1990.

Works translated and abridged:
Las aventuras de Tom Sawyer. Mark Twain, 1983.
Ivanhoe. Sir Walter Scott, 1984.
Oliver Twist. Charles Dickens, 1984.
Las aventuras de Gulliver. Jonathan Swift, 1984.
La isla misteriosa. Jules Verne, 1985.
David Copperfield. Charles Dickens, 1985.
Robin Hood. Anonymous, 1985.
La dama de blanco. Wilkie Collins, 1986.
La vuelta al mundo en 80 días. Julio Verne, 1987.
Azabache. Anne Sewell, 1988.
El último mohicano. J.F. Cooper, 1988.

A well-known writer in the Spanish language, Miguel Arteche has written poetry, novels, stories, autobiographic prose, essays, and anthologies; he has also translated poems and stories from English to Spanish. His most important poetry has been translated into English, French, Italian, German, Czechoslovakian, and Hebrew.

SIDELIGHTS: "I write because it is my vocation and because it is as necessary as breathing. I would not be able to breathe if I did not write. The sources of my inspirations and expirations are the fleetingness of life, time, human loneliness, human suffering, nature transfigured, and the sentiments of holiness or religion in a human being."

CRITICAL SOURCES:
Alfredo Lefebvre. *El Sur*, May 17, 1964.

ARTILES MACHADO, Freddy (1946-)

PERSONAL DATA: Born January 13, 1946, in Santa Clara, Villa Clara, Cuba. His parents are Sebastián and Ercilia Artiles. He is married to Mayra Navarro, and they have three children, Eric, Gabriel, and Adriana. *Education:* Holds a degree in the scenic arts (specializing in theater) from the Instituto Superior de Arte in Havana, Cuba.

ADDRESS: (Home) San Julio 316 (altos) e/Zapotes y San Bernardino, Santos Suárez, Havana, Cuba. Telephone: 406954.

CAREER: Dramatist and theatrical researcher; specialist in theater; national director of theater and dance, (1972-80); provisional director of culture for Havana, (1980-83); theatrical advisor to the Teatro Bertolt Brecht, 1983-89.

PROFESSIONAL ORGANIZATIONS: Unión de Escritores y Artistas de Cuba (UNEAC).

AWARDS, HONORS: UNEAC Award, 1971; La Edad de Oro Award, 1973, 1979; 13th of March Award, 1977; Theater Studies Prize, 1980; La Rosa Blanca Prize, 1990; La Edad de Oro Diploma, 1989, granted to outstanding persons in artistic creation for children and adolescents.

WRITINGS:
El conejito descontento. Havana: Gente Nueva, 1974; 1989.
El pavo cantor. Havana: Gente Nueva, 1980.
La actuación en el teatro de títeres. Havana: Extramuros, 1980.
Teatro para niños (selections, prologue, and notes). Havana: Letras Cubanas, 1981.
Aventuras en el teatro (selections, prologue, and notes). Havana: Letras Cubanas, 1988.
Teatro y dramaturgia para niños en la Revolución (essay). Havana: Letras Cubanas, 1988.
La maravillosa historia del teatro universal. Havana: Gente Nueva, 1989.

Additionally, Freddy Artiles is a well-known writer of works of theater for children and adults.

SIDELIGHTS: Concerning his involvement with the theater, Freddy Artiles remarks: "I have written theater for children and for adults for more than twenty years because I am fascinated with the art form that has held enormous prominence in Cuba since the 1960s. Then, as a professional, I began to gain interest in theatrical research in all aspects of theater for children, and at the time this was still unexplored territory.

My principal theme has always been that of the lives of people living in a social system that in spite of its many defects, I still consider to be more just and humane than capitalism."

CRITICAL SOURCES:
Elder Santiesteban. Verde Olivo. *October 1974.*
Nati González Freire. Bohemia. *June 12, 1981.*
Carlos Espinosa. Juventud Rebelde. *July 19, 1982.*
Vivian Martínez Tabares. Conjunto 53. *June 1982.*
José María Otero. Granma. *March 11, 1986.*
Amado del Pino. Revolución y Cultura 6. *June 1989.*
Osvaldo Cano. Revolución y Cultura 9. *September 1989.*
Antonio Orlando Rodríguez. Conjunto 82. *Winter 1990.*

ÁVILA GRANADOS, Jesús (1950-)

PERSONAL DATA: Born October 20, 1950, in Granada, Spain, the son of Jesús Ávila Martín and Purificación Granados Díaz, he is married to Josefa Artero Fernández and has two children; David and Alejandro. *Education:* Holds a degree in journalism from the Universidad Autónoma de Barcelona; holds a licentiate in informational sciences.

ADDRESS: (Home) Av. Gerona 42 B Urb. Terra Blanca 08130 Sta. Perpetua de Mogoda, Barcelona, Spain.

CAREER: Journalist; art critic; author of literature for children. He is now a correspondent for various magazines and journals, including *Arte y Cemente*, *Diario 16*, *L'Actualitat Flequera de Catalunya*, *Ser Padres*, and *Spic*.

PROFESSIONAL ORGANIZATIONS: Asociación Española e Internacional de Críticos del Arte, Madrid; FEPET (Spanish Federation of Journalists and Writers for Tourism).

AWARDS, HONORS: Second Prize, *Obra Sindical de Artesanía,* 1974; Special Award, *Bankunion,* 1975; Award from the city of Moia, 1975; *Comarca d'Olot* Award for Journalism, 1982; First Prize, France Awards, 1983, 1985; Europa Humana Award, 1984, 1985; Award for the Documentary from the Cinema Festival at Monte Carlo for *Rutas Andaluzas,* 1989; Award from the Office of Tourism of France, 1989; La Rosa del Azafrán de Oro, Medal, 1990.

WRITINGS:
La colegiata románica de Sant Pere de Ager. Lérida: Instituto de Estudios Ilerdenses, 1981.
Estambul. Barcelona: Salimos Ed., 1985.
Turquía. Barcelona: Salimos Ed., 1987.
La Granada nazarita. Madrid: Ed. Bruno, 1989.
Calafell, la sonrisa del Mediterráneo. Barcelona: Ed. Viceversa, 1989.
SALOU. Madrid: Ministerio de Transportes, Comercio y Turismo, 1991.
Els Balnearis de Catalunya. Barcelona: Ed. Labor, in print.
Valencia. Madrid: Ministerio de Transportes, Comercio y Turismo, in print.
La reforma agraria en Andalucía. Madrid: Ed. Bruno, in print.

SIDELIGHTS: "For me, literature is the principal source of intercultural communication; through it, it is possible to transmit the experiences of people around us while learning to better understand ourselves. It makes the cultural divisions more permeable and the ways people think and behave more accessible. When I was very young I became fascinated with the greatness of the Alhambra, among other reasons because I had a view of the largest Islamic monument in Spain from my bedroom window. I became interested in the study of the cultures that preceded our own. Because of this, cultural journalism has been and continues to be my philosophical interest and vocation. I specialize in Islamic countries, and I have written two books about Turkey, a country I have visited on four occasions, and more than 250 articles on the principal media of Spanish communication."

CRITICAL SOURCES: His works have been reviewed by critics such as: Robert Saladrigas, Ignacio Fernández Bayo, José Guerrero Martín, Agustín Bachs, and José Tomás Cabot. Reviews of his work have appeared in journals and magazines, including *La Vanguardia, Diario 16, Historia y Vida,* and *Cambio 16.*

BALCELLS, Jacqueline Marty de (1944-)

PERSONAL DATA: Born September 15, 1944, in Valparaiso, Chile, she is the daughter of Luis Marty Dufeu and María Magdalena Aboitz. She is married to Juan Ignacio Balcells Eyquem; their children are Olaya, Elvira, and Aurelia. *Education:* Journalism study at the Universidad Católica de Chile.

ADDRESS: (Home) Carlos Charlín 1456, Santiago, Chile. Telephone: 492151.

CAREER: Freelance journalist and writer, she writes special reports on topics related to literature.

PROFESSIONAL ORGANIZATIONS: IBBY, Chilean branch.

AWARDS, HONORS: IBBY Honors List, 1990.

WRITINGS:
El niño que se fue en un árbol. Chile: Ed. *Andrés Bello,* 1990.
El archipiélago de las puntadas. Chile: Ed. *Andrés Bello,* 1988.
El polizón de la Santa María. Chile: Ed. *Andrés Bello,* 1988.
La hacedora de claros y otros cuentos. Chile: Ed. Universitaria, 1990.
El país del agua. Chile: Ed. *Andrés Bello,* 1991.

Jacqueline Balcells has published stories in French and English.

SIDELIGHTS: "In general I am inspired by reality, and I then fill that reality with things magical or mysterious. I think that reality is full of wonder, a wonder that we need to bring to light."

CRITICAL SOURCES:
Ignacio Valente. *El Mercurio de Santiago.* Chile: 1991.
Booklist. United States: 1989, 1990.
Isabelle Audier. *El Mercurio de Antofagasta.* Chile: 1987, 1990.
Samuel Peña. *La Nación.* Chile, 1991.

BALCELLS KATZ, Alberto Ignacio (1918-)

PERSONAL DATA: Born June 3, 1918, in Santiago, Chile. His parents are Alberto Balcells Pi de la Serra and Olga Katz Brenner. He is married to Inés María Eyquem Astorga and has four children, Alberto, Ignacio, Pedro, and José Antonio. *Education:* Holds a degree in civil engineering from the Universidad de Chile in Santiago.

ADDRESS: (Home) Km. 4, Camino Concón Quintero, Chile. 812781 Viña. (Office) Casilla 1008, Concón, Chile.

CAREER: Engineer at a saltpeter construction plant in Puerto de Iquique, Chile, 1942-49; supervisor of engineers for construction, 1949-77; supervisor of engineers at Bethlehem Steel Corp., 1977-90; private consultant.

PROFESSIONAL ORGANIZATIONS: Instituto de Ingenieros de Chile; American Society of Civil Engineers.

WRITINGS:
Aventura en las estrellas. Chile: Ed. *Andrés Bello,* 1987.
Misión Alfa Centauro. Chile: Ed. *Andrés Bello,* 1988.
La rebelion de los robots. Chile: Ed. *Andrés Bello,* 1990.

SIDELIGHTS: "I have been an aficionado of science fiction for ten years. My favorite writers have been, in chronological order Jules Verne, H.G. Wells, and J.R.R. Tolkien."

BALLAZ ZABALZA, Jesús (1946-)

PERSONAL DATA: Born June 23, 1946, in Liedena, Navarra, Spain, he is the son of Saturnino and Cecilia Ballaz. With María Angels, his wife, he has two children, Xavier and Guillem. *Education:* History degree.

ADDRESS: (Home) Clavé 5, 08750 Molins de Rei, Barcelona, Spain. Telephone: 6686367. (Office) Rocafort 104, 08015 Barcelona, Spain. Telephone: 4233191.

CAREER: Has been a professor (1967-70) and an editor (1975-86). Since 1986 he has worked as editor in the literature for children and adolescents section at Ediciones B, where together with other European editors he has created the Europe Award for Literature for Children and Adolescents.

PROFESSIONAL ORGANIZATIONS: Asociación Colegial de Escritores de España.

AWARDS, HONORS: National Comic Award in children's reviews, 1975; Special Mention, Lazarillo Award, 1988 and 1990; National Translation Award (translating children's books into the Spanish language) 1982; National Critics Award for Literature for Children, 1983; Fellow of the Internationale Jugendbibliothek, Munich, Germany. Has been a judge for the Lazarillo Award and other literary awards, and he has been a bibliographic advisor to the Ministerio de Cultura in Spain for two years.

WRITINGS:
Una casa a la deriva. Barcelona: Ed. La Galera, 2nd ed., 1983.
Juanito Fuelle. Madrid: Ed. Espasa-Calpe, 3rd. ed., 1984.
Paloalto y los hombres extraordinarios. Ed. Labor, 1984.
El boquete. Barcelona: Ed. La Galera, 1985.
El baquero. Madrid: Ed. Escuela Española, 1986.
El misterio de la peña blanca. Barcelona: Ed. La Galera, 1987.

El árbol de los pájaros. Barcelona: Ed. La Galera, 1987.
Sin trompa y sin melena. Zaragoza: Ed. Edelvives, 1987.
El tambor de piel de piojo. Ed. Granica, undated.
Llums en el mar. Ed. La Magrana, 1987.
El collar del lobo. Madrid: Ediciones SM, 4th ed., 1987.
Autopista A-3. Barcelona: Ediciones B, 1988.
El picadero fantasma. Barcelona: Ed. Aliorna, 1988.
Maravillas. Madrid: Ed. Anaya, 1988.
La cueva del extranjero. Zaragoza: Ed. Edelvives, 1989.
El zoo Robaina. Gijón: Ed. Júcar, 1989.
La pareja indomable. Madrid: Ed. Anaya, 1989.
La jirafa que no llegaba al suelo. Gijón: Ed. Júcar, 1990.
Un conejo en el sombrero. Barcelona: Ed. Edebé, 1991.

Series:
Ibai. Ed. Tinum Mas (20 published titles).
Los BIT . . . Ed. Arín (4 published titles).
En el país de . . . Ed. Parramón (9 published titles).

SIDELIGHTS: I write children's literature "because I have stories to tell and the desire to tell them. I write about themes that illustrate to children the transformation of Spanish society in the last several years, in that Spain has passed from a rural society to a modern urban society. My roots are rustic (I am from Navarra) but almost all my life since my youth I spent in Barcelona and have witnessed its modernization. I have very clear double vision. The kinds of people I describe—those who are on the fringes of society or not—have a vision of people with strength and spirit. For certain critical observations of our society I use humor, irony, fantastic creations, and at times, dreams."

CRITICAL SOURCES:
María Solé. *Daily ABC.* Madrid.
Alfonso García. *Diario de León.* León, Spain.
José Luis Martín Nogales. *El Diario de Navarra.* Pamplona, Spain; this is perhaps the literary critic who knows most about the works of Jesús Ballaz.

BALLESTA, Juan (1935-)

PERSONAL DATA: Born May 2, 1935 in Almeria, Spain. *Education:* Graduate study in fine arts.

ADDRESS: (Office) Puerto Rico 11 28016, Madrid, Spain. Telephone: 5198489.

WRITINGS:
El lobito bueno. Co-written by José Agustín Goytisolo. Barcelona: Ed. Laia, 1983.
El príncipe malo. Co-written by José Agustín Goytisolo. Barcelona: Ed. Laia, 1983.
"Las parejas de J. B." Co-written by José Agustín Goytisolo. *Cambio 16,* 1983.
La bruja hermosa. Co-written by José Agustín Goytisolo. Barcelona: Ed. Laia, 1984.
El pirata honrado. Co-written by José Agustín Goytisolo. Barcelona: Ed. Laia, 1984.
Las hormigas de la belleza. Madrid: Ed. Novatex, 1985.

SIDELIGHTS: To write, "I need to feel that I live in contact with the world and with nature. If I write books for children it is because I consider them a blessing. If one of my works brings joy to a child, even if only to one, then my life on this Earth will be justified. Life inspires me every day: literature, friends, family, journeys and I try to transmit my feelings for life into my work; I find that it is worth the effort to live life in the here and now."

BALZOLA, Asun (1942-)

PERSONAL DATA: Born July 18, 1942, in Bilbao, Spain. Her parents are Martín and Mina Balzola.

ADDRESS: (Home) Clara del Rey 11, 28002 Madrid, Spain.

CAREER: Author and illustrator of books for children and adolescents.

PROFESSIONAL ORGANIZATIONS: Asociación de Ilustradores de Catalunya; Asociación de Ilustradores de Madrid; Asociación de Escritores de España.

AWARDS, HONORS: Lazarillo Award for Illustration, Madrid, 1965; Aigle d'Argent, from the Children's Festival at Niza, France, 1975; Second Place, National Award of Spain for the Illustration of Books for Children, 1978; List of the Most Interesting Books for Children, Ed. Altea, 1978; Janusz Korczak Prize (Poland) and Jane Adams Prize (U.S.A.), 1979; Honors List, Andersen Prize, 1980; Apelles Mestres Prize (illustration), Ed. Destino, Barcelona, 1981; Finalist, Catholic Award for Children, Cologne, Germany, 1985; The Golden Apple, (illustration), Bratislava, Czechoslovakia, 1985; National Award of Spain for Illustration, Barcelona, 1985;

People's Choice Award of Catalonia, 1988; Spanish Candidate for the Andersen Prize for Illustration, 1988, 1991; Critics' Award from *Serra d'Or* (illustration), 1988; Basque Government Award, 1990, 1991; Santa Maria Foundation Award (text and illustration), 1991.

ILLUSTRATIONS:
Mulder, Elizabeth. *Las noches del gato verde.* Madrid: Ed. Anaya, 1962.
Fernández Luna, Concha. *Pito va a la escuela.* Madrid: Ed. Anaya, 1962.
García Escudero, José María. *Mari Dos.* Madrid: Ed. Alameda, 1962.
Soler, Carola. *El pájaro pinto.* Madrid: Ed. Aguilar, 1964.
Cabodevilla, José María. *Nuestra Señora de cada día.* Valladolid: Ed. Marfil, 1964.
Gil Bonifacio. *Cancionero infantil universal.* Madrid: Ed. Aguilar, 1965.
Koenig, Lily. *Gringolo.* Madrid: Ed. Doncel, 1966.
Sanmartín, Carmela. *El perro milord.* Madrid: Ed. Doncel, 1970.
García Sánchez y Pacheco. *Soy una gota.* Madrid: Ed. Altea, 1974.
García Sánchez y Pacheco. *Soy un niño.* Madrid: Ed. Altea, 1974.
Cuadra, José María. *El trotamundos.* Madrid: Ed. Doncel, 1977.
Kunze, Rainer. *El león Leopoldo.* Madrid: Ed. Alfaguara, 1977.
García Sánchez y Pacheco. *La niña sin nombre.* Madrid: Ed. Altea, 1978.
García Sánchez y Pacheco. *El niño y el robot.* Madrid: Ed. Altea, 1978.
Jiménez, Juan Ramón. *Platero y yo.* Barcelona: Ed. Bruguera, 1980.
Parramón, Josep M. *La primavera.* Madrid: Parramón Ediciones, 1980.
Alcántara, Ricardo. *Pohopol.* Madrid: Ed. La Galera, 1980.
Lertxundi, Andu. *Negua.* San Sebastian: Ed. Erein, 1980.
Fernández Santos, Jesús. *El reino de los niños.* Madrid: Ed. Debate, 1980.
Conde, Carmen. *Cuentos de hoy.* Madrid: Ed. Escuela Española, 1980.
Del Amo, Monserrat. *Zuecos y naranjas.* Madrid: Ed. La Galera, 1981.
Retegui, Malencho. *El vagabundo y otros cuentos.* Valladolid: Ed. Miñón, 1981.
Roig, Monserrat. *Piripitusa.* Madrid: Ed. Noguer, 1981.
Vázquez Vigo, Carmen. *Guau.* Madrid: Ed. Noguer, 1981.
Puncel, María. *Dos cuentos de sirenas.* Madrid: Ed. Altea, 1981.
Robles, Antonio. *La bruja Doña Paz.* Valladolid: Ed. Miñón, 1981.
Balzola, Ana. *Los ángeles del Tíber.* Valladolid: Ed. Miñón, 1982.
Balzola, Ana. *El camisón bordado.* Valladolid: Ed. Miñón, 1982.
Balzola, Ana. *La playa de las conchas rosas.* Valladolid: Ed. Miñón, 1982.
Lertxundi, Andu. *Txalo Pin Txalo.* San Sebastian: Ed. Erein, 1982.
Atxaga, Bernardo. *Txitoen istorioa.* San Sebastian: Ed. Erein, 1984.
Nöstlinger, Christine. *Cosas de Franz.* Madrid: Ediciones SM, 1986.
Xirinachs, Olga. *Marina.* Ed. Ampurias, 1986.
Atxaga, Bernardo. *La cacería.* Madrid: Ed. Altea, 1986.
Quarenc, Antoni. *Genaro, la caracola y el mar.* Barcelona: Ed. La Galera, 1987.
Fortún, Elena. *Celia y la revolución.* Madrid: Ed. Aguilar, 1987.
Murciano, Carlos. *La niña enlunada.* Madrid: Ediciones SM, 1987.

Posadas, Carmen. *Hipocanta*. Madrid: Ediciones SM, 1987.
Hasler, Eveline. *El coleccionista de agujeros*. Madrid: Ediciones SM, 1988.
Serra i Fabre, J. *Lecturas*. Madrid: Ediciones SM, 1989.
Teixidor, Emili. *Las alas de la noche*. Madrid: Ediciones SM, 1989.
Landa, Mariasun. *Izeba txikia*. San Sebastian: Ed. Erein, 1989.
Landa, Mariasun. *Iholdi*. San Sebastian: Ed. Erein, 1989.
Machado, Ana María. *Un montón de unicornios*. Madrid: Ediciones SM, 1990.
Landa, Mariasun. *Alex*. San Sebastian: Ed. Erein, 1990.
Korchunowa, Irina. *Los babuchos del pelo verde*. Madrid: Ediciones SM, 1991.

ILLUSTRATED AND WRITTEN WORKS:
Historia del gran reino de la China. Madrid: Ed. Aguilar, 1965.
Sonatas 1, 2, 3, 4, 5 y 6. Madrid: Ed. Santillana, 1965.
Todos los niños del mundo seremos amigos. Barcelona: Ed. La Galera, 1965.
Historia de un erizo. Valladolid: Ed. Miñón, 1978.
Zenbakiak. San Sebastian: Ed. Erein, 1979.
Margoak. San Sebastian: Ed. Erein, 1979.
Itziar eta antton. San Sebastian: Ed. Erein, 1980.
Munia y la luna. Barcelona: Ed. Destino, 1982.
Lecturas. Madrid: Ed. Cincel, 1982.
Los zapatos de Munia. Barcelona: Ed. Destino, 1983.
Guillermo ratón de biblioteca. Madrid: Ed. Miñón, 1983.
Munia y la señora Piltronera. Barcelona: Ed. Destino, 1984.
La noche y el día. Madrid: Ediciones SM, 1985.
Las estaciones. Madrid: Ediciones SM, 1985.
Antes, ahora y después. Madrid: Ediciones SM, 1985.
Santino Pastelero. Barcelona: Ed. Destino, 1986.
El diario de Pepe. Madrid: Ed. Alhambra, 1986.
Los hijos de la abuela. Madrid: Ed. Alhambra, 1986.
Silvestrito. Valladolid: Ed. Miñón, 1986.
Leyendas vascas 1. San Sebastian: Ed. Erein, 1987.
Leyendas vascas 2. San Sebastian: Ed. Erein, 1987.
Leyendas vascas 3. San Sebastian: Ed. Erein, 1987.
La bufanda azul. Madrid: Ed. Alhambra, 1988.
Juanchu 4. Madrid: Ed. Alhambra, 1988.
El gato Bogart. Ed. Xerais, 1988.
Leyendas 4. San Sebastian: Ed. Erein, 1988.
La cazadora de Indiana Jones. Madrid: Ediciones SM, 1989.
Ala de mosca. Barcelona: Ed. Pirene, 1989.
Pablito. Madrid: Ediciones SM, 1989.
Munia y los hallazgos. Barcelona: Ed. Destino, 1990.
Historia de Nino. Zaragoza: Ed. Edelvives, 1990.
Por los aires. Madrid: Ediciones S.M., 1991.

Babi es Bárbara. Barcelona: Ed. Ampurias, 1991.
Partido de dobles. Barcelona: Ed. Ampurias, 1991.

SIDELIGHTS: It is said that Asun Balzola is "all but Basque, and the memories of her welcoming and friendly Basque origins surround and pervade her personality. She internalized the physical setting of her homeland and it has become an essential and vital part of her style. This style is straightforward and fresh, but is integrated with a Basque lyricism, and this lends her writing an effusiveness. Each patient and tentative observation reveals aspects of character that are in themselves grandly descriptive. Like the music which played an important role in her childhood, she extends and links images together with emptiness, like the pauses between beats, so that her books seem less written than composed."

CRITICAL SOURCES:
Maya Aguiriano. "Asun Balzola: ilustradora de libros infantiles." *El País*. Madrid: August 1979.
Rosana Torres. "Para los más pequeños." *El País*. Madrid: January 1981.
José Ignacio Aranes. "Asun Balzola: Dibujante de historias." *El Diario Vasco*. San Sebastian: January 1986.

BANACLOCHE PÉREZ-ROLDÁN, Julieta (1933-)

PERSONAL DATA: Born November 23, 1933, in Valencia, Spain. Her parents are Julio and Josefina Banacloche. She is married to Antonio, and their daughter is Julieta. *Education:* She holds a licentiate in U.S. history and general history from the Universidad Complutense in Madrid, Spain.

ADDRESS: (Home) Santo Reino 5, 4a. Jaen, Spain. Telephone: 255713.

CAREER: She is a professor at the Universidad Complutense de Madrid; college diocesan of Jaen.

PROFESSIONAL ORGANIZATIONS: Real Sociedad Económica de Amigos del País; Colegio Profesional de Doctores y Licenciados.

AWARDS, HONORS: Extraordinary Licentiate Award from the Faculty of Philosophy and Letters, Universidad Complutense de Madrid.

WRITINGS:
En vísperas del gran encuentro. Madrid: Ediciones SM, undated.

De aventurero a almirante. Madrid: Ediciones SM, undated.
¡Tierra a la vista! Madrid: Ediciones SM, undated.
La primera vuelta al mundo. Madrid: Ediciones SM, undated.
Gobierno y sociedad indianos. Madrid: Ediciones SM, undated.

CRITICAL SOURCES:
Reviews:
De Libros. 1989.
Quimera. 1990.
Platero. 1990.
El correo de América. 1990.
Mundo Cristiano. January 1990.
Biblioteca y Educación. February 1990.

Newspapers:
Diario 16. Madrid: October 12, 1989.
El Adelantado. Segovia: November 30, 1989.
El Correo Gallego. La Coruña: December 6, 1989.
La Crónica. León: January 28, 1990.
Diario de Extremadura. Cáceres: January 29, 1990.

BAQUEDANO AZCONA, Lucía (1938-)

PERSONAL DATA: Born December 18, 1938, in Pamplona, Navarra, Spain she is the daughter of Mateo Baquedano Ollacarizqueta and Francisca Azcona Cillero. She is married to Luis Costanilla Olave and is the mother of Luis, Ana, Fermín, and Lucía Costanilla Baquedano.

ADDRESS: (Home) Francisco Bergamín 27, 2° A, 31003 Pamplona, Navarra, Spain. Telephone: 240678.

CAREER: Secretary from 1957 to 1966.

AWARDS, HONORS: Barco de vapor, 1986; Finalist of the Barco de vapor Award, Gran Angular, and Infanta Elena award; CCEI Honors List, 1988; Honors List for the Jugendbibliothek, Munich, 1988.

WRITINGS:
Cinco panes de cebada. Madrid: Ediciones SM, 1981.

Fantasmas de día. Madrid: Ediciones SM, 1987.
De la tierra a Halley. Madrid: Ediciones SM, 1988.
Los candelabros de Santa Bárbara. Gijón: Ed. Júcar, 1988.
Los divertidos líos de la noche. León: Ed. Everest, 1988.
Nosotros, los otros y los demás. Madrid: Ed. Magisterio Español, 1991.
La casa de los diablos. Ed. Labor, 1992.
Los bonsais gigantes. Madrid: Ediciones SM, 1992.

SIDELIGHTS: "I began to write as a girl because of my love for literature, and I owe my best memories to this activity. My favorite theme is humor, although I like everything that can make my work more enjoyable to children. My source of inspiration is the world that surrounds me and my contact with children and young people."

BARTHE, Raquel Marta (1943-)

PERSONAL DATA: Born August 14, 1943, in Buenos Aires, Argentina, the daughter of Marcelo Fernando Barthe and Delia Marta Gualco, she is married to Juan Carlos García. She has two children, Mónica Susana and Diego Fernando García Barthe. *Education:* Primary teacher's certification in physical education for children; library science.

ADDRESS: (Home) Padre Montes Carballo 1596, 1407 Buenos Aires, Argentina. (Office) Entre Ríos 1349, 1133 Buenos Aires, Argentina. Telephone: 6822261.

CAREER: Writer and teacher.

PROFESSIONAL ORGANIZATIONS: Sociedad Argentina de Escritores; Asociación de Literatura Infantil y Juvenil Argentina; Asociación Argentina de Lectura- Asociación Amigos de la Biblioteca del Docente Municipal.

AWARDS, HONORS: Second Prize, Children's Story Competition from the Centro Cultural Docentes Argentinos; Second Prize, Raimundo Susaeta Awards; Children's Story Competition for the the Unión Trabajadores de Prensa de Buenos Aires; Band of Honor in Literature for Children and Young People, 1991-92.

WRITINGS:
Un cuento de yapa. Buenos Aires: Ed. Dimat, 1982.
10 cuentos para la imaginación. Buenos Aires: Ed. Dimat, 1985.

Cabeza de ratón, cola de león (anthology). Buenos Aires: Ed. Leo Lee, 1987.
Cuentos de papel (co-author). Buenos Aires: Ed. Susaeta, 1988.
La pandilla de Protón. Buenos Aires: Ed. Guadalupe, 2nd ed., 1991.
Abelardo, libretista genial. Buenos Aires: Ed. Guadalupe, 1991.
Audaz como un oso. Buenos Aires: Ed. Guadalupe, 1991.
Una extraña profecía. Buenos Aires: Ed. Magisterio, 1991.
El secreto de Rigoberta. Buenos Aires: Ed. Braga, 1991.
Antología cuentopibes. Buenos Aires: Ed. Utpba, 1991.
El sobre lacrado. Buenos Aires: Ed. Guadalupe, 1992.
Puerto Pirámide. Buenos Aires: Ed. Braga, 1992.
Valentina. Buenos Aires: Ed. Braga, 1992.
El escrófalo desrumbado y otros cuentos profundos. Buenos Aires: Ed. Braga, 1992.
La máquina de la travesura. Buenos Aires: Ed. Cástor y Polux, 1992.

SIDELIGHTS: "I write at the express demand of my daughter, who at five years of age solicited writings from me because she desired to read stories rather than listen to them. I discovered my vocation as a writer and so I wrote, and have been doing so for twenty years, for both children and for those who have retained something of their childhood. They are the source of my inspiration, and because of this, almost always my stories are realistic and the themes that I try to relate are of everyday life."

CRITICAL SOURCES:
Carlos Silveyra. *Clarín*. Buenos Aires: September 24, 1987.
Ruth Mel. *La Nación*. Buenos Aires: August 29, 1987.
Ana María Ramb. *Vivir* 143. Buenos Aires: April 1988.
Verónica Podestá. *La Nación*. Buenos Aires: August 4, 1991.
Daniel Kaplán. *Novedades Educativas* 9. Buenos Aires: June 1991.

BEDREGAL, Yolanda (1918-)

PERSONAL DATA: Born September 21, 1918, in La Paz, Bolivia, the daughter of Juan Francisco Bedregal and Carmen Iturri, she is married to Gert Conitzer and has two children, Juan-Gert and Rosángela. *Education:* Holds a degree from the Academia de Bellas Artes.

ADDRESS: (Home) Casilla Postal 149, La Paz, Bolivia. Telephone: 322851.

CAREER: Professor; senior advisor of culture, 1980-; author of literature for children.

PROFESSIONAL ORGANIZATIONS: Academia de la Lengua; Comité de Literatura Infantil-Juvenil.

AWARDS, HONORS: Honored with the creation of the Yolanda de Bolivia Awards for Education and Literature; numerous awards from the Ministerio de Cultura and the Bolivian Foundation for the Arts, as well as several international awards.

WRITINGS:
Nautragio.
Poemar.
Ecos.
Nadir.
El cántaro del Angelito.
Antologia de poesía boliviana. Edited by Yolanda Bedregal.

Yolanda Bedregal's numerous works of fiction, poetry, and nonfiction have been translated into languages as diverse as English, French, German, Hindi, and Urdu.

SIDELIGHTS: "Humanity, family, intimacy, children, motherhood, man, woman, landscape, the soul, God: It is difficult to define my reasons for writing. One writes from an internal necessity, maybe subconscious or unconscious or in order to communicate with others. I don't know. My father, a professor and a lawyer, was an author of sociological works, stories, and poetry. I was born into the environment and culture of writers."

CRITICAL SOURCES: There is a wealth of critical information concerning the works of this author that spans the last forty years. She has been the object of biographical and critical reviews in Bolivia, as well as in other South American and European countries.

BELLVER, Lourdes (1946-)

PERSONAL DATA: Born in Gandia, Valencia, Spain, in 1946. *Education:* Studied the applied arts at the Escuela de Artes y Oficios in Valencia.

CAREER: She is dedicated to the teaching profession and to illustrating books for children.

WRITINGS: La rata Marieta. Valencia: Ed. Tandem, 1990. The illustrated work of Lourdes Bellver is originally published in Valencian. The work cited here is a translation into Spanish.

SIDELIGHTS: "The level of illustration these days is very high. We have wonderful artists in this field. I think that Catalonia has created an excellent school, as good as that of Valencia; it has excellent creators, in illustration as well as in comic art. But I think that in contrast with other countries, illustrators here are not considered authentic artists. There are very few illustrated readings that follow a central character through different adventures in a series of books. It thus occurred to me to create a series of books directed toward children with Marieta as the protagonist."

BELPRÉ, Pura (1899-1982)

PERSONAL DATA: Born February 2, 1899, in Cidra, Puerto Rico, and died July 1, 1982, in the United States, she was married to Clarence Cameron White. *Education:* attended the School of Library Science of New York and Columbia University.

CAREER: Librarian; writer of literature for children; designer of marionettes.

AWARDS, HONORS: Mention in Brooklyn Art Books for Children, 1973; mention by the Instituto de Puerto Rico in New York for having introduced Puerto Rican folklore into the United States, 1978; Honorable Mention for her distinguished contribution to literature in Spanish, Bay Area Bilingual Education, 1978; Award of Honor for Arts and Culture from the Alcalde; Professional Award in the Field of Education, Colegio Baricus.

WRITINGS:
Pérez y Martina. Ed. Warne, 1966.
Santiago. Ed. Warne, 1971.
Libros en español: An Annotated List of Children's Books in Spanish. New York Public Library, 1971.

SIDELIGHTS: "At times I am asked, where do I get the ideas for my books. I do not have a specific answer. I take them from any place and any person, from conversations with others, from articles in the newspaper, from memories of people I once knew, from dreams, and (though rarely) from what I am asked to write about, or about something or some place special."

BENET ROQUÉ, Amelia (1914-)

PERSONAL DATA: Born January 10, 1914, in Ogassa, Catalonia, Spain, the daughter of Josep Benet and de Josepa Roqué, she is married to Joan Durán Veciana. Her children are Oriol, Juan, and Raimon. *Education:* Master's degree and higher studies in philosophy and letters, interrupted by the Spanish Civil War.

ADDRESS: (Home) General Mitre 218, 5° 2a., 08006 Barcelona, Spain. Telephone: 2374356.

CAREER: Professor, writer, teacher, editor, and journalist.

PROFESSIONAL ORGANIZATIONS: Asociación de Escritores de Lengua Catalana.

WRITINGS: More than 100 stories for children, published by Ed. Colón (Barcelona), 1945-63; writings in Castillian with translations into Portuguese, Italian, and French. These stories were published under pseudonyms: María Blanca Gil and Carmen del Valle. From 1965 to 1985, she published more than 100 books for children, edited by Teide, Juventud, La Galera, Betis, Salvatella, Anaya, and Publicaciones de Monserrat. Most of these works were published in Catalan and Castilian in separate editions.

SIDELIGHTS: "I write because since childhood I have enjoyed writing; I have always been given to writing, editing, and telling stories. My favorite theme has been nature, possibly because I was born in a small village high in the Pyrenees mountains and when I was a girl my family moved to a city (Barcelona). The nostalgia I felt for my life in the mountains caused me to appreciate and enjoy nature. I am inspired by listening to music, going to movies, seeing paintings, and being very observant."

BERTOLINO SIRITO, Roberto Noel (1944-)

PERSONAL DATA: Born October 22, 1944, in Carmelo, Uruguay, the son of Alfredo Bertolino and Genoveva Sirito, he is married to María Elena Depratti. His children are María Victoria, Mariana, Carolina, and Virginia.

ADDRESS: (Home) Catamarca 339, 4° 22, 1213 Buenos Aires, Argentina. Telephone: 938298. (Office) Bragado 6142, 1440 Buenos Aires, Argentina. Telephone: 6873758.

CAREER: Writer of literature for children and adolescents; educational advisor for editorial Kapelusz, 1975; editorial director for the *Lazarillo* Foundation, 1977-; screenwriter for television, 1975, 1986; elementary and professor of a teacher's college, high school teacher, director of a primary school.

PROFESSIONAL ORGANIZATIONS: Sociedad Argentina de Escritores; Asociación Argentina de Autores y Compositores; Asociación Uruguaya de Literatura Infantil; Nuevas Técnicas para la Promoción de la Lectura.

AWARDS, HONORS: First Prize for Uruguay, 1966, 1972, 1985, 1986; Ribbon of Honor, SADE, 1981; First Prize, Best Book for Adolescents, Argentina, 1981. Consultant to UNESCO for the project, "Campañas de lectura para América Latina."

WRITINGS:
Ramón. Montevideo: Ed. DISA.
Crónicas de niños. Montevideo: Ed. DISA.
Aprestamiento, Ciencias Naturales. Montevideo: Ed. DISA.
Anita y Pepín en vacaciones. Belgium: Ed. Hema.
Anita y Pepín: trabajos manuales. Belgium: Ed. Hema.
Anita y Pepín: en busca de trabajo. Belgium: Ed. Hema.
Anita y Pepín: trabajos en casa. Belgium: Ed. Hema.
Dampy: castillos en el aire. Holland: Ed. Mulder.
Dampy: los nuevos amigos. Holland: Ed. Mulder.
Dampy: la inundación. Holland: Ed. Mulder.
Dampy: los amigos del bosque. Holland: Ed. Mulder.
Cuentos del jardín (7 vols.). Japan: Ed. Froebel-Kant.
Consultorito (4 vols.). Spain: Ed. Ediexport.
A jugar (4 vols.). Buenos Aires: Ed. Gente Menuda.
Danilo. Buenos Aires: Ed. Juan Cruz.
Ayer. Buenos Aires: Ed. Plus Ultra.
Hoy. Buenos Aires: Ed. Plus Ultra.
Mañana. Buenos Aires: Ed. *Lazarillo.*
Vivir es . . . Buenos Aires: Ed. *Lazarillo,* 11th ed.
Hermanita, enséñame a leer. Buenos Aires: Ed. Betina.
Margarita. Buenos Aires: Ed. Betina.
Bimbo. Buenos Aires: Ed. Betina.
Tom. Buenos Aires: Ed. Betina.

SIDELIGHTS: "I write what I write because I think that to present the problems facing our children or our environment in a fresh, poetic form is the best way to bring them to the heart of the reader. My favorite themes are the world of children, the environment, and the spiritual development that comes from living life. I encounter these themes every day, then I look for inspiration in the solitude of my study in order to give them a poetic form."

BEUCHAT REICHARDT, Cecilia E. (1947-)

PERSONAL DATA: Born February 5, 1947, in Santiago, Chile, she is the daughter of Ernesto Beuchat and Erika Reichardt. She is married to Osvaldo Schencke and has two children, Pablo and Claudia. *Education:* Advanced studies in Castilian; Master's degree in letters, with emphasis in Hispanic literature.

ADDRESS: (Home) Orquídeas 973, Santiago de Chile 9, Chile. Telephone: 2317527. (Office) Diagonal Oriente 3300, Santiago de Chile, Chile. Telephone: 2744041.

CAREER: Professor of literature for children and Castilian methodology, Facultad de Educación, Pontificia Universidad Católica de Chile, 1966-.

PROFESSIONAL ORGANIZATIONS: IBBY Chilean Branch; International Reading Association; IRSCL.

AWARDS, HONORS: Mention at the International Library of Literature for Children in Munich.

WRITINGS:
La gallinita roja y otros cuentos. Co-written by Mabel Condemarín. Santiago: Ed. *Andrés Bello,* 1985.
Cuentos con algo de mermelada. Santiago: Ed. *Andrés Bello,* 1987.
Cuentos con olor a fruta. Santiago: Ed. *Andrés Bello,* 1989.
El lobo y el zorro y otros cuentos. Co-written by Mabel Condemarín. Santiago: Ed. *Andrés Bello,* 1990.
A ver, a ver, ¿vamos a leer? Co-written by Mabel Condemarín. Santiago: Ed. *Andrés Bello,* 1990.
Caracol, caracol, saca tu librito al sol. Co-written by Mabel Condemarín. Santiago: Ed. Universitaria, 1992.
Las cuatro estaciones. Co-written by Loreto Rodríguez. Santiago: Ed. *Andrés Bello,* 1992.
Un ratón de biblioteca. Co-written by Clementina Maldonado. Santiago: Ed. *Andrés Bello,* 1990.

She has also published complementary texts for basic education and books about teaching literature to children, as well as articles and reviews.

SIDELIGHTS: "I want to show the reality of my stories. My characters are children of flesh and blood, who have problems, and who interact with adults: parents, teachers, grandparents—in short—all kinds of people. I am inspired principally by reality; I think that it has its own magic. I can walk down the street or talk to someone and I will begin imagining things. I love to observe and to be nosey, and I never cease to be surprised with the beauty of being alive."

CRITICAL SOURCES:
Manuel Peña. *El Mercurio.* April 10, 1988; September 2, 1990.

BLANCO LÓPEZ, Cruz (1945-)

PERSONAL DATA: Born May 3, 1945, in Madrid, Spain, the daughter of Mateo and Rogelia. She has two children, Ana and Jorge. *Education:* Licentiate in educational sciences; journalism.

ADDRESS: (Home) Boileu U6-11, 3° INT, iz., Madrid, Spain. Telephone: 5471830.

CAREER: Journalist for the newspaper *El País*; director of the Office of Press and Publications at the Universidad Complutense de Madrid and the Politécnica in Madrid.

WRITINGS:
Velemiro. Madrid: Ed. Altea, 1970.
Adaptación de cuentos de hadas. Madrid: Ed. Bruguera, 1970.

SIDELIGHTS: Cruz Blanco López has written since childhood; he writes literature for children because he loves both children and psychology. His journalistic interests revolve around social themes.

BLÁNQUEZ PÉREZ, Carmen (1955-)

PERSONAL DATA: Born August 27, 1955, in Madrid, Spain. Her parents are Luis and Pilar Blánquez. *Education:* Ph.D. in philosophy and letters.

ADDRESS: (Home) Señores de Luzon 8, 1º A, 28013 Madrid, Spain. Telephone: 5420149. (Office) Departamento de Historia Antigua, Facultad de Geografía e Historia, Universidad Complutense de Madrid, 28040 Madrid, Spain. Telephone: 3945948.

CAREER: Professor of ancient history at the Universidad Complutense de Madrid.

PROFESSIONAL ORGANIZATIONS: Secretary of the association ARYS (prehistory, religion, and societies).

WRITINGS:
Telón en los juegos olímpicos. Madrid: Ed. Bruño, 1990.
El neolítico. Madrid: Ed. Bruño, in print.

She has also published books and articles about the histories of Greece and Rome.

SIDELIGHTS: "The themes that interest me are related to the world of ancient Greece and Rome, the topics that I research and teach at the Universidad Complutense de Madrid. I am inspired by these cultures, and I have written two stories about various aspects of the ancient world directed at children. I want to interest them in it, without making them feel that it is a subject of study, but only something that is fun and attractive."

BORNEMANN, Elsa (Isabel) (1952-)

PERSONAL DATA: Born February 20, 1952, in Buenos Aires, Argentina. Her father is Wilhelm Carl Heinrich Bornemann and her mother is Blanca Nieves Fernández Sánchez. She is married to Nobuyuki Adachi; Fernando and Isabel Toshie Adachi are their children. *Education:* She holds a National Primary School Teacher's certification; she graduated from the School of Philosophy and Letters at the Universidad Nacional de Buenos Aires; she obtained an advanced degree in English and German; she also took various courses concerning the arts and literature for children, both in Argentina and at foreign schools.

ADDRESS: (Home) Bulnes 1976, 5º A, 1425 Buenos Aires, Argentina. Telephone: 8352775.

CAREER: She has taught at the preschool, grammar, and high school levels; she has taught a creative writing workshop; she has also written screenplays for television programs for children.

PROFESSIONAL ORGANIZATIONS: Sociedad Argentina de Escritores; ARGENTORES; SADAIC (Society of Authors and Composers of the Republic of Argentina); YMCA (Young Men's Christian Association).

AWARDS, HONORS: Ribbon of Honor from the Sociedad Argentina de Escritores, 1972; Honors List for the International Hans Christian Andersen Prize, 1976, awarded by IBBY for the first time to an Argentinian writer; San Francisco de Asís, 1977; selected to represent Argentina in the International Expo for new tendencies and experiments in literature for children; Award, First National Competition of Stories for Children, 1983; *El libro de los chicos enamorados* considered one of the Ten Best Books, the International Library for Adolescents, 1982, and selected for Banco del Libro in Venezuela; Alicia Moreau de Justo Prize, 1985; ARGENTORES Prize, 1984; Special Mention, National Program of Literature for Children, 1986; Prize of the International Library for Adolescents, 1989; Reconocimiento Benito Lynch Award, Sociedad Argentina de Escritores, 1988.

WRITINGS:

Tinke Tinke: 55 versicuentos e historias en verso. Buenos Aires: Ed. Edicom, 1970.

El espejo distraído: 55 versicuentos. Buenos Aires: Ed. Edicom, 1971. Also: Buenos Aires: Ed. Plus Ultra, 1971.

El cazador de aromas. Illust. by Leonardo Haleblian. Buenos Aires: Ed. Latina, 1972.

El cumpleaños de Lisandro. Illust. by Kitty Lorefice. Buenos Aires: Ed. Latina, 1974.

Poemas para niños. Illust. by Alba Ponce. Buenos Aires: Ed. Latina, 1975.

Estudio y antología de la poesía infantil. Illust. by Guido Bruveris, Alba Ponce, and Clara Urquijo. Buenos Aires: Ed. Latina, 1976.

Cuadernos de un delfín. Illust. by Alberto Peri. Buenos Aires: Ed. Plus Ultra, 1976.

Cuentos a salto de canguro. Illust. by Julia Díaz. Buenos Aires: Ed. Fausto, 1977. Also illust. by Sergio Kern. Buenos Aires: Ed. Fausto, 1991.

Antología del cuento infantil. Illust. by Clara Urquijo. Buenos Aires: Ed. Latina, 1977.

El libro de los chicos enamorados. Buenos Aires: Ed. Fausto, 1977.

Bilembambudin o el último mago. Illust. by Guido Bruveris. Buenos Aires: Ed. Fausto, 1979. Also illust by Sergio Kern. Buenos Aires: Ed. Fausto, 1979.

El niño envuelto. Buenos Aires: Ed. Orión, 1981.

No somos irrompibles. Illust. by Guido Bruveris. Buenos Aires: Ed. Fausto, 1986. Also illust. by Sergio Kern. Buenos Aires: Ed. Fausto, 1986.

Disparatario. Illust. by Cristina Brusca. Buenos Aires: Ed. Orión, 1983.

Nada de tucanes. Illust. by Juan Carlos Marchesi. Buenos Aires: Ed. El Ateneo, 1985.

Los Josecitos. Illust. by Sergio Kern. Buenos Aires: Ed. Preescolar, 1986.

Lista de los paraguas. Illust. by Gustavo Macri. Buenos Aires: Ed. Preescolar, 1986.

De colores, de todos los colores. Illust by Juan Carlos. Buenos Aires: Ed. El Ateneo, 1986.

Puro ojos. Illust. by Elena Torres. Buenos Aires: Ed. El Ateneo, 1986.

Los Grendelines. Illust. by Sergio Kern. Buenos Aires: Ed. Fausto, 1987.

¡Socorro! Doce cuentos para caerse de miedo. Buenos Aires: Ed. Rei, 1988.

La edad del pavo. Illust. by Carlos Nine. Buenos Aires: Ed. Alfaguara, 1990.

Sol de noche. Canciones y cuentos de cuna para cantar y contar, Libro uno. Illust. by Mariel Ballester. *Libro dos*. Illust by Oscar Delgado. Buenos Aires: Ed. Losada, 1991.

Los desmaravilladores. Illust. by Diego Bianchi. Buenos Aires: Ed. Alfaguara, 1991.

Lobo rojo, Caperucita feroz. Illust. by Oscar Delgado. Buenos Aires: Ed. El Ateneo, 1991.

Queridos monstruos, diez cuentos para caerse de miedo. Illust. by Oscar Delgado. Buenos Aires: Ed. Alfaguara, 1991.

Corazonadas. Illust. by Carlos Nine. Buenos Aires: Ed. Fausto, 1992.

Cuento con miedo. Illust. by Oscar Delgado. Buenos Aires: Ed. El Ateneo, 1992.

SIDELIGHTS: "I decided during my adolescence to dedicate myself to the creation of books for children and young people, books like those that I had been exposed to, and this was still a practically unexplored genre in my country. Moreover, I feel that writing is an invaluable vocation: It is as if children's literature has chosen me and not I who chose it. Also, I am happy to know that I perform a service that our children need. With respect to my favorite themes, I try to synthesize love, absurd humor, and terror, always with a definite orientation toward the particular problems that confront our children. The most powerful source of inspiration for me comes from observation and contact (direct and through correspondence) with children, in addition to the events that reality presents to me daily. I am convinced that every theme can be emphasized in books for children, always, and that they can be clear so as to be apprehensible. For this reason, I am also a lover of poetry and songs directed toward childhood."

BORRELL, Joaquím (1956-)

PERSONAL DATA: Born in Valencia, Spain, in 1956. He is married and the father of four children.

CAREER: Notary public.

AWARDS, HONORS: Critics' Award from *Serra d'Or* for *El bes de la nivaira*, 1991.

WRITINGS:
Caballo verde. Valencia: Ed. Marí Montaña, 1983.
La esclava de azul. Barcelona: Ed. Círculo de Lectores, 1989.
El bes de la nivaira. Barcelona: Ed. Columna, 1990.

SIDELIGHTS: "I write for children without any conscious decision; at best because as an author I would like to continue being a child and even without trying to, I am aware of it. I think that basically everyone writes in order to create characters that one is attracted to, without risk, effort, or expense—that can with a little luck pay the bills—and above all, in order to arrange his characters' destinies in a way that in real life one cannot control."

BOSNIA, Nella (1946-)

PERSONAL DATA: Born February 3, 1946, in Milan, Italy, she is the daughter of Filippo and Alfonsina Bosnia. She is married to Friedmann Kaltbrunner and has one daughter, Elisa. *Education:* School of Professional Art.

ADDRESS: (Home) Via del Caravaggio 1, 20166 Milan, Italy.

CAREER: Illustrator of books for children. She also works as an advertising designer.

PROFESSIONAL ORGANIZATIONS: Associazione Illustratori.

ILLUSTRATIONS:
Los niños de los cuentos. 1978.
El zoo fantástico (14 vol.). 1979-84.

SIDELIGHTS: "In illustrating the books that I do, I want to be able to give children the smallest details, the most precise information about the past, because if they understand it they will have a better future. I think that my work, although it is entertaining to me, is done with an awareness and respect for children."

BRAVO-VILLASANTE, Carmen

PERSONAL DATA: Born in Madrid, Spain, the daughter of Juan and Carmen, she is married to Higinio and has four children, Juan Miguel, Carmen, Alvaro, and Arturo. *Education:* Doctorate in philosophy and letters.

CAREER: Author and professor of Spanish literature at Smith College, Middlebury, Lake Forest, and the Instituto de Cultura Hispánica.

ADDRESS: Arrieta 14, Madrid 28013, Spain.

PROFESSIONAL ORGANIZATIONS: Asociación Colegial de Escritores, Asociación de Traductores, Asociación de Escritores y Artistas.

AWARDS, HONORS: Award for Biographies, AEDOS, 1957; Fray Luis de León National Award for Translation, 1977; International Amade Award, 1979; National Award for the Investigation of Literature for Children, 1980; National Award for Literature, 1980.

WRITINGS:
Historia de la literatura infantil española. Madrid: Revista de Occidente, 1959.
Antología de la literatura infantil española, vol. I, II. Madrid: Ed. Doncel, 1962; 9th ed., 1989.
Historia y antología de la literatura infantil iberoamericana, vol. *I, II, III.* Madrid: Ed. Doncel, 1965; 3rd. ed., 1988.
Historia de la literatura infantil universal. Madrid: Ed. Doncel, 1971.
Antología de la literatura infantil universal. Illust. by Pacheco. Madrid: Ed. Doncel, 1971.
Vida y muerte del Doncel (book on tape). Illust. by Pacheco. Madrid: Video sistemas, 1973.
¿Qué leen nuestros hijos? Madrid: Magisterio Español, 1975.
Pecas, Dragoncín y el tesoro. Illust. by Jesús Gabán. Madrid: Ed. Almena, 1975; 4th. ed., 1989.
Una, dola, tela, catola. 1977.
Literatura infantil universal. Madrid: Ed. Almena, 1978.
Adivina, adivinanza. Illust. by Pacheco. Madrid: Ed. Interduc-Schroedel, 1978; 4th. ed., 1986.
Colección de libros infantiles antiguos de Carmen Bravo Villasante. Madrid: Artes Gráficas Iberomericanas, 1979.
Dos siglos de libro infantil. Madrid: Caja de Ahorros 1979.
Las tres naranjas del amor y otros cuentos españoles. Illust. by Carmen Andrada. Barcelona: Ed. Noguer, 1980; 3rd. ed., 1989.
China, china, capuchina. Illust. by Carmen Andrada. Valladolid: Ed. Miñón, 1981; 4th. ed., 1989.
El jardín encantado. Madrid: Ed. Emiliano Escolar, 1981.
La hermosura del mundo y otros cuentos españoles. Illust. by Carmen Andrada.

Barcelona: Ed. Noguer, 1981.

El libro de los 500 refranes. Illust. by Carmen Andrada. Valladolid: Ed. Miñón, 1982.

Colorín, colorete. Madrid: Ed. Didascalia, 1983.

El libro de las fábulas. Illust. by Carmen Andrada. Valladolid: Ed. Miñón, 1983.

Hermano Francisco. Valladolid: Ed. Miñón, 1983.

Arre, moto, piti, poto; arre moto, piti, pa. Madrid: Ed. Escuela Española, 1984.

Al corro de la patata. Illust. by Álvaro Donoso. Madrid: Ed. Escuela Española, 1984.

Cuentos populares de Iberoamérica. Madrid: ICI, 1984.

El principe oso y otros cuentos populares españoles. Barcelona: Ed. Noguer, 1984.

El libro de las adivinanzas. Illust. by Carmen Andrada. Valladolid: Ed. Miñón, 1985.

Diccionario de autores de la literatura infantil mundial. Madrid: Ed. Escuela Española, 1985.

El libro de los trabalenguas. Illust. by Carmen Andrada. Madrid: Ed. Gondomar, 1986.

Ensayos de literatura infantil. Murcia: Ed. Universidad, 1989.

The author of more than 800 publications, Carmen Bravo-Villasante has written essays, poetry, theater, literary criticism, and journalism as well as translations of both classic and modern works of literature.

CRITICAL SOURCES: José Antonio Ramírez Ovelar. *Bibliografía de Carmen Bravo Villasante.* Madrid: 1991. This book includes extensive and meticulous material about each publication, edition, and translation of her work, as well as criticism from books, journals, and magazines.

BUSTAMANTE DE ROGGERO, Cecilia (1949-)

PERSONAL DATA: Born July 9, 1949, in Georgia, U.S.A., of Peruvian nationality, she is the child of Luis Bustamante Pérez and Elsie Rodríguez. Cecilia is married to Mario Roggero Villena, and her children are Alonso, Sybila, and Chiara. *Education:* She studied literature at the Universidad Católica.

ADDRESS: (Home) Elias Aparicio 145, Rinconada Alta, La Molina, Lima, Peru. Telephone: 350464.

CAREER: She works at the Editorial Santillana on the selection and adaptation of texts for reading in the section on Peruvian educational techniques.

PROFESSIONAL ORGANIZATIONS: Instituto Altamira.

WRITINGS:
Garabatos. Lima: Ed. Arica, 1974.
Madrugada. España: Ed. Santillana, 1978.
Ida y vuelta. España: Ed. Santillana, 1978.
She has also collaborated on journals and children's reviews.

SIDELIGHTS: "I think that I write in order to transmit to children the richness of our world arranged in multiple manifestations of life: animals, persons and characters, animated objects. There is in my stories and poems a central prominence given to nature; to ourselves with our particular way of looking and feeling; to others, those that surround us and change; in all of this I find the confirmation and valorization of the creative imagination. Rain and tears, eyes and the sea, our yellow planet and a paper butterfly, all form aspects of the texts that can bring out the colors, music, enjoyment, and the awakening touch that frees our view from the real world which confines myths and poetry."

CABRÉ FABRÉ, Jaume (1947-)

PERSONAL DATA: Born April 30, 1947, in Barcelona, Spain, he is the son of Oriol Cabré and Leonor Fabré. He is married to Margarida Barba and has two children, Martí and Clara. *Education:* Licentiate in philology.

ADDRESS: (Home) Fogueroses 30 G Ap. 107, 08230 Matadepera, Spain. Telephone: 787568. (Office) Plaza Letamendi 37, 4a. 2a, 08007 Barcelona, Spain. Telephone: 4530594.

CAREER: Professor of language and literature; screenwriter for cinema and television; writer.

PROFESSIONAL ORGANIZATIONS: Catalan PEN Club.

AWARDS, HONORS: Catalan Critics' Award, 1981, 1985, 1992; Spanish Critics' Award, 1985, 1992; National Prize for Catalan Literature, 1992.

WRITINGS:
Libro de preludios. Madrid: Ed. Espasa-Calpe, 1989.
El extraño viaje que nadie se creyó. Barcelona: Ed. La Galera, 1981.

La telaraña. Barcelona: Ed. Argos-Vergara, 1984.
El hombre de Sau. Barcelona: Ed. La Galera, 1986.
Fray Junoy o la agonía de los sonidos. Madrid: Ed. Espasa-Calpe, 1988.

CRITICAL SOURCES:
Alex Broch. *Literatura catalana en los años ochenta.* Barcelona: Ediciones 62.

CALLEJA GUIJARRO, Tomás (1922-)

PERSONAL DATA: Born December 31, 1922, in Navares de Ayuso, Segovia, Spain, he is the son of Fermín Calleja Muñoz and Saturnina Guijarro de Frutos. He is married to Gregoria Martín and has four daughters, María del Rosario, María del Consuelo, María de las Mercedes, and María Jesús. *Education:* Master's degree, philosophy and literature; sociological study.

ADDRESS: (Home) Melilla 12, 6° B, esc. izqda. 28005 Madrid, Spain. Telephone: 4743559.

CAREER: Professor.

PROFESSIONAL ORGANIZATIONS: Asociación de Escritores y Artistas Españoles; Asociación Española de Amigos de la Arqueología; Sociedad Española de Estudios Medievales.

AWARDS, HONORS: ACCESIT National Award for Literature for Children and Adolescents; Poetry Prize from the municipality of Segovia; Fiction Prize from the municipality of Segovia; UNICEF Diploma—Spain; Golden Shield of Sepúlveda.

WRITINGS:
Dramatizaciones I. Madrid: Ed. Anaya, 1966.
Dramatizaciones II. Madrid: Ed. Anaya, 1966.
El mundo que ves vol. 1. Madrid: Ed. Hernando, 1966.
El mundo que ves vol. 2. Madrid: Ed. Hernando, 1967.
Poemas de amor y tierra. Author's edition, 1975.
Romances del tuerto de Pirón. Author's edition, 1981.
Leyendas de los santos segovianos. Author's edition, 1983.
Carrusel. Madrid: Ed. Escuela Española, 1982.
Girasol. Madrid: Ed. Escuela Española, 1982.
Aventuras en cuevas. Madrid: Ed. Edelvives, 6th. ed., 1988.

Sobresaltos en las cavernas. Madrid: Ed. Edelvives, Second. ed., 1991.
"Cuentos de navidad." *El Adelantado de Segovia.* 1983 to 1991.

He is also the author of instructional texts and scholarly investigation.

SIDELIGHTS: "I write as a vocation. It is part of the time that I have given to the children and young people with whom I have lived, as a professor, for forty-two years. My favorite themes are those that are more than merely entertainment for the readers, those that can help them benefit themselves and humanity. I especially emphasize in my works themes drawn from nature, so that young people will learn love and respect for it, the love of all types of life, friendship, honesty, etc. With my poetry for children, I try first to create and instill in youngsters from their first days in school a love for poetry so that they will continue to enjoy and read the greats. It is important to encourage the 'Cinderella-like' response that children have for the fine arts, rather than condemn it as we have been doing for so long. My favorite themes, then, are nature, children, and adults."

CRITICAL SOURCES:
Fernando Allue Morer. *La Estafeta Literaria.*
Pablo Martín Cantalejo. *El Adelantado de Segovia.*
José López Martínez. *Poesía Hispánica.*
Carlos Murciano. *ABC.*

CALNY, Eugenia (Fany Eugenia Kalnitzky de Brener) (1929-)

PERSONAL DATA: Born July 15, 1929, in San Juan, Argentina, the daughter of Abraham Kalnitzky and Rosa Costavesky, she is married to Carlos Brener and she has a daughter, Graciela Bertha Brener. *Education:* Self-educated.

ADDRESS: (Home) General Roca 2656, Florida, 1602 Buenos Aires, Argentina. 7607429.

CAREER: Editor and journalist. She has collaborated on literary supplements for children for various periodicals.

PROFESSIONAL ORGANIZATIONS: SADE (Argentina Society of Writers); and Gente de Letras.

AWARDS, HONORS: Honorable Distinction at the International Jugendliterathur,

Munich, Germany, 1988; other awards for her work for ecological development.

WRITINGS:
Conejita blanca y el viaje a la luna. Buenos Aires: Ed. Plus Ultra, 1976.
Osobel y la fantasía. Buenos Aires: Ed. Sigmar, 1977.
La gaviota perdida. Buenos Aires: Ed. Plus Ultra, 1978.
Morrongo, el gato sin botas. Buenos Aires: Ed. Guadalupe, 1979.
El congreso de los árboles. Buenos Aires: Ed. Plus Ultra, 1979.
Historias de ositos. Buenos Aires: Ed. Plus Ultra, 1980.
Toto el zorro y la fiebre del oro en California. Buenos Aires: Ed. Sudamericana, 1984.
El unicornio celeste y el caballito con alas. Buenos Aires: Ed. Acmé, 1984.
Poemas gatunos. Buenos Aires: Ed. Plus Ultra, 1986.
Gato rayado y Ratoncito lector. Buenos Aires: Ed. Plus Ultra, 1986.
La torre de Babel. Buenos Aires: Ed. Guadalupe, 1987.
La góndola y sus hermanos barcos. Buenos Aires: Ed. Plus Ultra, 1987.
Lágrimas de cocodrilo. Buenos Aires: Ed. Plus Ultra, 1987.
Gatimoreno y los molinos de viento. Buenos Aires: Ed. Plus Ultra, 1987.
Cuentos para soñar despierto. Magisterio del Río de la Plata, 1988.
Cuentos japoneses. Buenos Aires:1989.
Cuentos del dragón. Buenos Aires:1988.
El árbol del tronco inclinado. Ed. Errepar.
Los años de colores. Buenos Aires: Ed. Norte, 1990.
Cum, el joven guerrero celta. Buenos Aires: Ed. Braga, 1991.

SIDELIGHTS: "My literary vocation emerged very early in my life. At six years of age I was already inventing and writing stories. When I didn't know the words, I would draw pictures to convey my meanings and by fourteen years of age I won my first award. When I was about twenty I entered the field of journalism, but even then I was as interested in writing for youngsters as I was in writing for adults. I have published books of stories, novels, poetry, and drama. My literature for children includes messages of love, peace, liberty, respect for fellow humans and nature, but no violence. It is enriched with agile language, word games, humor, and careful documentation of personal histories, myths, and legends. I am very imaginative. I live in a continual state of creativity. I love my work. I have made a pact of love with children's literature: It gives me wonderful spiritual satisfactions and I give it the best part of myself."

CRITICAL SOURCES:
Solomon Lipp. "The Literary World of Eugenia Calny," in *Essays on Foreign Languages and Literatures.* New York: McGill University 1987.
Ernest H. Lewald. "Choque entre lo psicológico y lo social, clave de la literatura de Eugenia Calny." University of Tennessee.

CALVIMONTES SALINAS, Velia (1935-)

PERSONAL DATA: Born September 10, 1935, in Cochabamba, Bolivia, she is the daughter of Leónidas Calvimontes Carreño and Flora Salinas de Calvimontes. Her husband is Manuel Rodríguez, and they have two daughters, Lucía and Gissela. *Education:* Normal school certification; advanced study in grammar, phonetics, and linguistics.

ADDRESS: (Home) Calle Colombia 0457, Esq. Tarapcá, Cochabamba, Bolivia. (Mailing Address) Casilla Postal 980 Cochabamba, Bolivia. Telephone: 47123.

CAREER: Professor of Spanish and English.

PROFESSIONAL ORGANIZATIONS: Comité de Literatura Infantil/Juvenil; Unión Nacional de Poetas y Escritores de Cochabamba; ARGENTORES; Fundación Givré (Argentina); honorary president, Club del Libro María Quiroga Vargas, Cochabamba.

AWARDS, HONORS: Award from the Universidad Tomás Frías, 1977; Jorge Luis Borges Prize, 1979, 1982, 1986; Alfonsina Storni Prize, 1979; Honorable Mention, International Poetry Contest, Bilbao, Spain, 1981; Honorable mention, National Competition of Stories for Children, Cochabamba, 1988;   National Award, 1990.

WRITINGS:
Y el mundo sigue girando. Cochabamba: Ed. Imprenta Rocabado, 1975.
Rinconcuentos. Cochabamba: Ed. Talleres Gráficos Poligraf, 1988.
El uniforme. Cochabamba: Ed. Vendilusiones, 1991.
La ronda de los niños. Illust. by Gissela Rodríguez Calvimontes. Cochabamba: Ed. Vendilusiones, 1991.
Abre la tapa y destapa un cuento. Illust. by Rosario Moyano. Cochabamba: Ed. Imprenta H&P, 1991.
De la tierra y de las preguntas. Cochabamba: Ed. Colorgraf, Rodríguez, 1992.

SIDELIGHTS: "From childhood I knew I would be a writer. I loved to read stories, I was a tireless reader, and when I finished something that impressed me, I would say, 'I am going to write one day.' I write what I do because for me to write is a necessity. An act of injustice, as in *El uniforme*, or a happiness, a gesture of solidarity, they can be translated by my pen into the stories that I write. I enjoy writing for children, probably because inside me I still have a hidden child, and when I take the pen it is the child that awakens in me to write, and from my pen issue the words that she dictates. My source of inspiration? Everything. It can be a word that I hear as I walk down the street, an object, a tradition, or a legend of American Indians. The assassination of the scientist Dr. Noel Kempff Mercado (1986) gave me the theme of a story, a strong protest, in favor of the ecology."

CRITICAL SOURCES:
José Ortega and Rodolfo Cáceres Romero. *Diccionario de la literatura boliviana.* 1977.
Augusto Guzmán. *Biografías de la nueva literatura boliviana.* 1982.
Pedro de Anasagasti. *Presencia literaria.* La Paz, 1990.
Martha Urquidi Anaya. *Los Tiempos.* 1990.
Rosario Quiroga Urquieta. *Los Tiempos.* 1991.
Elizabeth Arrázola. *Los Tiempos.* February 1992.

CALZADILLA NÚÑEZ, Julia Lydia (1943-)

PERSONAL DATA: Born August 1, 1943, in Havana, Cuba. Her parents were Ramón and Julia. *Education:* She holds a licentiate in the history of art at the Universidad de La Habana; she has done postgraduate study.

ADDRESS: (Home) Calle 6a. 209, 6° piso Apto. 3, (entre 11 y Linea) Vedado, Municipio Plaza, Havana, Cuba. Telephone: 39605. (Office) Editorial José Martí, Calzada e/I y J, Vedado, Municipio Plaza, Havana, Cuba. Telephone: 329838.

CAREER: Editor and reviewer of Portuguese for Editorial José Martí; she is an interpreter and she translates from English, French, Portuguese, and Italian into Spanish, and from Spanish into Portuguese.

PROFESSIONAL ORGANIZATIONS: Unión de Escritores y Artistas de Cuba (UNEAC); Asociación de Escritores, Sección Literatura Infantil; IBBY of Cuba, president; Member of the Consejo Asesor for reviews in Zunzún, Arte y *Literatura*, Editorial Gente Nueva, and Editorial Abril.

AWARDS, HONORS: UNEAC Ismaelillo Prize, 1974, 1983; Children's Poetry Mention, Ed. Gente Nueva, Havana, 1974; Casa de las Américas Award in Literature for Children and Adolescents Prize, 1976, 1984; Mention, UNEAC Ismaelillo Competition, Ed. Gente Nueva, Havana, 1977; First Mention, UNEAC Ismaelillo Competition, Ed. Gente Nueva, Havana, 1981; selected for "The Most Beautiful Book," Havana, 1982; Mention, International Exposition of Art in Books, Leipzig, RDA, 1982; selected for Ten Best Books for Children, Banco del Libro, Caracas, Venezuela, 1982; Cuban Literature Forum comentator, 1983; Second Prize, Musical Show Competition, 1983; UNEAC La Rosa Blanca Prize, 1988, 1991; April Prize, 1989; *Cantares de la América Latina y el Caribe*, selected for the three best books edited in Cuba, International Library for Adolescents, Munich, 1986; Special Recognition, Ediciones Gente Nueva, Havana, 1989; Diploma Centenario *La Edad de Oro*, Minister of Culture, Havana, 1989; president, IBBY of Cuba, 1990.

WRITINGS:
Los poemas cantarines. Havana: Ed. Unión, 1975.
Cantares de la América Latina y el Caribe. Havana: Ed. Casa de las Américas, 1982. Also Havana: Ed. Pueblo y Educación, 1990.
Los alegres cantares de Piquiturquino. Havana: Ed. Gente Nueva, 1988. Co-written with Mary Nieves Díaz. *El escarabajo Miguel y las hormigas locas.* Havana: Ed. Unión, 1988.
Los Chichiricú del charco de la jícara. Havana: Ed. Casa de las Américas, 1988. Also *Os Chichiricos do Charco da Xicara.* Trans. to Portuguese by Ana María Machado. Sao Paulo: Ed. Klaxon, 1986.
Los pequeños poemas del abuelo cantarín. Havana: Ed. Gente Nueva, 1988.
Las increíbles andanzas de Chirri: Cuentos de detectives para niños. Havana: Ed. Gente Nueva, 1989.

SIDELIGHTS: "I write for children—poems and narrative—because of the necessity I feel to communicate with them, to affirm through poetic language in my fantastic and playful works universal moral truths, without falling into direct didactic speech or simple moralizing. My favorite themes and sources of inspiration are all things that are interesting, can make children smile, and can make them better people. Nevertheless, I prefer themes drawn from folklore because they do not have national or international boundaries, and because in folklore, as Gabriela Mistral says, one finds all the nourishment one needs to feed the minds of the young."

CRITICAL SOURCES:
Mirta Aguirre. *Casa.* 94-99, January-December 1976.
Jaime Sarusky. *Bohemia.* February 20, 1976.
Basilia Papastamatiu. *Juventud Rebelde.* March 9, 1982.
Enrique Pérez Díaz. *La Tribuna de La Habana.* July 20, 1982.
Alejandro G, Alonso. *Cartelera.* 107, March 15, 1984.
Dinorath do Valle. *Diário da Regiao.* 14/2, Sao Paulo, 1984.

Her work is discussed in numerous articles that have been published since 1990, principally in the newspapers and journals here cited, as well as in the journal *Granma.*

CANELA GARAYOA, Mercè (1956-)

PERSONAL DATA: Born July 11, 1956, in Sant Guim, Catalonia, she is the daughter of Magí Canela Gasol and María los Ángeles Garayoa Perdigó. *Education:* Graduated with a degree in philosophy and letters from the Universidad Autónoma de Barcelona.

ADDRESS: (Home) Avenue Slegers 108, 1200 Brussels, Belgium. Telephone: 7714893. (Office) Comission des Communautés Européennes, 200 rue de la Loi, 1049 Brussels, Belgium. Telephone: 2360567.

CAREER: Librarian at the Universidad Autónoma de Barcelona; document specialist for the Commission of European Communities.

PROFESSIONAL ORGANIZATIONS: Asociación de Escritores en Lengua Catalana; Sociedad Catalana de Arqueología; Asociación de Espectadores del Teatro Libre de Barcelona; Europe Tiers Monde; Médecins Sans Frontieres.

AWARDS, HONORS: Josep Ma. Folchi, Torres Prize, 1976; Critics' Award from *Serra d'Or*, 1981; L'Esparver Award, 1982; Guillem Cifré de Colonya Prize, 1983; Lola Anglada Prize, 1984; El Vaixell de Vapor Award, 1990.

WRITINGS:
  ¿De quién es el bosque? Trans. by María del Carmen Rute. Barcelona: Ed. La
    Galera, 1976.
  El anillo del mercader. Trans. by María Luisa Lissón. Barcelona: Ed. La Galera,
    1977.
  Utinghami, el rey de la niebla. Trans. by Joles Sennell. Barcelona: Ed. La Galera,
    1979.
  Eloy un día fue música. Trans. by José A. Pastor Cañada. Barcelona: Ed. La Galera,
    1981.
  En una mano el sol y en la otra la luna. Trans. by María Eugenia Rincón. Barcelona:
    Ed. Argos-Vergara, 1982.
  Asperú, juglar embrujado. Trans. by Jesús Ballaz Zabalza. Barcelona: Ed. La Galera,
    1983.
  Un gato en el tejado. Trans. by Mercedes Caballud. Barcelona: Ed. La Galera, 1983.
  Globo de luna llena. Trans. by Julia Goytisolo. Barcelona: Ed. Argos-Vergara, 1983.
  Pedro pícaro. Trans. by José A. Pastor Cañada. Barcelona: Ed. La Galera, 1983.
  Los siete enigmas del iris. Trans. by Angelina Gatell. Barcelona: Ed. La Galera,
    1984.
  La oca de oro. Trans. by José A. Pastor Cañada. Barcelona: Ed. La Galera, 1984.
  El huevo de cristal. Trans. by Angelina Gatell. Barcelona: Ed. La Galera, 1987.
  Nicolasa, muñeca de hierro. Trans. by Carme Pallach. Barcelona: Ed. Teide, 1987.

The work of Mercé Canela is originally written in Catalan. The books here cited are translations into Spanish. Her works have also been translated into Basque and Gallego.

SIDELIGHTS: "Each time I am asked, I hesitate more to try to give rational motives for the act of writing. The first answer that I am capable of giving must be that for me, writing is a pleasure and a necessity. I am interested in all themes and anything can serve me as a source of inspiration. Most of my work so far has been fantasy literature, and at times I have used the elements of popular narrative, but I have also written realistic and historical works."

CRITICAL SOURCES:
Pep Albanell. *Catalan Writing 4.* Barcelona: Institución de las Letras Catalanas, 1990.

CAÑIZO (PERATE), José Antonio del (1938-)

PERSONAL DATA: Born January 5, 1938, in Valencia, Spain, the son of José and Lucila. His wife is María Luisa Nadal; Miguel, Elena, and Carlos are his children. *Education:* Ph.D. in agricultural engineering.

ADDRESS: (Home) Navarra 18, 29017 Malaga, Spain. Telephone: 2292135. (Office) Avenida de la Aurora 47, 4a., 29002 Malaga, Spain. Telephone: 2324516.

CAREER: He has worked in his professional field as the director of Jardines Costa del Sol and the supervisor of sanitation for the Minister of Agriculture of Malaga.

PROFESSIONAL ORGANIZATIONS: Asociación Nacional de Amigos del Libro Infantil y Juvenil; founder of the Asociación Malagueña de Amigos del Libro Infantil y Juvenil (AMALIJ).

AWARDS, HONORS: Second Place, National Award for Literature, 1978; Second Prize, Gran Angular Competition, 1981; Lazarillo Prize, 1981; Third Prize, Gran Angular Competition, 1982; Elena Fortún Prize, 1990; included for six years in *White Ravens.*

WRITINGS:
Las fantásticas aventuras del caballito gordo. Barcelona: Ed. Noguer, 1980.
Las cosas del abuelo. Barcelona: Ed. Noguer, 1982.
El maestro y el robot. Madrid: Ediciones SM, 1983.
A la busca de Marte el guerrero. Barcelona: Ed. Noguer, 1984.
Un león hasta en la sopa. Madrid: Ediciones SM, 1984.
El pintor de recuerdos. Madrid: Ediciones SM, 1986.

Oposiciones a la bruja. Madrid: Ed. Anaya, 1987.
Con la cabeza a pájaros. Madrid: Ediciones SM, 1988.
Calavera de borrico y otros cuentos populares. Zaragoza: Ed. Edelvives, 1988.
Inventando el mundo. Madrid: Ed. Anaya, 1989.
Los jíbaros. Madrid: Ed. Alfaguara, 1990.

SIDELIGHTS: "I write because I enjoy doing it, because there are more than 600,000 people who have read my books, and because I believe that it is very important to promote a love of reading in the new generations. A person who speaks better, writes better, thinks better, and has more critical sense is more independent and definitely more free. In my books I combine my huge imagination, humor, fantasy, and poetry with the denouncement of some of the crimes of our age: dehumanization, the exchange of armaments for profit, dictatorship, terrorism, the abandonment of the elderly, and so on. These themes, sufficiently current for the realistic portrayal of children today, also deal with another current style, fantasy literature, which includes aspects of the absurd, or 'nonsense.' It is something that is becoming abundant and has been baptized 'uncompromising literature.' "

CRITICAL SOURCES: Cultural and literary reviews in newspapers and magazines, including *El País*, *ABC*, *Ya* of Madrid, and *Sur* of Malaga.

CAPDEVILA (i VALLS), Roser (1939-)

PERSONAL DATA: Born January 23, 1939, in Barcelona, Spain; Felip and Carmen are her parents; Joan is her husband; and Anna, Teresa, and Helena are her daughters. *Education:* Fine arts.

ADDRESS: (Home) Paseo San Gervasio 72, 08022 Barcelona, Spain. Telephone: 2119172.

CAREER: Teacher, painter, print designer, and illustrator of books for children.

PROFESSIONAL ORGANIZATIONS: Asociación Profesional de Ilustradores de Cataluña.

AWARDS, HONORS: People's Choice Award of Catalonia, 1977; *Serra d'Or* Award, 1975, 1976. She has also received various awards in Spain and Japan. Her work has been selected for several international expositions.

ILLUSTRATIONS:

Gaudrat, M. Agnes. *"Los días diferentes"* (6 titles). Barcelona: Ed. La Galera.

Ribas, Teresa. *"Miremos" (6 titles),* Barcelona: Ed. La Galera.

Ballestrín, Sergio. *Los Sarrampinas.* Barcelona: Ed. La Galera.

Ramón, Elisa. *La derrota de Gustavo.* Ed. Ángulo.

Company, Mercè. *"Las tres mellizas"* (10 titles). Ed. Planeta.

Company, Mercè. *"Las tres mellizas y . . ."* (9 titles). Ed. Planeta.

Larreula, Enric. *"La bruja aburrida"* (8 titles). Ed. Planeta.

Company, Mercè. *"La pandilla y la canguro"* (6 titles). Ed. Planeta.

Martínez, María. *"Hablemos de . . ."* (11 titles). Barcelona: Ed. Destino.

Lamuza, Ampar. *La familia feroz.* Barcelona: Ed. Aliorna.

Sennell, Joles. *La rosa de Sant Jordi.* Barcelona: Ed. Cruilla. Col. Barco de Vapor.

Larreula, Enric. M*elisa.* Barcelona: Ed. Argos-Vergara.

Sennell, Joles. *K.W.A.* Barcelona: Ed. Teide. Col. "La Peonza."

Larreula, Enric. *La familia de setas.* Barcelona: Ed. Teide. Col. "La Peonza."

De la Fontaine, Jorge. *El lobo y el caballo.* Parramón: Ed. Multilibro. Col. "Fábulas y Leyendas."

Cela, Camilo José. *Las orejas del niño Raúl.* Ed. Debate.

Cuadernos de verano 1 y 2. Madrid: Ed. Anaya.

WRITINGS AND ILLUSTRATIONS:

Capdevila, Roser. *¡No me dejes solo!* Barcelona: Ed. Destino.

Capdevila, Roser. *La máquina de coser.* Barcelona: Ed. Destino. Col. Apeles Mestres.

Capdevila, Roser. *La historia de botones.* Barcelona: Ed. Argos-Vergara. Col. "El Drac Vermell."

Capdevila, Roser. *La familia bus.* Tokyo: Ed. Gakken.

Capdevila, Roser. *"La jirafa Palmira"* (6 titles). Tokyo: Ed. Gakken.

Roser Capdevila has illustrated books for publishers in France, Germany, Austria, Italy, Canada, Belgium, Japan, and the Scandinavian countries. All of her work has been translated from Catalan, her native language, into various languages. The titles here cited are translations into Spanish.

SIDELIGHTS: Roser Capdevila has learned much about children; she has dedicated many years creating and teaching classes about drawing. Since 1980 she has dedicated herself exclusively to writing and illustrating books, preferably for children, although she at times illustrates popular works for adolescents and adults.

CARBÓ, Joaquím (1932-)

PERSONAL DATA: Born August 24, 1932, in Caldes de Malavella, Catalonia, Spain, the son of Francesc and María. He is married to María Rosa and he has one child, Maurici. *Education:* Holds a professorship in business.

ADDRESS: (Office) San Antoni M., Claret 324, puerta 48, 08026 Barcelona, Spain. Telephone: 4553920.

CAREER: Administrator at a savings and investment firm between 1949 and 1989.

PROFESSIONAL ORGANIZATIONS: Asociación de Escritores en Lengua Catalana; Catalan PEN Club; Asociación Catalana de Amigos del Libro Infantil.

AWARDS, HONORS: Josep Ma. Folch i Torres Prize, 1969; Critics' Award for *Serra d'Or*, 1978; People's Choice Award, 1981; Joaquím Ruyra Prize, 1981; Guillem Cifre de Colonya Prize, 1985; Critics' Award for *Serra d'Or*, 1991.

WRITINGS:

Novels:
La pandilla de los diez. Trans. by Emilio Sarto. Barcelona: Ed. La Galera, 1970.
Y tú, ¿qué haces aquí? Trans. by María del Carmen Rute. Barcelona: Ed. La Galera, 1970.
Los perros salvajes. Trans. Angelina Gatell. Barcelona: Ed. La Galera, 1983.
Miguel en el asfalto. Trans. by Angelina Gatell. Barcelona: Ed. La Galera, 1986.
Felipe Marlot investiga. Trans. by Jesús Ballaz, illust. by Mónica Echevarría. Zaragoza: Ed. Edelvives, 1988.
Felipe Marlot detective. Trans. by Jesús Ballaz. Barcelona: Ed. Edelvives, 1988.
La casa bajo la arena. Trans. by Inés Bayona. Barcelona: Ed. Aliorna, 1988.
¡Corre, Isabel, corre! Trans. by Isabel Abad. Barcelona: Ed. La Galera, 1989.
Operación Moscardón. Madrid: Ed. Anaya,1992.

Theater:
Las armas de Bagatela. Trans. by Antonio Redondo. Barcelona: Ed. La Galera, 1974.
El jardín de Hue-le-bien. Trans. by María José Hayles. Barcelona: Ed. La Galera, 1975.

Short novel:
Filo y su jardimóvil. Trans. by José A. Pastor Cañada. Barcelona: Ed. La Galera, 1982.

Comic book:
La casa bajo la arena. Trans. by D. Bas. Barcelona: Ed. Oikos-Tau, 1969.

Joaquím Carbó is also the author of anthologies, prologues, novels for adults, and adaptations of classical literature for children. He has written over 400 works, including stories, articles, interviews, and screenplays. His works are originally published in Catalan. The citations here listed are translations into Spanish.

SIDELIGHTS: "My literary vocation is, as is apparent, the product of much reading. One of my strongest influences, however, was outside literature: since I was very young I felt the need to participate in the communal life of my culture and I wanted to demonstrate that in my language—in Catalan—which was oppressed and marginalized by the Francoist dictatorship, we were yet able to express the same things as in any other language. Later, I converted this passion toward writing. Reality is the constant source of my stories. Everything that I see, feel, read, hear, observe, or imagine can serve as the basis for a story as long as I am capable of giving it narrative form. My imagination arranges it without diverting it toward the fantastic. I wish that I were a better narrator of adventures. In my books for adults I try to make adventures seem more difficult than simply to live: to make it to the end of the month, to survive."

CRITICAL SOURCES:
Albert Jané. "Joaquím Carbó, A Writer for an Audience," *Catalan Writing.* 4.
Albert Jané. "Narrador per a nois i noies," *Faristol.* 4.
Emili Teixidor. "La casa sota la sorra," *Catalan Writing.* 2.
Josep Faulí. "Una mosca apellidada Lovecraft," *La Vanguardia.* September 27, 1991.

CÁRDENAS (GARCÍA), Magolo (Magdalena Sofía) (1950-)

PERSONAL DATA: Born December 25, 1950, in Saltillo, Coahuila, Mexico. Her parents are Oscar R. Cárdenas and Carmen García. She is the mother of Esteban Sheridan Cárdenas. *Education:* She holds a licenciate in Hispanic language and literature.

ADDRESS: (Home) Francisco Coss y Alvaro Obregón, Saltillo, Coahuila, Mexico. Telephone: 173618. (Office) Dirección de Recreación y Cultura, Presidencia Municipal, Saltillo, Coahuila, Mexico. Telephone: 128766.

CAREER: Professor of literature, librarian, style advisor, editor, illustrator of books for children, and director of culture and recreation for the Municipality of Saltillo.

PROFESSIONAL ORGANIZATIONS: IBBY of Mexico.

AWARDS, HONORS: IBBY International Award to the Best Book for Children in Mexico, 1990.

WRITINGS:
Celestino y el tren. Ed. Novaro, 1982. Also Mexico: Secretaría de Educación Pública, 1986; Ed. Scott Foresman, 1985.
El tesoro de Don Te. Ed. Novaro, 1983. Also Ed. Houghton Mifflin, 1987.
Nuestros vecinos de ayer. Saltillo: Archivo Municipal, 1985.
La luna Iloteria. Mexico: Secretaría de Educación Pública, 1984.
Lucía y los cuarenta gordinflones. CIDCLI, 1987.
La zona del silencio. Ed. Patria, 1984.
Biografías inconclusas. Saltillo: Ayuntamiento de Saltillo, 1984.
Querido Señor Presidente. Saltillo: Ayuntamiento de Saltillo, 1984.
No era el único Noé. Mexico: Secretaría de Educación Pública, 1990.
Pero si a mí me gustaban los Panchos. Coahuila: Universidad Autónoma de Coahuila, 1989.

SIDELIGHTS: "I have written for children since my son was born in 1980. I think that I write fundamentally for nostalgia; through writing I try to recover something of my childhood, to bridge, if only for a moment, the chasm that separates me from it. I also write for the great pleasure that it gives to me. My favorite themes stem from history. I enjoy encountering little-known figures and scenes in actual history and recreating them; I invent a life, an atmosphere, a texture, a particular character."

CARVAJAL VALENZUELA, Víctor Enrique (1944-)

PERSONAL DATA: Born July 11, 1944, in Santiago, Chile. His parents are Víctor Carvajal and Niliana Valenzuela. He is married to Patricia Álvarez, and they have one child, Paulo. *Education:* Studies at the schools of journalism and audiovisual media at the Universidad Técnica Estado; studies of dramatic art at the Universidad de Chile.

ADDRESS: (Home) Los Espinos 3064 A, Macul, Santiago, Chile. Telephone: 2388365.

CAREER: Actor in independent companies and for television, now a full-time writer of literature for children and adolescents.

PROFESSIONAL ORGANIZATIONS: IBBY of Chile.

AWARDS, HONORS: Barco de Vapor Award, 1984; Honorable Mention, National Drama Competition, Universidad Católica de Chile, 1985; Honorable Mention, in the Theatrical Competition, Northeastern Illinois University, 1988.

WRITINGS:
Chante, chante Adriana (drama). Lyon: Cahiers du Soleil Debout, 1976.
Una muñeca llamada Esperanza. Berlin: Ed. Henschelverlag, 1977.
Cuentatrapos (cuento). Madrid: Ed. SM, 1985.
Chipana. Madrid: Ediciones SM, 1988.
Fray Andrés, otra vez. Santiago, Chile: Ed. Marasul, 1989.
Sakanusoyin, el cazador de tierra de fuego.

SIDELIGHTS: "I write from necessity. My themes are related to the works that have had the largest impact on me. They arise from life itself and from the things that I can see with my imagination—and those things I play with, because reality is as beautiful to me as fantasy and I do not write fantasy without relating it to reality. My characters are profoundly human. I am more interested in everyday heroes than in mythic or fantastic ones. At the moment, my great interest is the ecology and the preservation of the natural environment. Additionally, I want to increase the young reader's interest in the aboriginal cultures of my country and my continent."

CASTELLÓ YTURBIDE, Teresa
see CORONA, Pascuala (Teresa Castelló Yturbide)

CASTRILLÓN ZAPATA, Silvia (1942-)

PERSONAL DATA: Born December 5, 1942, in Medellin, Colombia, she is the daughter of Francisco Luis Castrillón and Ana Zapata. She has two children, Pablo and Manuela Miranda. *Education:* She holds a degree in library science.

ADDRESS: (Home) Carrera 24 no. 39A-36, Bogota, Colombia. Telephone: 2447885. (Office) Calle 74 no. 14-27, Bogota, Colombia. Telephone: 3107811, 3103332.

CAREER: Librarian and editor; executive director of FUNDALECTURA (Foundation for the Strengthening of Reading).

PROFESSIONAL ORGANIZATIONS: Asociación Colombiana de Bibliotecarios (ASCOLBI).

AWARDS, HONORS: Luis Florén Prize (library science).

WRITINGS:
Cúcuru mácara. Bogota: Ed. Norma, 1987.
Tope tope tun. Bogota: Ed. Norma, 1987.
Adivíname ésta. Bogota: Ed. Norma, 1988.

SIDELIGHTS: "Actually, my work in the field of literature for children is reduced to the investigation and compilation of rhymes, word games, riddles, and bits of popular folklore. I write it simply because I enjoy to and because there is a great lack of it in my country."

CELA, Camilo José (1916-)

PERSONAL DATA: Born May 11, 1916, in Iria Flavia, La Coruña, Spain, the son of Camilo and Camila Enmanuela. He is married to María del Rosario Conde Picavea and has a son, Camilo José. *Education:* Attended the University of Madrid from 1933 to 1936 and from 1939 to 1943.

ADDRESS: (Home) La Bonanova, 07015 Palma de Mallorca, Spain.

CAREER: Writer; publisher and editor of *Papeles de Son Armadans,*1956-79.

PROFESSIONAL ORGANIZATIONS: Real Academia Española; Real Academia Gallega; Hispanic Society of America; American Association of Teachers of Spanish and Portuguese.

AWARDS, HONORS: Nobel Prize for Literature, 1989; National Award for Literature, 1984; Critics' Award, 1955; Honorary Doctorates from Syracuse University, 1964, University of Birmingham, 1976, University of Santiago de Compostela, 1979, University of Palma de Mallorca, 1979, John F. Kennedy University, and Interamericana University.

WRITINGS:
Las orejas del niño Raúl. Illust. by Roser Capdevila. Madrid: Ed. Debate, 1985.
Vocación de repartidor. Illust. by Montse Ginesta. Madrid: Ed. Debate, 1985.

Camilo José Cela has written more than fifty novels, books of stories, plays, collections of essays, books of cultural criticism, and books of poetry. He is widely considered one of the most important writers to emerge in Spain in this century. The above-cited works are written and illustrated for children.

SIDELIGHTS: Cela's importance to the twentieth-century Spanish novel cannot be underestimated. He has virtually defined its place in world literature. His novels are uncompromising and difficult to classify: he utilizes styles including stream of consciouness, picaresque, realism, and existentialism, and created his own style, *Tremendismo.* He focuses, in a way often considered vulgar, on the marginal, loneliness, decay, and the grotesque, and his stories frequently follow vicious and remorseless characters. Nevertheless, he is supremely humane in his analyses of the human condition.

In *Forms of the Novel in the Work of Camilo José Cela*, David William Foster comments, that Cela "has chosen to make his career one of complete reexamination and reconsideration of the novel as an art form." The two works for which he has received the most critical acclaim have been *La familia de Pascual Duarte* and *La colmena*. His other works, however, have been equally ambitious in their investigation of narrative form and philosophical ideals. Foster notes that Cela's novels since *Mrs. Calwell habla con su hijo* have been experiments with a new kind of novel. These works deemphasize plot as the source of dramatic movement and instead favor a fragmentary or artificial pastiche of events.

Cela's name is synonymous with the experimental novel. He has been at the vanguard of writers who have revised traditional definitions of the novel to allow greater freedom of expression and greater social and political significance of subject.

CRITICAL SOURCES:
Kirsner, Robert. *The Novels and Travels of Camilo José Cela.* University of North
    Carolina Press. 1964.
Foster, David. William. *Forms of the Novel in the Work of Camilo José Cela.*
    University of Missouri Press, 1967.
McPheeters, D.W. *Camilo José Cela.* Twayne, 1969.

CERNA GUARDIA, Juana Rosa (1926-)

PERSONAL DATA: Born July 31, 1925, in Huaraz, Ancash (today, the Chavin Region), Peru, her parents were José Vidal Cerna González and Luisa Natalia

Guardia. *Education:* Studies in education and journalism.

ADDRESS: (Home) 28 de Julio 437, Barranco, Lima 4, Peru. Telephone: 671098.

CAREER: Professor at diverse institutions.

PROFESSIONAL ORGANIZATIONS: Instituto de Cultura Ancashina (INCA); Instituto de Nacional Mariscal Luzuriaga; Center of Information and Documentation of Peruvian Literature for Children and Adolescents.

AWARDS, HONORS: International Prize for Poetic Writing about Encyclica Pious XII, 1955; Award for Poetry, Piura, 1958; Honorable Mention, Teatro Escolar, 1963; National Award for Literature for Children, Juan Volatín, 1966; Second Prize for Poetry, NISEI, Peru, 1968; First Prize, International Competition of Literature for Children, CRAV, Chile, 1968; Second Prize, Lazarillo Awards, Spain, 1968; Honorable Mention for the Fomento a la Cultura José María Eguren Prize, 1968; Honorable Mention for the Juegos Florales Magisteriales, 1970; National Juan Volantín Prize, 1972; Second Prize, Ricardo Palma Awards, 1972; César Barranquino Prize, 1989; Laureles Magisteriales Ancashinos Award.

WRITINGS:
El Perú y sus recursos naturales. Peru: Ed. Ministerio de Educación, 1963.
Los días de carbón. Talleres Gráficos P.L. Villanueva, 1966.
El hombre de paja. Ed. Horizonte, 1973.
Los niños del Perú y sus poetas (anthology). Ed. Nueva Educación, 1976.
Tataramundo y Munduriviejo (oral tradition). Talleres Gráficos P.L. Villanueva, 1989.
Al alcance de los niños I y II. Talleres Gráficos P.L. Villanueva, 1990.
She has also published poetry for adults and instructional works.

SIDELIGHTS: "I was born with the undeniable vocation of a writer. I have written since I was a girl. My first works, anecdotes, prizes, and motivations date from primary school. The most valuable evidence of my early emerging vocation is that from my earliest writings, my professors did not believe that I accomplished my writing alone. I feel the urgency, the necessity, to write. From inside me there grows a taproot of emotion and love that is the source of my writing. I am thankful that I have an active imagination. I consider it one of the greatest gifts to humanity, without which nothing could come into being. As a child I was very receptive. To this I owe the ease and candor with which I write."

CLEMENTE, Horacio (Domingo) (1930-)

PERSONAL DATA: Born November 25, 1930, in Buenos Aires, Argentina. His parents are Carmelo and Juana Catalina. He is married to Estela Ida Espezel, and they have two children, Marina and Pablo.

ADDRESS: (Home) Virrey Olaguer y Feliú 2628, 13 B, 1426 Buenos Aires, Argentina. Telephone: 7835335. (Office) Billinghurst 228, 1174 Buenos Aires, Argentina. Telephone: 8627233.

CAREER: Journalist and photographer; has worked for the Centro Editor de América Latina. Also works freelance.

AWARDS, HONORS: Fellowship from the National Fund for the Arts; Third Prize, Municipal Poetry Award; selected by the ALIJA as one of the best works of literature for children of the past five years.

WRITINGS:
El ojo (poems). Ed. Seijas-Goyanarte, 1964.
Cuentos de Las mil y una noches (adaptation for children). Centro Editor, 1967.
Festival de Walt Disney. Ed. Sigmar, 1967.
Fotografiando en Buenos Aires. 1987.
Historias de perros y otras personas. Buenos Aires: Ed. Libros del Quirquincho, 1988.
El obelisco de Buenos Aires y otras extravagancias. Buenos Aires: Ed. Libros del Quirquincho, 1990.
El zoológico por afuera. Buenos Aires: Ed. Libros del Quirquincho, 1991.
Vidas de artista. Buenos Aires: Ed. Libros del Quirquincho, 1992.
La gallina de los huevos duros. Buenos Aires: Ed. Sudamericana, 1990.

Horacio Domingo Clemente has also published two collections of letters.

SIDELIGHTS: "I am concerned with the power of delinquents, the advance of dehumanization, the flagrance and crimes of the powerful. Many things occupy my thought: the ideal of utopia, ingenuity of the disenfranchised, the faith of those without strength. My sources of inspiration are life, humanity, my own experiences, and dreams. My favorite theme is that of the everyday hero."

CLIMENT (CARRAU), Paco (Francisco) (1945-)

PERSONAL DATA: Born January 25, 1945, in Valencia, Spain, the son of Francisco and María. He has a son, Jaime. *Education:* Teacher's certification.

ADDRESS: (Home) Lagasca 131, 28006 Madrid, Spain. Telephone: 4114853. (Office) TVE, Emisora s/n, Pozuelo de Alarcón, 28023 Madrid, Spain. Telephone: 3469161.

CAREER: Programmer for Spanish television; he has worked in the Department of Programs for Children since 1975.

PROFESSIONAL ORGANIZATIONS: OEPLI, Madrid; Antislavery Society, London.

AWARDS, HONORS: Second Place, National Award for Literature for Children, Spain, 1980; Lazarillo Award for Literature for Children and Young People, Spain, 1985.

WRITINGS:
La gripe del Búfalo Bill. Illust. by Ángel Esteban. Valladolid: Ed. Miñón, 1981.
Las otras minas del Rey Salomón. Illust. by Ángel Esteban. Madrid: Ed. Escuela
    Española, 1985.
El tesoro del Capitán Nemo. Barcelona: Ed. Noguer, 1986.
Picasso pinta a Pinocho. Zaragoza: Ed. Edelvives, 1987.
Potón el gato no quiere pato. Madrid: Ed. Magisterio, 1987.
Potón el gato y la escuadrilla gansa. Madrid: Ed. Magisterio, 1990.
Potón el gato y los niños mapaches. Madrid: Ed. Magisterio, 1993.

SIDELIGHTS: "A pen and a blank piece of paper are all that are required to create whatever the imagination can supply. Anything can be written. If you decide that stones can talk, they talk; if horses need to appear green, they are green. No, there are no limits to this vocation, and it allows a stupendous amount of entertainment and liberty, difficult to find in other activities. But then writing is difficult, physically as well as mentally."

CRITICAL SOURCES:
Reseña. March 6, 1983.
El País. June 30, 1985; July 21, 1985; December 28, 1985.
Pilar Ortega. *Ya.* December 10, 1985.
Carlos Murciano. *ABC.* July 14, 1986; March 10, 1990.
Antonio García Tejeiro. *Faro de Vigo.* October 14, 1986.
Jesús Ballaz Zabalza. *J20.* Barcelona: October 1986.
Comunidad Escolar. December 2, 1987.

Marta Prieto Sarro. *Diario de León*. March 1, 1987.
Boletín de la Asociación Española de Amigos del Libro Infantil y Juvenil 2. March 1990.
Francisco Cubells Salas. *Comunidad Educativa* 187. April 1991.

COLCHADO LUCIO, Oscar (1947-)

PERSONAL DATA: Born November 14, 1947, in Huallanca, Ancoshi, Peru, he is the son of Ambrosio and Justa. His wife is Irene, and they have three daughters, Marlene, Patricia, and Jessica.

ADDRESS: (Home) Fray Bartolomé Herrera 132, Urb. Ingeniería, 5a. etapa San Martín de Porres, Peru. Telephone: 33471056.

CAREER: Professor of language and literature.

PROFESSIONAL ORGANIZATIONS: APLIJ (Peruvian Association of Literature for Children and Adolescents).

WRITINGS:
Cholito en los Andes mágicos. 1986, 1988, 1990.
Tras las huellas de Lucero. 1980, 1990.

COLUCCIO, Félix (1911-)

PERSONAL DATA: Born August 23, 1911, in Buenos Aires, Argentina; his parents were Vicente Coluccio and Catalina Nasso; his wife is María Mercedes Blanco, and his children are Jorge Raúl, Amalia Mercedes, Susana Beatriz, and Marta Isabel. *Education:* Professor of geography and physical education.

ADDRESS: (Home) Hipólito Irigoyen 1796,7° piso O, 1089 Buenos Aires, Argentina. Telephone: 408493.

CAREER: Professor; director of the National Fund for the Arts, 1973-76 and 1984-89; Undersecretary of Culture for the Nation, 1974 -75.

PROFESSIONAL ORGANIZATIONS: Academia Nacional de Geografía; Comisión

Internacional Permanente de Folklore; Círculo de Ministros, Secretarios y Subsecretarios de Cultura de la Nación; Fondo Nacional de las Artes.

AWARDS, HONORS: Second Prize shared with National Konnex, literature of folklore, 1960; Decoration from the government of Brazil, 1960; Silvio Romero Medal, Brazil, 1965; Diploma of Honor, International Congress of Folklore, Peru, 1985.

WRITINGS:
Diccionario folklórico argentino. Buenos Aires: Ed. El Ateneo, 1948. Also Buenos Aires: Ed. Plus Ultra, 7th ed., 1992.
Folklore de las Américas (anthology). Buenos Aires: Ed. El Ateneo, 1949.
Cuentos folklóricos. Buenos Aires: Ed. Plus Ultra, 1985.
Cuentos folklóricos iberoamericanos. Buenos Aires: Ed. Plus Ultra, 1988.
Cuentos de Pedro Urdemalas. Buenos Aires: Ed. Plus Ultra, 1989.
Diccionario de creencias y supersticiones argentinas y americanas. Buenos Aires: Ed. Corregidor, 1991.
Diccionario de juegos infantiles tradicionales de América Latina. Buenos Aires: Ed. Corregidor, 1988.
Fiestas y costumbres de Latinoamérica. Buenos Aires: Ed. Corregidor, 1956; 3rd ed., 1992.
Cultos y canonizaciones populares de Argentina. Ediciones del Sol, 1986.
Los potros de la libertad (stories for children and adolescents). Buenos Aires: Ed. Plus Ultra, 1988.
Llamar el alma (stories for adolescents). Buenos Aires: Ed. Braga, 1992.

SIDELIGHTS: "I have always been interested in popular and traditional culture because for fifty years I have been exposed to and have gathered folklore phenomena from Argentina and Latin American, much of which fundamentally constitutes the stories that I write, or various specialized works, as well as the dictionaries used all over Latin America and the greater part of Europe. Our works about folklore have required us to travel to many countries. I have worked in collaboration with my daughters, Marta Isabel, a graduate of folklore and folk dance, Susana Beatriz, a graduate of educational science, and Amalia Mercedes, a professor of geography. Jorge Raúl, a graduate in sociology, has also been entirely dedicated to this profession."

CRITICAL SOURCES:
Horacio Carballal. *La Capital.* Mar del Plata.

Critical works about his writings have also been published by Ñusta de Piorno, from Argentina; Altimar Pimentel, Mario Sputomaior, and Veríssimo de Melo, from

Brasil; and Celso Lara, from Guatemala.

COMPANY (I GONZÁLEZ), Mercè (1947-)

PERSONAL DATA: Born May 19, 1947, in Barcelona, Spain. Her parents are José Company i Torras and Enriqueta González del Egido; she is married to Agustí Asensio i Saurí and has two children, Gisel-la and Nona. *Education:* Academic training achieved through a self-devised curriculum comprised of courses and seminars in drawing, painting, sculpture, the history of art, literature, philosophy, photography, aesthetics, English, Catalan, advertising, marketing, sales, public relations, and screenplay writing for the radio, cinema, and television.

ADDRESS: (Home) Puigmartí 40, 2° 2a., 08012 Barcelona, Spain. Telephone: 2190101. (Office) Puigmartí 22, ent. 2°, Barcelona, Spain. Telephone: 2843721, 2105853. Fax: 2105853

CAREER: Public relations executive and fashion reviewer; journalist; photographer, editor, and screenwriter; writer of literature for children and adolescents. She is the creator and designer of a series of programs for public television directed toward children and young people; she created the *Technical Narratives* method for adults; she participates in debates and discussions on the radio and television, is a juror for numerous literary award organizations, and acts as literary advisor for publishers.

PROFESSIONAL ORGANIZATIONS: Asociación de Escritores en Lengua Catalana; Asociación de Amigos del IBBY. She is a collaborating member of the Casal d'Infants del Raval; the Consell Catalá del Llibre per a Infants, 1984, 1985; and the Junta de l'AELLC, 1987-88.

AWARDS, HONORS: First Prize for Adolescent Painting, Molins de Rei, 1964; Second Prize, Adolescent Painting Competition, Barcelona, 1964; Ciutat d'Olot Award, 1982; Jacme March de Gavá Prize, 1982; Critics' Award from *Serra d'Or*, 1983, 1986; Enric Valor Prize, 1983; Distinction from the Minister of Culture, 1983; White Raven Selection, 1985, 1987, 1990; People's Choice Award of Catalonia, 1986; Award for the Book Best Edited, Ministery of Culture, 1986; Finalist, Vaixell de Vapor Award, 1988; Fellowship for Cinematic Creation from the Institución de Letras Catalanas for writing the screenplay of her novel *La dama del medallón*, 1989.

WRITINGS:
Collections for children,
Los cuentos del tío Agus (4 titles). Trans. by Mercé Company, illust. by Agustí

Asensio. Barcelona: Ed. Eurocromo, 1973.

Ana y Víctor (8 titles). Trans. by Mercé Company, illust. by Agustí Asensio. Barcelona: Ed. Bruguera, 1981.

"Las tres mellizas" (9 titles). Trans. by Mercé Company, illust. by Roser Capdevila. Barcelona: Ed. Arín-Planeta, 1985. Also Trans. into English as *Meet the triplets*. New York: Ed. Derrydale, 1986.

"Los birimboyas" (7 titles). Trans. by Mercé Company, illust. by Agustí Asensio. Barcelona: Ed. Arín, 1986.

"Las tres mellizas y . . ." (10 titles). Trans. by Mercé Company, illust. by Roser Capdevila. Barcelona: Ed. Arín Planeta, 1988.

"Santi y Nona" (10 titles). Trans. by Mercé Company, illust. by Horacio Elena. Barcelona: Ed. Timun Mas, 1992.

"El canguro de la panda pequeña" (7 titles). Trans. by Mercé Company, illust. by Roser Capdevila. Barcelona: Ed. Planeta, 1990.

"En el corazón del bosque" (5 titles). Trans. by Mercé Company, illust. by Agustí Asensio. Barcelona: Ed. Timun Mas, 1990.

"La granja de los artistas" (4 titles). Trans. by Mercé Company, illust. by Mercé Aránega. Barcelona: Ed. Timun Mas, 1990.

"Nana Bunilda" (6 titles), Trans. by Mercé Company, illust. by Agustí Asensio. Barcelona: Ed. Cruilla, 1992.

For youngsters seven to ten:

"Los dos + una" (6 titles). Trans. by Mercé Company, illust. by Agustí Asensio. Barcelona: Ed. Timun Mas, 1989.

"El dragón rojo en acción" (3 titles). Trans. by Mercé Company, illust. by José María Lavarello. Barcelona: Ed. Toray, 1991.

Picture Books:

Bamba, el rey gordo. Illust. by Agustí Asensio. Madrid: Ed. Alfaguara, 1990.

El prisionero del gigante. Trans. by Josep Serret i Grau, illust. by Agustí Asensio. Barcelona: Ed. HYMSA, 1982.

Don Gil y el paraguas mágico. Trans. by Mercé Company, illust. by Agustí Asensio. Mexico, 1990.

La bruja Carracuca. Trans. by Josep Serret i Grau, illust. by Francesc Rovira. Barcelona: Ed. HYMSA, 1983.

La ciudad de las estrellas. Trans. by Julia Goytisolo, illust. by Valentina Cruz. Barcelona: Ed. Argos-Vergara, 1983.

Las peripecias de Don Paco Pelacañas. Trans. by Josep Serret i Grau, illust. by Francesc Rovira. Barcelona: Ed. Destino, 1983.

Historia del paragua. Trans. by Julia Goytisolo, illust. by Agustí Asensio. Barcelona: Ed. Argos-Vergara, 1983.

Charlot. trans. by Josep Serret i Grau, illust. by Violeta Denou. Barcelona: Ed. HYMSA, 1984.

La noche. Trans. by Manuel Serrat, illust. by Valentina Cruz. Barcelona: Ed. Argos-Vergara, 1984.

Don Remigio el campañero. Illust. by Agustí Asensio. Madrid: Ed. Alfaguara, 1984.

Los dientes del león. Trans. by Mercé Company, illust. by Paula Reznicková. Barcelona: Ed. Argos-Vargara, 1984.

Nana Bunilda come pesadillas. Trans. by Manuel Fernández. Madrid: Ediciones SM, 1985; 3rd. ed., 1988.

La estrellita. Trans. by Pilar Giralt, illust. Violeta Denou. Barcelona: Ed. Argos-Vergara, 1985.

El mundo de las cosas perdidas. Trans. by Mercè Company. Ed. Ultramar, 1986.

Las viejecitas del museo. Trans. by Mauricio Wiesenthal, illust. by Valentina Cruz. Barcelona: Ed. HYMSA, 1986.

Guillermo, el deshollinador. Trans. by Mercè Company, illust. by Agustí Asensio. Barcelona: Ediciones HYMSA, 1987.

Ángela Ratón, mensajera exprés. Trans. by Mercè Company, illust. by Agustí Asensio. Gijon: Ed. Júcar, 1987.

En la buhardilla. Trans. by Mercè Company, illust. by Agustí Asensio. Barcelona: Ed. Parramón, 1988.

Huele a primavera. Trans. by Mercè Company. Madrid: Ediciones SM, 1989.

Mmm. Qué rica manzana. Illust. by Agustí Asensio. Madrid: Ediciones SM, Second. ed., 1991.

El gato y el pájaro. Trans. by Mercè Company, illust. by Roser Capdevila. Barcelona: Ed. Toray y RTVE, 1991.

Stories for children seven to ten:

La casa del gatus. Trans. by de Angelina Gatell, illust. by Montse Ginesta. Barcelona: Ed. La Galera, 1984.

La historia de Ernesto. Trans. by Mercè Company. Madrid: Ediciones SM, 7th. ed., 1986.

La reina calva. Trans. by Mercè Company, illust. by Mercè Aránega. Madrid: Ediciones SM, 1988.

Una jaula en el comedor. Trans. by Mercè Company, illust. by Francesc Rovira. Barcelona: Ed. Teide, 1988.

Novels for children over eleven years:

Mi hermano mayor. Trans. by Eric Parellada, illust. by Francesc Rovira. Barcelona: Ed. La Galera, 1985.

¡Los bichos unidos, jamás serán vencidos! Trans. by Mercè Company, illust. by Irene Bordoy. Barcelona: Ed. Plaza & Janés, 1990.

Pegando brincos por ahí. Illust. by Francesc Rovira. Madrid: Ediciones SM, 1989.

Una mentira larga y gordita. Trans. by Mercè Company, illust. by J.M. Lavarello. Barcelona: Ed, Plaza & Janés, 1990.

Stories and novels for young people over fourteen:
La imbécil. Trans. by Mercè Company. Salamanca: Ed. Lóguez, 1987.
Quique, hijo único. Trans. by Mercè Company. Ed. Empuriés-Paidós, 1990.
La presencia. Trans. by Francesc Sales. Barcelona: Ed. Timun Mas, 1989.
La dama del medallón. Trans. by Francesc Sales. Barcelona: Ed. Timun Mas, 1989.
El aviso. Trans. by Francesc Sales. Barcelona: Ed. Timun Mas, 1989.
El mago. Trans. by Francesc Sales. Barcelona: Ed. Timun Mas, 1990
La voz. Trans. by Francesc Sales. Barcelona: Ed. Timun Mas, 1991.

Dramatic works for boys and girls:
La furia de los elementos. Madrid: Ediciones SM, 1991.
Muchos demonios y una bruja. Madrid: Ediciones SM, 1991.
Adivina quién soy. Madrid: Ediciones SM, 1991.
Quiero un bicho que me haga compañía. Madrid: Ediciones SM, 1991.

Screenplays and television series:
¿Quién te quiere, Babel? 1989.
Los cuentos de Nana Bunilda (series: 26 episodes of five minutes each). 1991.

The extensive work of Mercè Company is written in Catalan, with some exceptions in Castilian.

SIDELIGHTS: "When I decided to embark on a literary career, the decision to write for children and young people was made for the following reasons:

—Because I could communicate well with them; I could "feel" what they thought, how they felt, by the way they acted. When introduced to someone five, seven, ten years old I could empathize with that person without the least effort. Thus I thought that I should have particular success in reaching out to them.
—Because I thought that I could contribute much to new minds, the young people, and the enthusiasts who retain part of their childhood. I thought that I could contribute different ways of seeing and understanding life and the world. And above all, I wanted to reaffirm their appreciation of themselves, so they could be who they were, could know and see that the strength, in every sense of the word, was a part of themselves and not foreign to them.
—I wanted to make sure that they would not be left with a single version of facts, as if everything was obvious, analyzable, and apprehensible; there are always more than two points of view.
—I also wanted to give them the concept of liberty, not abstractly, as something far out of reach, but as something that is inside ourselves, that is born within people.
—I wanted to give them alternatives and success in the face of contradiction, if possible; to awaken doubts, give them something to think about.

All of this is what I wanted to give to young people. For the young, at the base of all my stories there lies this very project: to stimulate their boundless imaginations. I play with ideas, situate them in environments, and let my readers have them as their own.

Perhaps this combination is successful, for one can see by my bibliography that the children of Barcelona read with as much enthusiasm as the Japanese, the Germans, or the French. I hope so. I do not, I must stress, dedicate my efforts or my literary creations to adults. Their chronic fear of change and their general apathy strongly encourages me to continue my writing."

CRITICAL SOURCES:
El Periódico. April 26, 1990.
CLIJ 17. May 1990.

CONDEMARÍN, Mabel 1931-

PERSONAL DATA: Born November 3, 1931, in Chile, she is the daughter of Guillermo Condemarín and Amalia Grimberg. She is married to Felipe Alliende and has two children, Felipe and Mabel Alliende Condemarín. *Education:* Secondary school developmental reading California State College, Los Angeles, 1967; master's in educational science, Pontificia Universidad Católica de Chile; candidate for a doctorate in education, University of Wales, Cardiff.

ADDRESS: (Home) Pedro Torres 330, Santiago, Chile. Telephone: 2230120. (Office) Universidad Católica de Chile, Facultad de Educación, Campus Oriente, Santiago, Chile. Telephone: 6983351.
*CAREER: Associate professor in the departm*ent of special education, Universidad Católica de Chile, 1972-92; coodinator of the oral and written language program in the Program for Bettering the Quality of Special Education, 1990-92.

PROFESSIONAL ORGANIZATIONS: International Reading Association; Centro de Estudios y Atención del Niño y la Mujer.

AWARDS, HONORS: Diploma of Recognition and Merit, Universidad de Antioquia, Colombia, 1985; Diploma of Honor, Cámara del Libro, 1991.

WRITINGS:
Hurganito. Santiago, Chile: Ed. Universitaria, 1974.

Lectura temprana. Santiago, Chile: Ed. *Andrés Bello,* 1989.

¿A ver, a ver, vamos a leer? Co-written with C. Beuchat. Santiago, Chile: Ed. Universitaria, 1990.

Juguemos a leer. Santiago, Chile: Salo Editores, 1990.

El zorro, el lobo y otros cuentos. Co-written with C. Beuchat. Santiago, Chile: Ed. *Andrés Bello,* 1990.

Juguemos a escribir, Co-written with V. Galdames and A. Medina. Santiago, Chile: Salo Editores, 1991.

Hato Ambó: Lecturas para niños del jardín infantil. Co-written with R. Morán and S. Martínez. Panamá: Ed. Norma, 1991.

Caracol, caracol, saca tu librito al sol. Co-written with C. Beuchat. Santiago, Chile: Ed. Universitaria, 1992.

She has also published numerous books and articles concerning reading techniques.

SIDELIGHTS: "The principal contents of my works envelop the methodological aspects of developing oral and written language. Works of literature for children are usually referred to as 'easy reading,' that is to say, as reading for children, in that linguistic and conceptual elements are controlled for easier readability, coupled with the selection and/or creation of entertaining plots. My principal interest in writing is to emphasize literacy as a medium for bettering the quality of education for Spanish speaking children."

CORONA, Pascuala (Teresa Castelló Yturbide) (1917-)

PERSONAL DATA: Born March 21, 1917, in Mexico, D.F. Her parents were Alfonso Castelló and Teresa Yturbide. She is married to Mauricio de María y Campos, and they have three children, Teresa, Beatriz, and Alfonso. Education: Advanced studies in plastic arts.

ADDRESS: (Home) Andes 330, Lomas de Chapultepec, 11000 Mexico, D.F. (Office) Telephone: 5202252.

*CAREER: Inves*tigator.

PROFESSIONAL ORGANIZATIONS: PROSEDA.

AWARDS, HONORS: Award from the Mesa Redonda Panamericana for two books of stories.

WRITINGS:
La presencia de la comida prehispánica. Mexico: Edited by BANAMEX.
Los colorantes. Mexico: Edited by Resistol.
Historia y arte de la seda en México.
Sangalote. CIDCLI, 1987.
Cuentos de rancho.
Fiesta.

SIDELIGHTS: "I write because of children and for children."

CRITICAL SOURCES:
Justino Fernández. *Folletín de Investigaciones Estéticas.*

CUADROS LÓPEZ, Luis Alexander (1942-)

PERSONAL DATA: Born May 7, 1942, in Coracora, Ayacucho, Peru. His parents are Luis and Delfina. He is married to Amada and has three children, Nieves, Emma, and Alex. *Education:* Doctorate in education.

ADDRESS: (Home) Avenida N. Ayllón, Mz. F, Lote 22, Chaclacayo, Peru. Telephone: 910052.

CAREER: University professor.

PROFESSIONAL ORGANIZATIONS: APLIJ; Colegio de Doctores en Educación; Asociación Peruana de Estudios Psicopedagógicos.

WRITINGS:
Cuentos paranicochanos.

SIDELIGHTS: "I write because it is necessary to rescue and to preserve the literature of the Andes regions, and of Peru."

CRITICAL SOURCES: Hildebrando Pérez and Huilfredo Capsol value his work for the knowledge and thought related to the Andes and to Quechuan mythology.

DA COLL (RÖSTRÖM), Ivar (1962-)

PERSONAL DATA: Born March 13, 1962, in Bogota, Colombia, he is the son of Alberto Da Coll Cian and Annemarie Röström Trujillo.

ADDRESS: (Office) Calle 80A No. 6-41, Apto. 402, Edificio Santa Mónica, Bogota, Colombia. Telephone: 2175859.

CAREER: Drafting, design, and collaborations for the review of literature for children.

AWARDS, HONORS: Award for the Best Book for Children, FUNDALECTURA, 1989.

WRITINGS AND ILLUSTRATIONS:
Colección "Chigüiro" (6 vols.). Bogota Ed. Norma, 1986.
"Historias de Eusebio" (3 vols.). Bogota Ed. Carlos Valencia, 1989.
"Historias de Hamamelis" (2 vols.). Caracas: Ed. Ekaré, in print.
"Nuevas historias de Chigüiro" (2 vols.). Ed. Norma, in print.

SIDELIGHTS:
"I like ideas that are clear and simple. Everything that one can feel: sadness, happiness, in short, emotions. I like to convert these emotions into stories and to tell them (at least I try to do this) in the simplest form possible. I am inspired by ideas that can help children, by life's experiences, and by my memories of childhood."

DAROQUI, Julia Carmen (1915-)

PERSONAL DATA: Born July 24, 1915, in Ramos Mejía, Buenos Aires, Argentina, she is the daughter of Alberto Daroqui and María Taberner. *Education:* Fine arts and courses in literature.

ADDRESS: (Home) Perón 2527, Buenos Aires, Argentina.

WRITINGS:
Los pollitos que perdieron su voz. Buenos Aires: Ed. Sigmar.
El río que no quiso andar. Buenos Aires: Ed. Sigmar.
Los dos amigos. Buenos Aires: Ed. Sigmar.
Mi primer diccionario. Buenos Aires: Ed. Sigmar.

SIDELIGHTS: "I write children's stories because I like to be around children. My favorite themes derive from this preference, and my source of inspiration is also children. To visit them, to speak to them, to listen to them, to hear their most candid reflections, sincere and ingenious, this is an invaluable source of inspiration. I also love nature, so the magical world of animals will at times invade the realm of my stories. Nature has always been another of my favorite themes."

CRITICAL SOURCES:
El Mundo. October 13, 1963.
Angel Mazzei. *La Nación.* August 7, 1977.
Clarín. October 13, 1977.
La Nación. October 22, 1977.

DE LA CRUZ YATACO, Eduardo Francisco (1944-)

PERSONAL DATA: Born December 21, 1944, in Lima, Peru, he is the son of Félix and Felícita. He is married to Miriam and has four children, César, Alicia, Helena, and Rosa Carla. *Education:* Undergraduate study at the Universidad Mayor de San Marcos, master's degree from the Universidad Garcilaso de la Vega; postgraduate study in Madrid and Malaga, Spain.

ADDRESS: (Home) Prolongación Ayacucho 483-4i, Lima-San Miguel, Peru. Telephone: 639036.

CAREER: University professor, author, and editor.

PROFESSIONAL ORGANIZATIONS: APLIJ; SOPERARTE (Peruvian Association for Education about the Arts); APELEC (Peruvian Association for the Promotion of Reading).

AWARDS, HONORS: INLIL Award for Creative Works for Children.

WRITINGS:
Literatura fantástica del niño. SAGSA, 1988.
Cómo enseñar poesía a niños de 2 a 6 años. EDIPROCSA, 1989.
Razonamiento verbal. EDIPROCSA, 1990.
Cuadernos de creatividad (series: from 2 to 6). EDIPROCSA, 1990.
Lenguaje y literatura, razonamiento verbal y creatividad. EDIPROCSA, 1992.

SIDELIGHTS: "I write from an inclination toward children, education, and the arts. I write in order to spread my thoughts among children, to diseminate these thoughts by creative techniques. I write from an eagerness to bring art, reading, and literature to children. Finally, I write because it is the height of my academic calling."

CRITICAL SOURCES:
Jesús Abel. *La literatura infantil de Perú, América y Europa.*
Roberto Rosario. *La literatura infantil en la educación inicial.*
Luis Chiroque. *Autoeducación.*
Danilo Sánchez. *Literatura infantil, magia y realidad.*

DE SANTIS, Pablo (Ulises María) (1963-)

PERSONAL DATA: Born February 27, 1963, in Buenos Aires, Argentina, the son of Ulises de Santis and Elvira Cazzulino. He has two children, Paulo and Francisco De Santis. *Education:* Letters, Faculty of Philosophy and Letters, Universidad de Buenos Aires.

*ADDRESS: (*Home) Yerbal 969, 6ª 1405 L, Buenos Aires, Argentina. Telephone: 4331347. (Office) Ediciones de la Urraca, Venezuela 842, Buenos Aires, Argentina. Telephone: 3345063.

CAREER: Journalist; screenwriter of short dramas and comedies; editorial supervisor.

AWARDS, HONORS: Award for Short Stories for "Fierro busca dos manos," 1985.

WRITINGS:
Espacio puro de tormenta. Buenos Aires: Ediciones de la Serpiente, 1985.
El palacio de la noche. Buenos Aires: Ediciones de la Flor, 1987.
Desde el ojo del pez. Buenos Aires: Ed. Sudamericana, 1991.
La sombra del dinosaurio. Buenos Aires: Ed. Colihue, 1992.
Pesadilla para hackers. Buenos Aires: Ed. Colihue, 1992.
Historieta y política en los 80 (essay). Buenos Aires: Ed. Letra Buena, 1992.

SIDELIGHTS: "I am interested above all in whatever crosses popular genres (science fiction, terror, fantasy, crime stories) with writing that is as finely crafted as possible, however simple. This makes literature intense. And in regard to literature for young people, I want to write stories that do not make concessions to form or type;

I want them to be 'literature' before they are 'literature for children.' "

DEL AMO (Y GILI), Montserrat

PERSONAL DATA: Born in Madrid, Spain. Her parents are Alvaro del Amo Martínez and Juana Gili Roig. Education: She holds a degree in philosophy and letters, with emphasis in Hispanic literature, from the Universidad Complutense de Madrid.

ADDRESS: (Home) Calle Pilar de Zaragoza 24, 28028 Madrid, España. Telephone: 3568043.

PROFESSIONAL ORGANIZATIONS: Colegio Oficial de Licenciados y Doctores de Madrid; Asociación de Escritores y Artistas Españoles; Asociación Española de Amigos del Libro Infantil y Juvenil.

AWARDS, HONORS: April and May Prizes for the Novel for Adolescents, 1956; Award, 1960; Doncel Award, 1969; Theater Award from AETIJ, 1970; Silver Chest Award, 1970; Golden Ring Award, Popularity of Spanish Television, 1971; CCEI Award for the Best Book of the Year, 1971, 1991; New Futures Award, 1974; National Award for Literature for Children and Adolescents, 1978; nominated for the International Hans Christian Andersen Prize, 1979.

WRITINGS:
Zuecos y naranjas. Barcelona: Ed. La Galera, 1975; 5th. ed., 1990.
La fiesta. Barcelona: Ediciones Edebé, 1982.
Chitina y su gato. Barcelona: Ed. Juventud, 1982.
Me gusta escribir. Madrid: Fundación Germán Sánchez Ruipérez, 1985.
Cuentos para contar. Barcelona: Ed. Noguer, 1986.
Cuentos para bailar. Barcelona: Ed. Noguer, 1987.
El nudo. Barcelona: Ed. Juventud, 1988.
Historia mínima de Madrid. Madrid: Ed. Avapiés, 1988.
Montes, pájaros y amigos. Madrid: Ed. Anaya, 1989.
El fuego y el oro. Barcelona: Ed. Noguer, 1989.
Soñado mar. Madrid: Ed. Susaeta, 1990.
La piedra y el agua. Barcelona: Ediciones Noguer, 1990.
Tres caminos. Madrid: Ed. Susaeta, 1990.
La piedra de toque. Madrid: Ediciones SM, 1991.
La torre. Madrid: Ed. Susaeta, 1990.

Velero de tierra y mar. Madrid: Ed. Magisterio Español, 1990.
Tranquilino rey. Barcelona: Ed. Noguer, 1990.
La casa pintada. Madrid: Ediciones SM, 1990.
La encrucijada. Madrid: Ediciones SM, 1991.
El abrazo del Nilo. Madrid: Ed. Bruño, 1991.
Rastro de Dios. Madrid: Ediciones SM, 1991.
Siempre toca. Madrid: Ediciones Bruño, 1991.

She has also published theater, biographies, works of popular history, and essays.

SIDELIGHTS: "In the moment of creation, I am thinking only of how to achieve a good story, good writing, authentic quality literature. Deciding the age of the readership for a work, classifying it for a specific group of possible readers, these are later decisions, and we are not always succsessful in predicting who will enjoy a particular book. We usually have to adapt once we see who is reading it, and anyway, it is not the author's job to select the reader. I will never ask the age of those who choose my books: all are welcome. The riches of a literary work are manifested in the multiplicity of its possible interpretations. Adult readers can find profound significance in a story that is ostensibly for children, in relation to their sensibilities, their life experiences, or their preferred level of reading. Always in my works there is the valorization of symbolism, the presence of oral narration underlying its written form, and the wish for universal solidarity."

DEL BURGO GONZÁLEZ DE LA ALEJA, Miguela (1953-)

PERSONAL DATA: Born May 16, 1953, in Daimiel, Ciudad Real, Spain, the daughter of Jesús del Burgo Marchán and Miguela González de la Aleja Moreno. She is married to Juan Francisco Madrid González and has one daughter, Lara Magdalena. *Education:* Professor of E.G.B., and education.

ADDRESS: (Home) Alcorisa 49, 28043 Madrid, Spain. Telephone: 7591009, 3880472. (Office) C.P. Vicente Aleixandre Valdemoro, Madrid, Spain. Telephone: 8952919.

CAREER: Professor in several schools.

PROFESSIONAL ORGANIZATIONS: Antiguos Alumnos de la Escuela del Magisterio.

AWARDS, HONORS: Finalist for the Gran Angular Award for the Novel, Ediciones SM, 1987.

WRITINGS:
Adiós, Alvaro. Madrid: Ediciones SM.

She has also published articles in Spanish reviews, including *Alacena*, which specialize in literature for children and young people.

SIDELIGHTS: "My source of inspiration is life. And my life everyday is school and the boys and girls who are my students. My contact with them enriches me greatly, and not only by keeping me up-to-date with their language, pleasures, and intensities . . . (although these are important; our readers must believe in the authenticity of our material) but because by carefully and respectfully observing these developing personalities, these fresh adolescent minds, I see qualities that many believe are lost to the younger generations: loyalty, honor, generosity, friendliness . . . , lives full of strength and impulsiveness. Children fill me with the desire, the motivation, and the themes about which I write."

CRITICAL SOURCES:
Emilio Ortega. *100 Gran Angular.* Madrid: Ediciones SM, 1989.

DEL RÍO, Jocelyn (1950-)

PERSONAL DATA: Born July 27, 1950, in Mexico, D.F., the daughter of Ricardo del Río and Valerie Porter. She is married to Ignacio Gómez-Palacio and has five children, Antonio, Ricardo, Carlos, Bryony, and Branko. Education: Plastic arts.

ADDRESS: (Home) Telephone: 5200292. (Office) Monte Everest 1020, 11000 Mexico, D.F. Telephone: 5206141. Fax: 5206140.

PROFESSIONAL ORGANIZATIONS: SOMART, PRO-AMATE.

AWARDS, HONORS: Antonio Robles Award for Children's Stories, granted by IBBY of Mexico, 1989.

WRITINGS:
El amate. Mexico: Ed. Patria.

SIDELIGHTS: "Being basically a painter and sculptor, I find my work in books is more enjoyable than illustration; but the last book that I wrote interested me outside of any artistic perspective. It was largely concerned with the ecology and with culture. Writing it as a book directed at children was at best a tertiary consideration."

DELGADO CAVILLA, Pedro E(ugenio) (1953-)

PERSONAL DATA: Born March 29, 1953, in Tangier, Morocco, the son of José María and Pilar. He is married to Aranzazu Soler Garijo. *Education:* Three years' study of philosophy and letters, with emphasis on the history of art; two years' study of journalism.

ADDRESS: (Home) Avenida de la Coruña 2, 4° A, San Fernando de Henares, Madrid, Spain. Telephone: 6737667.

CAREER: Cartoonist; illustrator for *El País* and *Atlántida*, illustrator of the publisher Rialp; director of production of a series of animated drawings.

PROFESSIONAL ORGANIZATIONS: Unión de Consumidores de España (UCE); Presencia Gitana; Aldeas Infantiles.

WRITINGS:
Esos adorables monstruos. Ed. Palabra, 1987.
Los buenos modales o cómo impresionar a los demás. Barcelona: Ed. Destino, 1990.
Héroe o la fascinación por la bestia (essay). Ed. Casset.

SIDELIGHTS: "I write for pure enjoyment. My favorite themes are humor, history, and science fiction adventures. Literature and the cinema are my sources of inspiration."

CRITICAL SOURCES:
C. Albert. *Telva.*
C. Palacios. *El País.*
Cuadernos de Literatura Infantil. CLIJ.
Ya.
Mundo Cristiano.

DELGADO MERCADER, Josep Francesc (1960-)

PERSONAL DATA: Born February 6, 1960, in Barcelona, Spain, the son of Francisco and Josefina Delgado.

ADDRESS: Lepant 380, 6° 1a., 08025 Barcelona, Spain.

CAREER: Professor of Catalan language and literature; writer.

PROFESSIONAL ORGANIZATIONS: Asociación de Escritores en Lengua Catalana.

AWARDS, HONORS: Ruyra Award for Literature for Adolescents; Amadeu Oller Prize, Poetry; María Manent Prize, Poetry; Pretérit Incert Prize, Fiction; Al Vent Award, Fiction.

WRITINGS:
Las noches del Everest. Trans. into Spanish by the author. Madrid: Ediciones SM.

Josep Delgado writes in Catalan and has written five other books in that language.

SIDELIGHTS: Josep Delgado writes principally about his travels and mountaineering.

DÍAZ, Gloria Cecilia (1951-)

PERSONAL DATA: Born September 21, 1951, in Calarca, Quindio, Colombia, the daughter of Humberto Díaz and María Helena Ortiz de Díaz. *Education:* She holds a degree in modern languages from the Universidad del Quindio and a doctorate in letters from the Sorbonne in France.

ADDRESS:(Home) 59 rue de Babylone, 75007 Paris, France. Telephone: 47530313.

CAREER: Professor of literature and Spanish at the Universidad de Colombia (1973-82); editor at various publishing houses.

PROFESSIONAL ORGANIZATIONS: Centre de Recherches Interuniversitaires sur del Champs Culturels en Amerique Latine (CRICCAL).

AWARDS, HONORS: Second Prize, Rafael Pombo National Competition, Colom-

bia; First Prize, Barco de Vapor International Competition, Spain, 1985; Second
Prize, Barco de Vapor International Competition, Spain, 1992.

WRITINGS:
El secreto de la laguna. Barcelona: Ed. Argos-Vergara, 1982.
Es el amor que pasa (poems for children). Edited by Ramón Zubiría. Bogota: 1984.
La hora de los cuentos. "La concha de caracol." Colombia: Instituto Colombiano de
   Bienestar Familiar, 1984.
El valle de los cocuyos. Madrid: Ediciones SM, 1986.
La bruja de la montaña. Madrid: Ediciones SM, 1990.

Her stories and poems are included in various literary anthologies.

SIDELIGHTS: "At times I think that literary creation is a mystery. I do not think that
I have a favorite theme or a specific source of inspiration. I love people, nature, and
everything that can help bring humanity toward a true evolution."

DÍAZ (GONZÁLEZ), Joaquín (1942-)

PERSONAL DATA: Born May 14, 1942, in Zamora, Spain, the son of Germán and
Luisa Díaz González. *Education:* Philosophy and letters.

ADDRESS: (Home) Real 4, 47862 Ureña, Valladolid, Spain. Telephone: 983717472.

CAREER: Director of the Center of Ethnography; folklorist and writer.

PROFESSIONAL ORGANIZATIONS: Real Academia de Bellas Artes de la Purísima
Concepción (Valladolid); Sociedad Ibérica de Etnomusicología; Sociedad Española
de Musicología.

AWARDS, HONORS: Doctorate *honoris causa* from the University of Saint Olaf,
Minnesota; Gold Record from the Bienal Internacional del Sonido.

WRITINGS:
Cien temas infantiles. Valladolid: Centro de Estudios Folklóricos y Ayuntamiento,
   1982.
Otros cien temas infantiles. Valladolid: Centro de Estudios Folklóricos y
   Ayuntamiento, 1983.
Cuentos castellanos de tradición oral. Co-written with Maxime Chevalier. Valladolid:

Ed. Ámbito, 1983.
Adivinanzas de Castilla y León. Co-written with Modesto Martín Cebrián. Valladolid: Ed. Nueva Castilla, 1984.
Trabalenguas de Castilla y León. Co-written with Modesto Martín Cebrián. Valladolid: Ed. Nueva Castilla, 1985.
¡Qué zorro eres! Valladolid: Ed. Paulinas, 1991.

He has published more than thirty-five books of lyrical narrative, fiction, romance, and folk songs. His collection of folk music contains more than twenty-five songs.

SIDELIGHTS: "My favorite themes are those that refer to cultural traditions and folklore. When I was very young I began to write articles about this theme. In particular, I am interested in the cultural environment of children, and I have dedicated works about tongue twisters, stories, puzzles, songs, games, and pastimes in an effort to elucidate that environment."

CRITICAL SOURCES:
Peter Kien. *El Norte de Castilla.* June 6, 1992.

DÍAZ MENDEZ, María Nieves (1951-)

PERSONAL DATA: Born March 9, 1951, in Cienfuegos, Cuba, the daughter of Isidro and Rosalina. *Education:* Medical degree, specializing in endocrinology.

ADDRESS: (Home) Calle C 360-4, entre 15 y 17, Vedado, Municipio Plaza, Havana, Cuba. Telephone: 304501. (Office) Hospital Eusebio Hernández. Departamento de Endocrinología. Municipio Marianao, Calle 31, entre 84 y 86; Havana, Cuba. Telephone: 205911.

CAREER: Supervisor of the Provincial Department of Endocrinology, Ciego de Ávila, Cuba, 1983-88; supervisor of the Department of Endocrinology, Hospital Eusebio Hernández, 1988.

PROFESSIONAL ORGANIZATIONS: UNEAC; Unión de Periodistas de Cuba (UPEC); Asociación de Escritores, Sección Literatura Infantil; various medical organizations.

AWARDS, HONORS: First Mention, First of January Competition, 1980; Honorable Mention, *La Edad de Oro* Competition, 1981; First Prize, First of January Competition, 1981; *La Edad de Oro* Award, 1982; Award, at the National Competition of Screenplays for Musicals, 1983; UNEAC Ismaelillo Award, 1983.

WRITINGS:
La extraña ciudad de los pequeños habitantes. Havana: Ed. Gente Nueva, 1983.
Aunabay en el país de los pájaros y frutas. Havana: Ed. Gente Nueva, 1985.
El escarabajo Miguel y las hormigas locas. Co-written with Julia Calzadilla.
     Havana: Ed. Unión de Escritores y Artistas de Cuba, 1988.
De Paula 41 al Museo Casa Natal José Martí. Havana: Ed. Letras Cubanas, 1988.

SIDELIGHTS: "I do not write around a single specific theme, although I incline toward historical fiction and the popularization of science. I write about whatever holds my interest and about what I think should be passed on to children, as much for them to remember as to dream about."

CRITICAL SOURCES:
Diana Sosa. *Granma.* January 26, 1982.
Juventud Rebelde. May 19, 1982; July 19, 1989.
Mariano Rodríguez Solveira. *5 de Septiembre.* Cienfuegos: September 30, 1983.
Fanny Abramovich. *Folha de São Paulo.* April 8, 1984.
Amelia Roque. *5 de Septiembre.* Cienfuegos: May 25, 1984.
Cartelera 214. April 3, 1986.
Granma. April 5, 1986.
Amelia Roque. *5 de Septiembre.* Cienfuegos: July 22, 1986.
E. Labrada. *Adelante.* Camagüey: January 24, 1988.
Waldo González. *Tribuna de La Habana.* November 27, 1988.

DÍAZ PLAJA, Aurora (1913-)

PERSONAL DATA: Born August 7, 1913, in Barcelona, Spain. Her parents were Francisco Díaz Contestí and Josefina Plaja Ibran. She is the widow of Federico Ulsamer Puiggari and has four children, Isabel, Federico, Fernando, and Aurora. *Education:* Degrees from the Escuela Superior de Bibliotecarias and the Escuela Oficial de Periodistas; she holds a diploma in journalism for children and adolescents.

ADDRESS: (Home) Casa Alegre 12, 08023 Barcelona, Spain. (Office) Ateneo Barcelonés, Canuda 6, 08002 Barcelona, Spain. Telephone: 3174904.

CAREER: Director of various libraries, 1933-88; critic of literature for children 1958-; professional advisor at the International Center for Books for Children and Adolescents of the Foundation Germán Sánchez Ruipérez at Salamanca, 1986-. She is also a professor of literature for children.

PROFESSIONAL ORGANIZATIONS: Asociación Nacional de Bibliotecarios y Archiveros; Asociación Española de Amigos del IBBY; Colegio de Periodismo; Colegio de Bibliotecarios; Asociación Española de Críticas Literarias.

AWARDS, HONORS: National Award for the Best Book for Children, 1955; Bibliography Award, 1961; National Critics' Award for Literature for Children; Award from the Journal for Children Project, 1966; Antoni Balmanya Prize, 1969; Award to the Best Critic of Literature for Children, 1978.

WRITINGS:
El rey negro. Ed. Artigas, 1953.
Tres rondalles de Nadal. Barcelona: Casa del Libro, 1954.
La niña de los sueños de colores. Ed. Ferma, 1959.
Los mejores cuentos del mundo. Ed. De Gassó, 1963.
La ruta del sol. Barcelona: Ed. La Galera, 1964.
Entre juego y juego ¡un libro! Barcelona: Ed. La Galera, 1967.
La isla llena (anthology). Barcelona: Ed. Teide, 1967.
La rana que salta. Ediciones B. Igreca, 1968.
La llamita que quería ducharse. Ed. Igraca, 1968.
La hoguera de San Juan. Barcelona: Ed. La Galera, 1969.
Cuento de los meses. Ed. Martín Casanovas, 1972.
El ciempiés descalzo. Producciones Editoriales, 1973.
Cuentos de sol y de sal. Ed. Roma, 1983.
Tres animales chiquitos. Madrid: Ed. Escuela Española, 1984.
Tres juegos del fuego. Barcelona: Ed. HYMSA, 1984.
Aventuras de Till Eulenspiegel. Ed. Lumen, 1987.

SIDELIGHTS: "When I was writing my first stories I had already been published for books about library science. It was my first daughter that provoked my writing books for children. I write what I do because I enjoy it—as much as I enjoy trying to entertain the reader. But I have had to fit the writing of books for children with my works of literary criticism, and have done so in an effort to inspire this: reading for reading's sake. My favorite themes for children are those that are fantastic, and for adolescents they are novelized biographies."

CRITICAL SOURCES:
Fernando Cedán. *Medio siglo de libros infantiles y juveniles en España.*
Autores españoles de literatura infantil. Asociación Española de Amigos del IBBY.

Cien autores de literatura infantil. Asociación de Amigos del IBBY. *Diccionario de autores.* M. Fundación Germán Sánchez Ruipérez, 1986.

DOMÍNGUEZ (HERNÁNDEZ), Carlos Guillermo (1925-)

PERSONAL DATA: Born January 10, 1925, in Gran Canaria, Canary Islands, Spain, the son of Rafael Domínguez Escudero and Catalina Hernández Ojeda; he is married to Mercedes Hernández Martín and has three children, María de la Paz, María de las Mercedes, and Carlos Guillermo. *Education:* Specialist in children's and adolescents' press from the Escuela Oficial de Periodismo.

ADDRESS: (Home) Sorolla 7, Tafira Alta, 35017 Las Palmas de Gran Canaria, Canary Islands, Spain. Telephone: 928350717.

CAREER: Director of several supplements for children in periodicals, including *Diario de la Provincia* and *Diario de Las Palmas*; founder of the journal *Aguayro*, 1976; supervisor of the Gabinete de Prensa, 1981-86; commentator and journalist; full-time writer,1986.

PROFESSIONAL ORGANIZATIONS: Sociedad General de Autores de España; Asociación de la Prensa de España; Member of the Museo Canario de Las Palmas de Gran Canaria.

AWARDS, HONORS: First Prize, National Theater Competition, 1956; International Narration Award from the Instituto de Cultura Hispánica, 1959; Silver Antenna for Radio and Television, 1963; First Prize for Supplements for Children in Adult Press, 1965; Quijote de Plata, 1968; Almendro de Oro, Municipality of Tejada, 1962; National Emilio Freixas Prize, 1977; Third Prize, Gran Angular de Literatura Juvenil, 1984; CCEI Honors List, 1986; Second Prize, Gran Angular de Novela Juvenil, 1986; CCEI Award , 1986.

WRITINGS:
Garapiña. Madrid: Ed. Nacional, 1967.
Paraíso atlántico. Milan: Ed. Sinet, 1972.
Nuestras islas, Las Palmas de Gran Canaria. Ed. Caja Insular, 1982.
Constitución española para niños. Excelentísima Mancomunidad Provincial de Cabildos de Las Palmas, 1983
Atacayte. Madrid: Ediciones SM, 1985.
Sosala. Madrid: Ediciones SM, 1987.

Gran Canaria. Santa Cruz de Tenerife: 1989.
Tenerife. Santa Cruz de Tenerife: 1989.
El hombre de otra galaxia. Madrid: Ediciones SM, 1989.
Bencomo. Madrid: Ediciones SM, 1992.

RECORDED WORKS:
El enanito Tip; El gorrión que no quería estudiar; El espantapájaros; El soldadito feo;
    El rey del mar; Tripucho. Barcelona: Compañía del Gramófono Odeón, 1957.
Pepillo el pobre. Madrid: Fonópolis, 1957.
El oso que buscaba la felicidad. Madrid: Fonópolis, 1957.

THEATER:
Presentations of theatrical works in Madrid (1958-71), Las Palmas and Santa Cruz
de Tenerife (1968-74).

SPANISH TELEVISION: Escuadrilla (Madrid), 1965; *Los diez duendecillos* (Madrid),
1971; *Mis amigos* (Canarias), 1968-71.

SIDELIGHTS: "For me, to write is a vital necessity, like breathing or feeling . . . As
a boy, I was immersed in a brutal war; surrounded by fear, hunger, and death, I sought
refuge in reading and through it traveled through time and space by the hands of
authors from all races. When stampeding through the canyons of the American West,
the sound of the chains rattling against the tanks could never reach me. I was far away.
Led by Jules Verne, I was visiting the center of the earth or the surface of the moon;
together with Huck Finn and Tom Sawyer, guided by Mark Twain, I was exploring
the Mississippi; I was riding with Don Quixote and Sancho across the plain of La
Mancha, and dreaming with Rabindranath Tagore about the knowledge of children's
souls. One day I decided that I wanted to write too, and so I did. I wanted to give back
to others what these and many other authors had given to me."

"I am a native of a land that the poets of antiquity named the Paradise of Man, the
Fortunate Islands, the Land of Blessedness. But these, my islands, do not only have
beautiful beaches, mysterious peaks, and a wonderful climate. They are also the
cradle of a noble and unique race of people. This land, the men and women that live
and have lived here, they are my source of inspiration, and thus, like Tagore told me
so long ago, "I love what is good and what is beautiful.""

CRITICAL SOURCES:
Dolores Campor Herreros. *Canarias.* 7.
Antonio Cruz, Chisco, and David Hatchuel. *La Provincia.* Gran Canaria.
Luis Doreste Silva. *El Eco.* Gran Canaria.
Juan del Río Ayala. *El Eco.* Canarias.
Orlando Hernández, Fernando Díaz Cutillas, Agustín Quevedo and Antonio

Lemus. *Diario de las Palmas.*
Alfredo Marquerie. *Ya.* Madrid.
Montserrat Sarto. *Mini Ya.* Madrid.
Heraldo de Aragón.
CLIJ.

DOUMERC DE BARNES, Beatriz (1928-)

PERSONAL DATA: Born December 14, 1928, in Buenos Aires, Argentina, the daughter of Guillermo Doumerc and Micaela Vázquez, she is married to Ayax Barnes and has six children, Gabriel, Sebastián, Cristóbal, Santiago, Guillermo, and Mariana.

ADDRESS: (Home) Marqués de Barberá 1, 2° 2a., 08001 Barcelona, Spain. Telephone: 318001.

AWARDS, HONORS: Award, World Organization for Preschool Education (OMEP), Argentinian branch, 1972; Linder Award, Milan, 1981; Third Prize, Barco de Vapor Awards, 1985; Apelles Mestres Award, 1985; Lazarillo Award, 1987.

WRITINGS:
Tatarafábulas. Buenos Aires: Ed. Latina, 1967.
Un cuento muy blanco. Buenos Aires: Ed. Latina, 1967.
Así se hacen los niños. Buenos Aires: Ed. Shapire, 1972.
El pueblo que no quería ser gris. Buenos Aires: Ed. Rompan Filas, 1975. Also
	Caracas: Ed. Alfadil, 1984. Also Milan: Ed. Ottaviano, 1978. Also Stockholm:
	Ed. Nordan, 1982.
La fábula de las fábulas. Barcelona: Ed. Bruguera, 1981.
El viaje de ida y regreso. 1982.
Aserrín, aserrán. 1984.
La familia Claroscuro. Stockholm: Ed. Nordan, 1987.
Caramelo de paseo. Madrid: Ed. Espasa-Calpe, 1985.
Las cosas de gusano y mariposa. Madrid: Ed. Espasa-Calpe, 1985.
Versión del Popol Vuh. Barcelona: Ed. Lumen, 1988.
De puerta en puerta. Madrid: Ed. Espasa-Calpe, 1987.
Tal para cual. Barcelona: Ed. Destino, 1987.
Daniel y los reyes. Barcelona: Ed. Destino, 1987.
Un cuento grande como una casa. Madrid: Ed. Anaya, 1988.
Versión de Gargantúa y Pantagruel. Barcelona: Ed. Lumen, 1986.

El espejo del agua. Barcelona: Ediciones B, 1988.
Todo pasa volando. Madrid: Ed. Edelvives, 1988.
El pájaro Federico. Madrid: Ed. Edelvives, 1990.
Una pluma con historia. Madrid: Ed. Edelvives, 1990.
¿Quién llegará primero? Madrid: Ediciones SM, 1990.
Simón el dragón. Madrid: Ediciones SM, 1990.
"Truck" (4 titles). Barcelona: Ed. Juventud, 1986.

SIDELIGHTS: "I write what I write because it is a way of accompanying children through the walkways of the imagination. Both theirs and mine. Along these walkways, nature is always present, with its brightnesses and its shadows, yet in its smallest forms and its most ephemeral manifestations. Many things occupy and merit my attention. Others are stored away in my memory, and I call them when they are needed. Thus, everything and anything can serve as an invaluable source of inspiration."

ECHEVARRÍA (MOLINA), Pablo (1963-)

PERSONAL DATA: Born March 26, 1963, in Bilbao, Spain, the son of José Luis Echevarría and Ana María Molina. *Education:* He studied interior design at the Escuela de Artes Decorativas in Madrid and publicity art at the Escuela de Nuevas Profesiones in Madrid.

ADDRESS: (Home) La Masó 4, 4c, 28034 Mirasierra, Madrid, Spain. Telephone: 7351567.

CAREER: Has worked at several publicity presses and in the department of design at various magazines; illustrator of books for children.

PROFESSIONAL ORGANIZATIONS: Jersey Wildlife Preservation Trust.

AWARDS, HONORS: Apelles Mestres Award, 1988; Lazarillo Award for Illustration, 1989; Euskadi Award for Illustration, 1990; Diploma IV International Catalonia Prize for Illustration, 1990; IMFE Award Instituto Nacional del Fomento de la Exportación, 1985.

ILLUSTRATIONS:
Popoty. Madrid: Ed. Espasa-Calpe.

Carola. Madrid: Ed. Espasa-Calpe.
Miwi. Barcelona: Ed. Destino.
Yaga y el hombrecillo de la flauta. Madrid: Ediciones SM.
Agustina la payasa. Madrid: Ediciones SM.
Yo la quería. Madrid: Ediciones SM.
Uno, dos, tres. Madrid: Ediciones SM.
Don Gato. Madrid: Ed. Ciclo.

SIDELIGHTS: "My source of inspiration is the many facets of nature. I want to fuse nature with scenes of everyday life (as in Oriental art). I am also inspired by open spaces—like the desert. The flight of birds across the sky gives a feeling of liberty and purity. I enjoy trying to capture their fierce movement on the page."

CRITICAL SOURCES:
Iñigo de Barrón. *DEIA.*
Ana D'Atri. *El Correo Español.*
M.Z. *La Vanguardia.*
Gabriel Keselman. *Ser Padres.*
Agustí Famcelli. *El País.*
Concha A. *Telva.*
Jesús Zatón. *La Nueva España,* Oviedo.

ESCARDÓ I BAS, Mercè (1948-)

PERSONAL DATA: Born August 14, 1948 in Barcelona, Spain; her parents are Joan and Mercè. She is married to Albert and has three children, Albert, Mercè, and Jordi. *Education:* Holds a degree in library science and documentation from the Escuela Universitaria Jordi Rubio de Barcelona.

ADDRESS: (Home) Sant Genis 5, 08480 L'Ametlla del Vallés, Spain. Telephone: 8432576. (Office) Biblioteca Infantil y Juvenil Can Butjosa, La Salut 52, 54, 08150 Parets del Vallés, Spain. Telephone: 5622353.

CAREER: Librarian.

PROFESSIONAL ORGANIZATIONS: Asociación de Escritores en Lengua Catalana.

AWARDS, HONORS: Critics' Award from *Serra d'Or,* 1991.

WRITINGS:
Miguel el dormilón. Illust. by Ricard Recio. Barcelona: Ed. La Galera, 1987.
Una carta para Marta. Illust. by Ricardo Recio. Barcelona: Ed. La Galera, 1989.
La luna y los espejos. Illust. by Gemma Sales. Barcelona: Ed. La Galera, 1991.

SIDELIGHTS: "I have a habit, good or bad, of transforming my responses to everyday life into the material of my stories. It is my way of expressing my feelings, my opinions about everything that surrounds me, worries me, touches me, and gives me life. In my stories there are always children (who are happy and have great confidence in others) who move back and forth across the tenuous line that separates fantasy from reality."

CRITICAL SOURCES:
Aurora Díaz Plaja. *Serra d'Or.*
Pep Duran. *Recull de Llibres.*
Avui.

ESCRIVÁ, Viví (1939-)

PERSONAL DATA: Born in Valencia, Spain, in 1939. *Education:* Holds a licentiate in fine arts.

CAREER: Has enjoyed several successful expositions of painting and sculpture, and has created a cartoon television show; began illustrating books for children in 1976. At present Viví Escrivá divides her time between illustration and creating various kinds of puppets.

AWARDS, HONORS: Lazarillo Award, 1980; Austral Award, 1991.

ILLUSTRATIONS:
La Biblia para todos. Madrid: Ed. Santillana, 1969.
Mañana de parque. Madrid: Ed. Anaya, 1972.
El lago y la corza. Madrid: Ed. Escuela Española, 1980.
Dos cuentos de princesas. Madrid: Ed. Altea, 1982.
Un millón de cuentos de un molinero y sus tres hijos. Madrid: Ed. Altea, 1982.
Aire de colores. Valladolid: Ed. Miñón, 1987.
Los cristales de colores. Madrid: Ed. Santillana, 1989.
Cipi. Madrid: Ed. Alfaguara, 1990.
Cuando Lía dibujó el mundo. Madrid: Ed. Espasa-Calpe, 1991.

SIDELIGHTS: "I entered the world of publishing very casually, although I had always respected illustrating as a profession. I had been a professional painter for a few years, and had had a few modest successes at art expositions, when one day a painter friend called me to ask if I would work with him on the publication of an illustrated Bible. It wasn't aimed specifically at children, but I enjoyed working on it. After we completed it, the publishers asked me to illustrate a book for children. For the next few years I balanced painting with illustrating children's books. I didn't actually dedicate myself to illustration until later, after I won the *Lazarillo* Award. Publishers began calling and little by little, illustrating took the place of painting in my life. Nowadays, I rarely find time to paint."

ESTEBAN NOGUERA, Asunción (1948-)

PERSONAL DATA: Born September 20, 1948, in Gerona, Spain, the daughter of Julio and Asunción, she is married to Francisco and has two children, Clara and Francisco. *Education:* Holds a degree in graphic design.

ADDRESS: (Home) Ribatallada 31 C-2, 5a. 3a. 08009 Barcelona, Spain. Telephone: 6747797. (Office) Plaza Lesseps 2, 5o. 3o. Telephone: 2374949.

CAREER: Designer, illustrator, and author.

PROFESSIONAL ORGANIZATIONS: Asociación de Ilustradoras de Catalunya; Asociación de Padres CIC y AUENC.

AWARDS, HONORS: Finalist for the Apelles Mestres Award, 1984; Critici in Erba Award, 1978; Universidad de Trento Award; Distinction from the Minister of Culture, Spain; Special Mention at the IX Europe Awards for Literature.

WRITINGS:
Dany Duende. Madrid: Ed. Alfaguara, 1981.
El astro azul. Madrid: Ed. Alfaguara, 1982.
El hallazgo de Gwin. Ed. Destino, 1982.
¿Dónde has estado Aldo? Barcelona: Ed. Juventud, 1986.
El viaje de los pájaros. Barcelona: Ed. Juventud, 1986.
Teo descubre el mundo. Co-written with Violeta Denou. Barcelona: Ed. Timun Mas.

SIDELIGHTS: "I write for the youngest readers. I am attracted to the child's fantasy. All of my books are based on my own fantasies and experiences as a child. I also want to have everyday life presented to the young in detail and with expressivity."

CRITICAL SOURCES:
El Periódico.
Los Sitios. Gerona.
La Vanguardia.

FABREGAT, Antonio-Manuel (1936-)

PERSONAL DATA: Born November 17, 1936, in Orihuela, Alicante, Spain. His parents were Manuel and Josefa. He is married to Esperanza and has five children, Antonio Manuel, Santiago, Jesús, Ana, and Esperanza. *Education:* He is a professor of primary education and of Spanish as a second language; he holds a technical degree in audiovisual methods and a doctorate in Hispanic philology.

ADDRESS: (Home) Melilla 5, 7° A, 28005 Madrid, Spain. (Offices) Escuela Universitaria Don Bosco, Universidad Complutense de Madrid. Also María Auxiliadora 9, Madrid, Spain. Telephone: 4745203.

CAREER: Professor of primary and secondary education. He is the chairperson of his department at the Universidad Complutense de Madrid.

PROFESSIONAL ORGANIZATIONS: Profesores de Secundaria; FERE (Association of Professors of Formative Courses).

AWARDS, HONORS: Award from the Municipality of Madrid, for his labor as a teacher.

WRITINGS:
Fantasía y realidad (7 vol.). Madrid: Ed. Rosas.
Oso panda (7 vol.). Madrid: Ed. Rosas.
Cuentos de mi escuela. Madrid: Ed. Bruño, 1990; 3rd. ed., 1992.
Cuentos para hablar. Madrid: Ed. Bruño, 1990; 3rd. ed., 1992.
Cómo crear cuentos. Buenos Aires: Ed. GRAM Argentina, 1991.
Para dormir a la abuela. Barcelona: Ed. Edebé, 1992.
El encuentro gozoso con los libros. Madrid: Ed. Bruño, 1992.

SIDELIGHTS: "I am a teacher. Life at school allows me to spend time observing and listening to the marvelous creations of students. My source of inspiration is school. My stories and books have enabled me to travel throughout Spain and talk to girls and boys about the wonder of reading . . . to introduce the joys of reading to those who read a little or not at all. My favorite themes involve how absurd and senseless things create fantastic situations and ideal stories."

FARÍAS, Juan

CAREER: He has published several books of memoirs and short novels.

AWARDS, HONORS: National Award for Literature for Children, 1980.

WRITINGS:
Algunos niños, tres perros y más cosas. 1981.
Un tiesto lleno de lápices. 1982.
Años difíciles. 1982.
El barco de los peregrinos. 1984.
La isla de las manzanas. 1985.

FERNÁNDEZ VALDÉS, Olga (1943-)

PERSONAL DATA: Born September 6, 1943, in Santa Clara, Villaclara, Cuba. Her parents are Francisco and Margarita. She is married to Agenor and has two children, Agenor and Claudia. *Education:* Holds a degree in history and journalism from the Universidad de La Habana.

ADDRESS: (Home) Avenida 21 7613, entre 76 y 78, Playa Maríanao 14, 11400, Havana, Cuba. Telephone: 291510. (Office) Ed. de Publicaciones en Lenguas Extranjeras "José Martí," Calzada 269, entre H e I, Vedado, Havana, Cuba. Telephone: 329838.

CAREER: Writer, journalist, and editor. She is also a musicographer, specializing in the folk music of Cubans and Afro-Cubans. She has studied the rumba, the son, and the origin of puppet theater in Havana and in Santiago de Cuba.

PROFESSIONAL ORGANIZATIONS: Unión de Escritores y Artistas de Cuba.

AWARDS, HONORS: La Edad de Oro Award for Historical Stories; National Competition of Literature for Children, 1980, 1986, 1989; Fiction Prize, 1983; Commentary Award, Union of Cuban Journalists, National Journalism Competition, 1977, 1980; 13th of March Award for Reporting, Universidad de La Habana, 1980, 1983; 13th of March Award for Articles, 1982; Press Award, Journalism Contest, 1982; 13th of March Award for Interviewing, 1984; Finalist in short story award Casa de las Américas, 1988; 26th of July Award for Fiction, 1988; Special La Rosa Blanca Prize, 1989, 1991.

WRITINGS:
Los frutos de una mañana. Havana: Ed. Universitaria, 1981.
Por esta independencia. Havana: Ed. Universitaria, 1982.
Cuba a simple vista. Havana: Ed. Universitaria, 1984.
Dos días con el general Antonio. Ed. Gente Nueva, 1985.
La mujer y el sentido del humor (anthology). Ed. Letras Cubanas, 1986.
A pura guitarra y tambor. Santiago de Cuba: Ed. Oriente, 1984.
En do mayor. Havana: Ed. Universitaria, 1985 .
Con mi abuelo y sus amigos. Ed. Gente Nueva, 1988.
Niña del arpa. Ed. Union, 1989.
La otra carga del capitán Montiel. Ed. Letras Cubanas, 1990.
A la vanguardia, el general. Ed. Gente Nueva, 1990.
Mi amigo José Martí. Caracas: Ed. Alfadil, 1991; Ed. Gente Nueva, in print.
El abanderado. Ed. Gente Nueva, in print.
Circo del Nuevo Mundo. Ed. Teduca, in print.

More than twelve of her stories have been included in literary anthologies, and over ten have been published in Cuban journals and magazines.

SIDELIGHTS: "I began writing for children and adolescents possibly because of the pleasure I took in being a teacher for several years. Then I began writing for adults as well, especially stories (I am just now finishing my first novel) because certain themes haunt me and some characters dwell in my mind. History clearly takes precedence in my work as a whole. It attracts me not only because it locates in the past the events that determine the outcome of a plot, but also because it delineates the process by which these causes influence us as closely as they do. The present and the past interact in ways that circumscribe the possibilities of the future. The past can also determine the behavior and the trajectory of characters. Moreover, history can be used by the author as an instrument, a system of reference that allows the reader to critically assess the conduct of the characters, to understand them in relation to a greater awareness of reality."

CRITICAL SOURCES:
Roberto Pérez Laón. *Tribuna de La Habana*. December 21, 1984.
Ilse Bulit. *Bohemia*. February 22, 1985.
Pedro Herrera. *Juventud Rebelde*. April 3, 1986.
Carlos Sánchez. *Semanario Cartelera*. March 26, 1989.
Marcos Pineda. *Correo*. Mérida, Venezuela: April 22, 1989.
Sergio Adricaín. "Revolución y cultura." *Granma*. May 5, 1989.
Magaly Sánchez. *Semanario Cartelera*. July 27, 1989.
Madeline Cámara. *Letras Cubanas*. November 1992.

FERRÁN, Jaime (1928-)

PERSONAL DATA: Born in Cervera, Lerida, Spain. *Education:* Holds a law degree from the Universidad de Madrid.

CAREER: Has been a professor at the Universidad de Madrid and at Colgate University in the United States.

AWARDS, HONORS: Adonis Award, 1953.

WRITINGS:
Ángel en España. 1960.
Ángel en Colombia. 1967.
Historias de mariposas. 1966.
Ángel en USA (Norte). 1971.
Ángel en USA (Sur). 1971.
Tarde de circo (poetry). 1981.
La playa larga (poetry). 1981.
Cuaderno de música (poetry).

FERRER BERMEJO, José Francisco (1956-)

PERSONAL DATA: Born January 18, 1956, in Alcala de Henares, Madrid, Spain.
Education: Studies in history and geography.

ADDRESS: (Home) Paseo de la Ermita del Santo 15, 2° D Madrid, Spain.

CAREER: Postal official.

WRITINGS:
Incidente en Atocha. Madrid: Ed. Alfaguara, 1982.
El increíble hombre inapetente. Alcala: Ed. Alcalá Narrativa,1982.
El globo de la trapisonda. Madrid: Ed. Alfaguara, 1985.
El ídolo de Aruba. Madrid: Ed. Anaya, 1991.
La música de Ariel Caamaño. Navarra: Ed. Hierbaola, 1992.

SIDELIGHTS: "I don't know why I write, only that I have always invented and told stories. My favorite themes are adventure, fantasy, and science fiction."

CRITICAL SOURCES:
Joaquín Arnaiz. *Diario 16.* Madrid: October 31, 1982.
Luis Suñen. *El País.* Madrid: November 21, 1982.
Ramón Acin. *Quimera.* Barcelona: December 1982.
Luis Mateo Díez. *Guía del Ocio.* Madrid: February 1983.
James J. Abbot. *World Literature Today.* University of Oklahoma Press, Winter 1984.

FIERRO, Julieta (1948-)

PERSONAL DATA: Born February 24, 1948, in Mexico, D.F. Her parents are Leonel Fierro and Joan Gossman. Her children are Agustín and Luis Rayo. Education: Master's degree in science.

ADDRESS: (Home) Copilco 300 13-504, Universidad de Coplico, 04563 Mexico, D.F. Telephone: 6584838. (Office) Instituto de Astronomía, Universidad Nacional Autónoma de México, Ap. 70 264, 04563 Mexico, D.F. Telephone: 5505922.

CAREER: Investigator at the Institute of Astronomy and professor for the Faculty of Sciences at the UNAM since 1972. She has numerous publications in magazines and journals.

PROFESSIONAL ORGANIZATIONS: Unión Astronómica Internacional y Sociedad Mexicana de Física.

WRITINGS:

Astronomía para niños. Co-written with D. Dultzin, et al. Mexico: CIDCLI, 1984.

El cometa Halley. Co-written with Estrella Burgos. Mexico: Secretaría de Educación Pública, 1985.

El cometa Halley. Co-written with Miguel Ángel Herrera. Fondo Educativo Interamericano, 1985.

La tierra. Co-written with Miguel Ángel Herrera. Fondo Educativo Interamericano, 1986.

El sistema solar. Co-written with Miguel Ángel Herrera. Fondo Educativo Interamericano, 1986.

Las estrellas. Co-written with Miguel Ángel Herrera. Fondo Educativo Interamericano, 1986.

El cosmos. Co-written with Miguel Ángel Herrera. Fondo Educativo Interamericano, 1986.

El eclipse. Co-written with Jesús Galindo, and Daniel Flores. Mexico: CONAFE, 1990.

El eclipse del 11 de julio de 1991. SITESA, 1991.

La familia del sol. Mexico: Fondo de Cultura Económica, 1989.

¿Cómo acercarse a la astronomía? Mexico: Ed. LIMUSA y Consejo Nacional para la Cultura y las Artes, 1991.

El día y la noche. Mexico: CUCC, in print.

SIDELIGHTS: "I write science books for children because I believe that science is a road leading us toward a better future."

CRITICAL SOURCES:
Héctor Gally. Unomasuno. May 13, 1989.
Héctor Ceceña. El Universo.
Eduardo Camacho Suárez. Excelsior. June 13, 1991.
Walter Ramírez Aguilar. El Nacional. June 13, 1991.
Gaceta UNAM. June 1991.
Malena Mijares. Supplement for La Jornada. July, 1991.

FRAIRE, Isabel (1934-)

PERSONAL DATA: Born in Mexico, D.F. Education: Advanced studies at the Faculty of Philosophy and Letters at the Universidad Nacional Autónoma de México.

ADDRESS: (Home) Puebla 41, Col. Roma, zona postal 7, Mexico, D.F. (Office) Telephone: 5285165.

CAREER: She directed several poetry workshops and formed part of a group that edited such magazines as *Mexicana de Literatura*. Aditionally, she has written collaborative works for *Katarsis, Revista de la Ciudad de México, La Semana de Bellas Artes, Proceso*, and *Diálogos*, among others.

AWARDS, HONORS: Fellowship awarded by the Guggenheim Foundation, 1977.

WRITINGS:
Sólo esta luz. Mexico: Ed. Era, 1969.
Seis poetas de lengua inglesa. Mexico: Secretaría de Educación Pública, 1974.
Poemas de Isabel Fraire. United States: Ed. Prensa Mundus Arquium, 1975.
Poemas en el regazo de la muerte. Mexico: Ed. Joaquín Mortiz, 1977.

FUERTES, Gloria (1918-)

PERSONAL DATA: Born in Madrid, Spain, in 1918.

WRITINGS:
Canciones para niños. 1952.
Don Pato y Don Pito. 1971.
El camello cojito. 1973.
El hada acaramelada. 1973.
La gata chundarata y otros cuentos. 1974.
Cangura para todos. 1977.
La oca loca. 1977.
El dragón tragón. 1978.
La momia tiene catarro. 1978.
Las tres reinas magas. 1980.
El libro loco de todo un poco. 1981.
Pío, pío Lope, el pollito miope. 1981.
El domador mordió el león. 1982.
Plumilindo. 1982.
Coleta, la poeta. 1983.
Coleta, la payasa. 1984.
El abecedario de Don Hilario. 1984.
Yo contento, tú contenta, qué bien me sale la cuenta. 1984.

SIDELIGHTS: She writes popular and traditional poetry, as well as fiction, for children and adults.

GALLEGO ALFONSO, Jacoba Emilia (1946-)

PERSONAL DATA: Born May 27, 1946, in Havana, Cuba, the daughter of Bernabé Agustín and María Hortensia. *Education:* Licentiate in Hispanic language and literature from the Universidad de la Habana, 1974; postgraduate studies in aesthetics and aesthetic education, theory of communication, drama and direction, scenic arts, methodology of social investigation, North American literature, and Hispanic-American literature.

ADDRESS: (Home) Calle M 103, entre 13 y 15, Vedado, Plaza, Havana, Cuba. Telephone: 326747. (Office) Dirección de Programación. Televisión Cubana, Edificio del Instituto Cubano de la Radio y la Televisión, Calle 23, Esq. M, 6° Havana, Cuba. Telephone: 322944.

CAREER: Teacher, 1965-74; university professor, 1974-80; researcher for the Instituto Central de Ciencias Pedagógicas, 1980-89. Since 1989 she has worked for television and as a professor of Cuban culture at the Facultad de Comunicación Social of the Universidad de La Habana.

PROFESSIONAL ORGANIZATIONS: Asociación de Pedagogos de Cuba; Asociación de Escritores de Cuba; Cátedra Martiana de la Universidad de La Habana; vice-president of the IBBY of Cuba.

AWARDS, HONORS: 13th of March Award for Poetry for Children, 1981; *La Edad de Oro* Award for Poetry for Children, 1982, 1985; Frank País Award for the Essay and Poetry for Children, 1982; Methods of Teaching Award for the Best Book for Preschool Students, 1984; Medal for Alphabetization, 1989; National Order of Education, 1991.

WRITINGS:
Para un niño travieso. Havana: Ed. Universitarias, 1981.
El arte de ver y escuchar. Havana: Ministerio de Educación, 1981.
Y dice una mariposa. Havana: Ed. Gente Nueva, 1982.
El ánima encantada de la literatura infantil: esa otra dimensión. Havana: Ed. Gente Nueva, 1986.

La magia en "La Edad de Oro". Havana: Ed. Letras Cubanas, 1986.
Un acercamiento necesario a "Cartas a Elpidio". Havana: Ed. Ciencias Sociales, 1988.
Para un estudio comparativo entre las "Cartas a Elpidio" y "La Edad de Oro". Havana: Ed. Universidad de La Habana, 1989.
Apuntes sobre la presencia de la magia en "La Edad de Oro". Havana: Ed. Letras Cubanas, 1989.
Poemas y narraciones en libros de lectura. Havana: Ministerio de Educación, 1990.
Sol sin prisa. Havana: Ed. Gente Nueva, in print.
¿Para quién se escribe "La Edad de Oro"? Havana: Ed. Universitarias, in print.
Leo, luego existo. Colombia: CERLAC, in print.

SIDELIGHTS: "I write because I cannot avoid it. My sources of inspiration in regard to poetry and fiction are life itself and the attitude we need to assume in the face of it, disjointed, contradictory, and difficult as it is. Nowadays, love and the defense of nature are being reasserted as fundamentally important, and they influence my own work as well. In regard to the essay, I have worked to integrate literature and illustration into an ethic and aesthetic for children. I have closely studied the works of Padre Félix Varela and José Martí, giants of Cuban and American thought, whose contributions to educational theory, ideas of independence, liberty, the best forms of government, art, literature, and the identity, thought, and culture of societies constitute paradigms of such brilliance and complexity that they deserve close attention. Their works propose philosophical and humanistic evolutions of profound importance, even more so in our times."

GANGES, Montserrat (1964-)

PERSONAL DATA: Born in Malgrat de Mar, Barcelona, Spain, in 1964. *Education:* Holds a degree in Catalan philology.

AWARDS, HONORS: Apelles Mestres Award (shared with Imma Pla), 1991; Honorable Mention for the Illustration Award from the Bologna Children's Book Fair, 1992.

WRITINGS:
Una mosca a la sopa. Barcelona: Publicaciones de l'Abadía de Montserrat, 1989.
Zip y el dragón fanfarrón. Barcelona: Ed. Destino, 1991.
Zip y la oveja del sueño. Barcelona: Ed. Destino, 1992.

SIDELIGHTS: "I write for children because I feel able to, and because I enjoy it. I chose literature for children for the same vague and strange reasons that cause anyone to choose any other profession. I did not start out with the idea of writing and then try to choose a specific genre; for me the choice derived from my long-time attraction to literature for children. The other genres feel as remote and strange to me as professions that I do not know."

GARCÍA JAMBRINA, Luis M(iguel) (1960-)

PERSONAL DATA: Born July 30, 1960, in Zamora, Spain, the son of Teodoro García Benavente and María Luisa Jambrina Velázquez. *Education:* Holds a degree in Hispanic philology from the Universidad de Salamanca; degree in French philology; advanced studies in psychology.

ADDRESS: (Home) San Pablo 54-56, 3° H. 37008 Salamanca, Spain. Telephone: 923263575. (Office) Departamento de Literatura Española, Facultad de Filología, Plaza de Anaya, s/n 37008, Universidad de Salamanca, Salamanca, Spain. Telephone: 923294400, extension 1711.

CAREER: Research Fellowship at the University of Salamanca, 1989-92; fellowship for the inventory and cataloging of Miguel de Unamuno Library-Museum, 1989; professor of secondary education, 1987-88.

PROFESSIONAL ORGANIZATIONS: Asociación Internacional del Siglo de Oro; Instituto de Estudios Zamoranos "Florián de Ocampo."

WRITINGS:
Claudio Rodríguez para niños. Co-edited by Luis Ramos de la Torre. Madrid: Ediciones de la Torre, 1988.
Guía de lectura para Claudio Rodríguez Co-edited by Luis Ramos de la Torre. Madrid: Ediciones de la Torre, 1988.
"Literatura." *Zamora.* Madrid: Ed. Mediterráneo, 1991.
"Las promociones poéticas de los años 50 y 60." *La poesía de postguerra* 47. Edited by Ricardo de la Fuente.
Historia de la literatura española. Madrid: Ediciones Júcar, in print.

SIDELIGHTS: "I receive inspiration in three ways:
—I study poetry in general and poetic language in particular and ways in which to use them for teaching.

—I study and play with songs and games for children.
—I am influenced by the songs and games for children from several authors of Spanish literature (Claudio Rodríguez, Agustín García Calvo, etc.)."

CRITICAL SOURCES:
Rosa Lanoix. *Ya.* February 4, 1989.
Ana Garralón. *Educación y Biblioteca.* 2, July-September 1989.
Juan Carlos Suñén. *El País.* October 29, 1989.
J. Hernández. *El Correo de Zamora.* August 8, 1989.
Tomás Sánchez Santiago. *Boletín de la Asociación de Jóvenes Investigadores "Benito Pellitero".* 3, Zamora: 1990.

GARCÍA MARTÍN, Pedro (1957-)

PERSONAL DATA: Born February 1, 1957, in Béjar, Salamanca, Spain. His parents are Simón García Morato and Margarita Martín Calderón. *Education:* Doctorate in modern history.

ADDRESS: (Home) Arechavaleta 30, 4° D, 28041 Madrid, Spain. Telephone: 7966444. (Office) Universidad Autónoma de Madrid, Facultad de Filosofía y Letras, Departamento de Historia Moderna, Ciudad Universitaria de Cantoblanco, 28049 Madrid, Spain. Telephone: 3974130.

CAREER: Has been a professor at the Universidad Autónoma de Madrid since 1984.

WRITINGS:
Los comuneros. Madrid: Ed. Bruño, Col. "Pueblos y Gentes," 1990.
Las plantas. Madrid: Ed. Bruño, Col. "Historia del Planeta Azul." 1992.
El agua. Madrid: Ed. Bruño, Col. "Historia del Planeta Azul." 1992.

He has also published more than ten historiographic books and articles.

SIDELIGHTS: "My involvement with literature for children is the result of my principal professional interest, history. Since I made various incursions into other genres, such as journalism, the essay, etc., and because of the excellent reception my first story received, I proceeded with this line of narrative, adding other themes, from ecology to classical adventure. Although I have consigned my existing body of writing to this genre, I have other books as yet unpublished, in which I take on a variety of places and characters in order to continue expanding my range of themes."

GERBER (FETENSE), Thomas (Rudolf) (1959-)

PERSONAL DATA: Born March 24, 1959, in Santiago, Chile, the son of Klaus Gerber and Mónica Fetense. He is married to María Soledad Zenteno; and they have four children, Danae, Vanesa, Valentina, and Cristóbal. *Education:* Holds a licentiate in art from the Universidad Católica de Chile.

ADDRESS: (Home) Camino de la Luna, Parcela s/n, Peñalolen, Santiago, Chile. Telephone: 2233079. (Office) Don Carlos 3075, Depto. 5A, Las Condes, Santiago, Chile. Telephone: 2314013.

*CAREER: Illustrato*r since 1986.

AWARDS, HONORS: First Prize at the National Illustration Competition.

ILLUSTRATIONS:
Hechos. Ed. Publicidad y Ediciones, 1987.
Antología del cuento chileno de ciencia ficción y fantasía. Santiago, Chile: Ed. Andrés Bello, 1988.
La familia del barrio chino. Santiago, Chile: Ed. An*drés Bello*, 1988.
La cabaña del tío Tom. Santiago, Chile: Ed. An*drés Bello*, 1989.
Cuando Dios caminó por el mundo. Santiago, Chile: Ed. An*drés Bello*, 1989.
La rebelión de las masas. Santiago, Chile: Ed. An*drés Bello*, 1989.
Cuentos cortos de la tierra larga. Santiago, Chile: Ed. An*drés Bello*, 1989.
La última bruja. Santiago, Chile: Ed. An*drés Bello*, 1990.
Alí Baba y los cuarenta ladrones. Santiago, Chile: Ed. An*drés Bello*, 1991.
Aladino. Santiago, Chile: Ed. An*drés Bello*, 1991.
El cazador de cuentos. Santiago, Chile: Ed. An*drés Bello*, 1991.
Pupi. Santiago, Chile: Ed. An*drés Bello*, 1992.
Cuentos del fin del mundo. Santiago, Chile: Ed. An*drés Bello*, 1992.
El pato Renato. Santiago, Chile: Ed. An*drés Bello*, 1992.
El duende Pin Pon. Santiago, Chile: Ed. An*drés Bello*, 1992.
Tres príncipes. Santiago, Chile: Ed. An*drés Bello*, 1992.

SIDELIGHTS: "To illustrate books for children implies communication and fantasy.

Reality is transformed into an infinitude of fantastic worlds, and I transform myself into the imagination of the child: if a character is happy, I must feel that. This I enjoy! My favorite theme is history (especially in relation to pre-Columbian America). My favorite kind of characters are witches, ghosts, hairy monsters, and princes, and my sources of inspiration are my travels around the world and the inventions of my mind."

GEVERT, Lucía (1932-)

PERSONAL DATA: Born August 2, 1932, in Santiago, Chile. Her parents are Enrique Gevert and Marta Parada. Married to Igor Saavedra, she has two children, Pablo and Pedro Elster. *Education:* Journalist, Universidad Católica de Chile.

ADDRESS: (Home) Nueva Costanera 3470, Santiago, Chile. Telephone: 2283376.

CAREER: Editor of *El Mercurio* 1964-73; director of the women's magazines *Eva* and *Saber Comer y Vivir Mejor* 1969-73; director and producer of national television; cultural attaché to the press in Germany and later an embassador to that country, 1973-78.

PROFESSIONAL ORGANIZATIONS: President IBBY of Chile since 1979; director of the National Association of Female Journalists; vice-president of the Chilean-German Cultural Institute.

AWARDS, HONORS: Honorable Mention for the John Reitemeyer Prize, 1969; Lenka Franulic Prize, 1970; Great Cross Decoration from the Federal Republic of Germany, 1978.

WRITINGS:
El puma. Ed. Zig-Zag, 1969.
El gatito que no sabía ronronear. Santiago, Chile: Ed. Andrés Bello, 1985.
El pato y el río enfermo. Santiago, Chile: Ed. Andrés Bello, 1987.
Cuentos cortos de la tierra larga. Santiago, Chile: Ed. Andrés Bello, 1989.
La tierra nuestra. Santiago, Chile: Ed. Andrés Bello, 1991.
Cuentos de príncipes, garzas y manzanas. Madrid: Ediciones SM, 1991.
El mundo de Amado. Santiago, Chile: Pehuén Editores, 1991.
El caballo tordillo. Santiago, Chile: Ed. Andrés Bello, 1992.
Aguas oscuras. Salao Editores, in press.

SIDELIGHTS: "I want to familiarize children with nature. I want them to feel that they are parts of a whole, and I want them to understand that knowledge about themselves can be obtained from the world around them. In the same way I think that the legends and myths of our aboriginal cultures are of great importance to all of us, for our knowledge about ourselves and our histories. The interior landscape of each child must be nourished, not with didactic lectures, but with adventures that give children a strong base and form of knowledge."

CRITICAL SOURCES:
El Mercurio. August 1969.
Hernán del Solar. *El Mercurio.* June 29, 1969.
Braulio Arenas. *Las Últimas Noticias.* September 1969.
Raúl Silva Castro. *El Mercurio.* October 1, 1969.

GIL GRIMAU, Rodolfo (1937-)

PERSONAL DATA: Born August 1, 1937, in Madrid, Spain. His parents are Rodolfo and Emilia. He is married to Pilar, and they have two children, María and Daniel. *Education:* Ph.D. in Arabic and Islamic philology.

ADDRESS: (Office) Instituto Cervantes Centro Cultural Español, Calle Mohamed Torres 3, Tetuan, Morocco. Telephone: 95239.

CAREER: Director of the Hispanic Cultural Center in Cairo; director of the Spanish Culture Center in Tetuan.

PROFESSIONAL ORGANIZATIONS: Asociación Española de Orientalistas; Real Academia de Ciencias, Nobles Artes y Bellas Letras de Córdoba.

AWARDS, HONORS: Outstanding Distinction for Doctoral Study, Universidad Autónoma de Madrid; awarded to the Order of Civil Merit, Spain.

WRITINGS:
Que por la rosa roja corrió mi sangre. Colección de narraciones orales marroquíes.
    Co-written with Muhammad Ibn Azzuz Hakim. Madrid: Instituto Hispano
    Árabe de Cultura, 1977.
Los cuentos de hadas: historia mágica del hombre. Madrid: Ed. Salvat, 1982.
Magia, adivinación y alquimia. Madrid: Ed. Salvat, 1982.
Cuentos al sur del Mediterráneo. Madrid: Ed. La Torre, 1987.

SIDELIGHTS: " 'Once upon a time, goodness came for everyone and those who sought evil sought elsewhere.' This is a typical magic formula that opens the eyes and ears of the reader to a world of imagination and history. Here, also, Rodolfo Gil Grimau introduces his collection of stories, which are adaptations of stories and tales of Berber, sub-Saharan, and Arabic origin. The literary transcription of these stories in all their richness and beauty of images and myths has been possible thanks to the author's profound knowledge of the Arabic language and culture, in which environment he lived since childhood achieving academic and professional success."

GIMÉNEZ PASTOR, Marta (1923-)

PERSONAL DATA: Born December 23, 1923, in General Pico, La Pampa, Argentina, the daughter of Carlos Giménez and Sara Aragón. She is the widow of José Daniel Viacova and has three children, Conrado Martín, María Alejandra, and Clara Mireya. *Education:* Professor of primary education.

ADDRESS: (Home) Arenales 3207, 7°R, Buenos Aires, Argentina. (Office) Magisterio del Río de la Plata (Ed.), Viamonte, 1674 Buenos Aires, Argentina. Telephone: 497446.

CAREER: Teacher (1948-76), editorial director, journalist, editor, and critic of books and theater for children.

PROFESSIONAL ORGANIZATIONS: SADE; ARGENTORES; SADAIC.

AWARDS, HONORS: Award of Honor from SADE, 1950; National Foundation for the Arts Award for Literature for Children, 1967; Municipality Award for Theater for Children, 1990.

WRITINGS:
Canciones. Published by the author, 1948.
Acaso follaje. Published by the author, 1950.
Después noviembre. Ed. Balcón de Madera, 1953.
El campeón. Ed. Trayectoria, 1960.
Cuentos. Buenos Aires: Ed. Latina, 1960.
Versos en sube y baja. Ed. Huemul, 1967.
Cuento. Buenos Aires: Ed. Latina, 1972.
Cosas de la vida. Ed. Huemul, 1975.
Literatura infantil. Buenos Aires: Ed. Plus Ultra, 1975.

Literatura infantil. Centro Editor de América Latina, 1976.
Cuentos. Ed. El Hogar Obrero, 1984.
Cuentos. Ed. Corregidor, 1987.
Libros de lectura. Ed. Abril, 1982.
Literatura infantil. Buenos Aires: Ed. Magisterio Río de la Plata, 1986.
Cuentos. Buenos Aires: Ed. El Ateneo, 1989.
Cuentos. Buenos Aires: Ed. Guadalupe, 1990.
Libros de cuentos. Ed. Sigmar, 1990.
Cuento. Buenos Aires: Ed. Braga, 1992.
Libro de lectura. Buenos Aires: Ed. El Ateneo, 1992.
Cuentos. Ed. Renglón, 1992.
15 leyendas americanas. Buenos Aires: Ed. Magisterio Río de la Plata, 1992.
El alma que canta. Ed. Corregidor, 1992.

SIDELIGHTS: "My start in literature came with a book of poetry published in 1948 and again in 1960. I became interested in children's literature through my children. As they began to read, I began to write. My first stories appeared in the weekly supplement to *La Nación*, and I continued to contribute to it for the next six years. I feel that I have strong communication with my readers, and this stimulates my creativity. I enjoy sifting through my memories of childhood in a small village, and selecting the themes of my stories from them. My stories always pay attention to animals, nature, and games. I try to make them poetic, humorous, and tender."

GISBERT (PONSOLE), Joan Manuel (1949-)

PERSONAL DATA: Born October 16, 1949, in Barcelona, Spain, the son of Manuel and Montserrat. He is married to Agustina. *Education:* Electronic engineering degree.

ADDRESS: (Home) Grassot 39, 3° 3a., 08025 Barcelona, Spain. Telephone: 2071460.

CAREER: Advisor for Editorial Labor, 1973-90; writer.

PROFESSIONAL ORGANIZATIONS: Asociación de Amigos del Libro Infantil y Juvenil; Asociación Colegial de Escritores de España (Autonomous section of Catalonia).

AWARDS, HONORS: CCEI Award, 1979; Lazarillo Award, 1980; IBBY Honors List, 1982; Book of Interest for Children, 1983; Critics' Award from *Serra d'Or*,

1984; National Award for Literature for Children and Young People, 1985; Gran Angular Award, 1989; Barco de Vapor Award, 1990.

WRITINGS:
Escenarios fantásticos. Barcelona: Ed. Labor, 1979.
El misterio de la isla de Tökland. Madrid: Ed. Espasa-Calpe, 1981.
El extraño adiós de Odiel Munro. Barcelona: Ed. Labor, 1982.
Leyendas del planeta Thámyris. Madrid: Ed. Espasa-Calpe, 1982.
El museo de los sueños. Madrid: Ed. Espasa-Calpe, 1984.
La noche del viajero errante. Barcelona: Ed. Labor, 1984.
La aventura inmortal de Max Urkhaus. Madrid: Ed. Alfaguara, 1985.
La sonámbula en la Ciudad-Laberinto. Barcelona: Ed. Labor, 1985.
El mago de Esmirna. Madrid: Ed. Anaya, 1987.
El arquitecto y el emperador de Arabia. Zaragoza: Ed. Edelvives, 1988.
El talismán del Adriático. Madrid: Ediciones SM, 1988.
La mansión de los abismos. Madrid: Ed. Espasa-Calpe, 1988.
La noche del eclipse. Madrid: Ediciones SM, 1990.
El misterio de la mujer autómata. Madrid: Ediciones SM, 1991.
La frontera invisible. Madrid: Ediciones SM, 1992.

SIDELIGHTS: "I try to create fantastic narrations, written with the idea that at times the fantastic is an extension or exploration of aspects of reality. I like characters who confront situations head on, and I like to create situations that demand the best of them, sometimes requiring strength and resolve that they did not know they possessed. I also appreciate the element of imagination. I would like to take the imagination of my readers to new places and new ideas. In the same way, I enjoy all that involves the investigation and resolution of enigmas of a certain complexity or scope."

CRITICAL SOURCES: There are two doctoral theses in progress assessing the works of Joan Manuel Gisbert, one from the Universidad de Madrid and the other from the Universidad de Granada. The critical reviews of his work are extensive and have appeared in the major newspapers and journals of Spain.

GÓMEZ CERDÁ, Alfredo (1951-)

PERSONAL DATA: Born July 6, 1951, in Madrid, Spain. *Education:* Holds a degree in Spanish philology.

ADDRESS: (Home) Illescas 211, 12° D, 28047 Madrid, Spain. Telephone: 7180095.

PROFESSIONAL ORGANIZATIONS: ACE; Asociación Española de Amigos del Libro Infantil y Juvenil.

AWARDS, HONORS: Altea Prize, 1984; Second Prize, Gran Angular Award, 1983; Second Prize, Lazarillo Award, 1985; Second Prize, Barco de Vapor Award, 1985; First Prize, Barco de Vapor Award, 1989; CCEI Honors List, 1987, 1989, 1991.

WRITINGS:
Las palabras mágicas. Illust. by Margarita Puncel. Madrid: Ediciones SM, 1983.
La ciudad que tenía de todo. Illust. by Teo Puebla. Madrid: Ed. Altea, 1985. Also
    Madrid: Ed. Anaya, 1990.
La casa de verano. Madrid: Ediciones SM, 1985.
Macaco y Antón. Illust. by Margarita Menéndez. Madrid: Ediciones SM, 1986.
Un amigo en la selva. Illust. by Juan Manuel Menéndez. Zaragoza: Ed. Edelvives,
    1988.
Timo rompebombillas. Illust. by Jesús Gabán. Barcelona: Ed. Noguer, 1986.
Cha ca pun. Illust. by José Pérez Montero. Leon: Ed. Everest, 1987.
El árbol solitario. Illust. by Jesús Gabán. Madrid: Ediciones SM, 1987.
El puente de piedra. Illust. by Antonio Tello. Madrid: Ed. Susaeta, 1987.
Un barullo en mi cabeza. Illust. by Margarita Puncell. Ed. Altea, 1987.
Nano y Esmeralda. Illust. by Carmen Lucini. Madrid: Ediciones SM, 1987.
El cartero que se convirtió en carta. Illust. by Ignacio Oliva. Zaragoza: Ed.
    Edelvives, 1987.
Jorge y el capitán. Illust. by Margarita Menéndez. Madrid: Ediciones SM, 1988.
Alejandro no se ríe. Illust. by Viví Escrivá. Madrid: Ed. Anaya, 1988.
La princesa y el pirata. Illust. by Teo Puebla. Mexico: Fondo de Cultura Económica,
    1991.
Pupila de águila. Madrid: Ediciones SM, 1989.
Luisón. Illust. by Teo Puebla. Madrid: Ed. Bruño, 1990.
Apareció en mi ventana. Illust. by Jesús Gabán. Madrid: Ediciones SM, 1990.
El volcán del desierto. Illust. by Juan Manuel Cicuéndez. Zaragoza: Ed. Edelvives,
    1990.
La guerra de nunca acabar. Illust. by Alfredo Gómez Cerdá. Gijon: Ed. Júcar, 1990.
El laberinto de piedra. Illust. by Juan Manuel Cicuéndez. Madrid: Ed. Bruño, 1991.
La sexta tele. Illust. by Jesús Gabán. Madrid: Ed. Susaeta, 1991.
El monstruo y la biblioteca. Illust. by Ma. Luisa Torcida. Barcelona: Ed. Noguer,
    1991.

SIDELIGHTS: "At the moment I begin writing I look at two things:1) at my environment, the world, and the people who surround me; 2) and at myself. I take a glance inside. These two views provide me with my themes and my sources of inspiration. There is more realism in my stories than fantasy, but realism interpreted and modified by my imagination. I recognize the difference between imagination and fantasy, and of course I stay with the former."

CRITICAL SOURCES:
Anabel Sáiz Ripoll. *Tesis doctoral.* Universidad de Barcelona.

GÓMEZ YEBRA, Antonio A. (1950-)

PERSONAL DATA: Born March 25, 1950, in Almoharín, Caceres, Spain, the son of Agustín Gómez Collado and Hortensia Yebra Somoza, he is married to Carmen Jiménez Fernández and has three children, Javier, Irene, Marta. *Education:* Ph.D. in Hispanic philology.

ADDRESS: (Home) C/ Santa Elena, 20, 8-B 29007 Malaga, Spain. (Office) Departamento de Filología Española II, Facultad de Filosofía y Letras, 29071 Malaga, Spain.

CAREER: University professor of Spanish since 1984.

PROFESSIONAL ORGANIZATIONS: Asociación Española de Amigos del IBBY; AMALIJ (Málaga Association of IBBY); Sociedad General de Autores de España; Asociación Colegial de Escritores de España.

AWARDS, HONORS: Third Place, Calderi Story Competition, Barcelona, 1974; Second Place, Teatro Guiñol, Malaga, 1975; First Prize, Los Llanos National Literary Awards, Albacete, 1980; Runner-up, First Competition for Stories at the Universidad Popular de Yecla, 1984; First Prize for Poetry, Algeciras, 1990.

WRITINGS:
Algo de teatro infantil. Malaga: Ed. Universidad, 1978.
Travesuras poéticas. Malaga, Ed. Universidad, 1979.
Versos como niños. Ronda: Sagrada Familia, 1983.
Mi mejor amigo. Malaga: C. Ahorros Provincial, 1983.
Pequeños poemas y cuentos. Publicaciones Librería Anticuaria Guadalhorce, 1985.
Animales poéticos. Madrid: Ed. Escuela Española, 1987.
Aventuras con tito Paco. Zaragoza: Ed. Edelvives, 1988.
Osaba, Joseba, argaletan argalena. Ed. Edelvives Bizkaia, I.K.A., 1991.
Mario, Neta y la nube roja. Madrid: Ed. Escuela Española, 1988.

El juicio de Salomón. Madrid: Ed. Escuela Española, 1989.
Muñeco de nieve. Madrid: Ed. Escuela Española, 1992.

Antonio Gómez Yebra has written numerous other works, including stories, novels, essays, criticism, and historical investigations.

SIDELIGHTS: "With books one is able to make many children more happy than they would otherwise be. Books are an antidote for boredom, complacency, and the loss of human and moral values. I write prose, poetry, and theater. My theme is the world of children, their accoutrements, their friends—and among their friends, animals. Many of my poems for children have animals as their protagonists. My sources of inspiration are children themselves, their phrases, their games, their way of expressing themselves, their restlessness, their humor. On occasion, I have taken ideas from *Arabian Nights* and the *Bible*, as well as from the works of Chekov, García Lorca, and Jorge de Guillén. Humor is always present in my work."

CRITICAL SOURCES:
González, C. "Antonio A. Gómez Yebra, escritor." *Sur*. March 21, 1980.
Bustos, C.I. "Gómez Yebra: nadie se atreve a editar poesía para niños." *ABC*. December 30, 1981.
Quiles Faz, A. *Hora de Poesía*. 57-58, May 1988.
Garrido, A. "*Aventuras con tito Paco* de Antonio Gómez Yebra." *Canopus*. 20, December 1988.

GRANATA, María (1924-)

PERSONAL DATA: Born September 3, 1924, in Buenos Aires, Argentina, the daughter of Miguel Ángel Granata and Rosa Luisa Schiaffino, she is married to Ramón Prieto and they have one child, Rafael.

ADDRESS: (Home) Potrerillos y Lamadrid, Alejandro Korn, Argentina.

PROFESSIONAL ORGANIZATIONS: Sociedad Argentina de Escritores.

AWARDS, HONORS: National Award for Literature; Award from the city of Buenos Aires; Dedication Award from the city of Buenos Aires; Emecé Award; Strega Award of Argentina; Person of Letters Prize; Grand Award of Honor from the Sociedad Argentina de Escritores.

WRITINGS:
El ángel que perdió un ala. Ed. Acme, 1974.
El bichito de luz sin luz. Buenos Aires: Ed. Sigmar, 1976.
El gallo embrujado. Ed. Acme, 1980.
El cazador de zorros azules. Ed. Acme, 1980.
La ciudad que levantó vuelo. Ed. Abril, 1984.
Pico de cigüeña. Buenos Aires: Ed. Sigmar, 1982.
Cien cuentos. Buenos Aires: Ed. Sigmar, 1985.
El perro sin terminar. Buenos Aires: Ed. Plus Ultra, 1984.
El tren que aprendió a jugar. Ed. Emecé, 1987.
Mambrú se fue a la guerra. Buenos Aires: Ed. El Ateneo, 1990.
El viaje de Colón contado por un pájaro. Buenos Aires: Ed. Sigmar, 1991.
El pizarrón viajero. Buenos Aires: Ed. Sigmar, 1991.
Primeras letras (collection). Buenos Aires: Ed. Sigmar, 1991.

SIDELIGHTS: "In my literature for adults, I try to explore the human condition. In my literary work for children, I want to exhalt peace, happiness, and love in an atmosphere of entertainment and adventure. The many manifestations of nature are a favorite theme of mine. I write because when I do, I am happy (although when I don't, I am also happy)."

CRITICAL SOURCES: Horacio Rega Molina, Nicolás Olivari, Delfín Leocadio Garasa, Alicia Dujovne, and Emilio Zolezzi, among others, have written about her work in newspapers, including *El Mundo, La Nación, Clarín*, and in the literary journal *Raíces*.

GREGORI, Josep (1959-)

PERSONAL DATA: Born in Alzira, Valencia, Spain, in 1959.

CAREER: Teacher, editor, and writer.

AWARDS, HONORS: Ciutat de València Award, 1985; Enric Valor Prize, 1988; Josep Ma. Folchi i Torres Prize, 1991.

WRITINGS:
Tereseta la brujita. Barcelona: Ed. La Galera, 1992.

The work cited here is a translation into Spanish from Catalan. The author has published two other books in Catalan.

SIDELIGHTS: "I think that writing for young people is more important than writing for adults because it establishes a relationship between the author and the reader that is more immediate and vital than is possible in adult fiction. It is necessary to bear in mind that youngsters, especially children, are open to new ideas and are in the process of making decisions that will profoundly affect the rest of their lives. If, as a writer, you can gain their trust and affection, it is assured that you have secured a place in their hearts forever. Who can resist that?"

GUERRA CÁCERES, Juan (1943-)

PERSONAL DATA: Born March 14, 1943, in Navia, Asturias, Spain, the son of Eugenio and Mercedes, he is married to Soledad and they have one child, Juan. *Education:* Holds a degree in economics; also studied psychology.

ADDRESS: (Home) Francisco Santos 10, Madrid, Spain. Telephone: 3553293. (Office) Castellana 160, 2a., 28071 Madrid, Spain. Telephone: 3494567.

CAREER: Economist in the service of the state administration.

WRITINGS:
Cuentos del abuelo. Madrid: Ed. Paulinas, 1988.
Fábulas del duende sabio. Barcelona: Ed. Obelisco, 1990.
Fábulas para pequeños y grandes. Barcelona: Ed. Obelisco, 1991.

SIDELIGHTS: "I write works with characters that are designed to edify. I also try to include essential ethics. All of my writings are aimed toward a world that is more united, beautiful, just, and fraternal. They are all aimed at making the reader more joyful. I am inspired by nature."

GUSTI (Gustavo Ariel Rosemffet)

PERSONAL DATA: Born in Buenos Aires, Argentina, in 1963. He lives in Sitges, Barcelona, Spain. *Education:* Technical studies in design and publicity.

CAREER: Worked for Catú Cine Animación as an assistant animator; worked as a promoter; later studied the animated films of Hanna Barbera. For the last several years he has dedicated himself to illustrating books for children.

AWARDS, HONORS: Austral Award, 1987; Pomme d'Or Bratislava Award, 1989; Edelvives Award, 1989; Apelles Mestres Award, 1989; National Award for Illustration, 1990; Lazarillo Award for Illustration, 1991.

ILLUSTRATED WORKS:
Un caballo azul. Madrid: Ed. Espasa-Calpe, 1987.
Colección "Pip". Publicacions de l'Abadía de Montserrat, 1987.
Un miedo de risa. Madrid: Ediciones SM, 1988.
Tomás y el lápiz mágico. Madrid: Ed. Edelvives, 1988.
Camilón, Comilón. Madrid: Ediciones SM, 1989.
El pirata valiente. Madrid: Ediciones SM, 1989.
Sorpresa, sorpresa. Madrid: Ediciones SM, 1989.
¿Quién recoge las cacas del perro? Madrid: Ediciones SM, 1989.
La estrella de Jacinto. Tokyo: Ed. Gakken, 1989.
Uña y carne. Barcelona: Ed. Destino, 1990.
Gustavo y los miedos. Madrid: Ediciones SM, 1990.
¿Quién usa las papeleras? Zaragoza: Ed. Edelvives, 1991.
La pequeña Wu-Li. Madrid: Ediciones SM, 1991.

SIDELIGHTS: "Everything began one autumn when I opened the door of my home and found a white speckled cat on the doorstep. It arched its back, purring for a stroke and begging for food. Three years later, our cat Blanqui,—what we named it,—was an active part of our family. It had two homes at the time, ours and next door at the home of a friend, Ricardo Alcántara, who had named it Wu-Li. I think that this is the origin of Alcántara's story, *La pequeña Wu Li*. However, any similarity it has to reality is, of course, pure fiction."

GUTIÉRREZ (OVIEDO), Douglas (Miguel) (1955-)

PERSONAL DATA: Born October 19, 1955, in San Felipe, Yaracuy, Venezuela, he is the son of Miguel Gutiérrez and Norma Antonia Oviedo. He is married to Ingrid Z. Quintero and has a daughter, Maríalucia. *Education:* Advanced study at the Instituto Pedagógico in Caracas, Venezuela.

ADDRESS: (Home) Urbanización Marylago, calle 8, casa y taller "El sol de las botellas." Itsmo Caribe, Estado Anzoátegui, Venezuela. Telephone: 7518495.

CAREER: From 1975 to 1987 he was a professor of physical education and sports for the Ministerio de Educación; from 1987 to 1990 he was the coordinator of sports in Lagoven, an affiliate of Petróleos de Venezuela; Since 1990, he has conducted an art workshop, "El sol de las botellas."

PROFESSIONAL ORGANIZATIONS: Colegio de Profesores de Venezuela.

AWARDS, HONORS: Best Books for Children Award, awarded by Banco del Libro of Venezuela and the Instituto Autónomo Biblioteca Nacional, 1988; participant in the Ninth Annual Exposition of Illustrated Books, Biblioteca Nacional de Venezuela, 1988.

WRITINGS:
Educación física I. Ed. Larense, 1987.
Educación física II. Ed. Larense, 1988.
La noche de las estrellas. Illust. by María Fernanda Oliver. Ed. Ekaré, 1987.

SIDELIGHTS: Concerning his motivation to write, Douglas Gutiérrez tells us: "I don't know exactly. I suspect it is from a need to present to the world the manner in which I perceive existence." He is inspired by "solitude; silence; a clean, ventilated, attractive place; reflection."

HERNÁNDEZ CARDONA, Francesc Xavier (1954-)

PERSONAL DATA: Born December 17, 1954, in Barcelona, Spain, the son of Juan and Lina, he is married to Montserrat and has two children, Guillem and María del Mar. *Education:* Licentiate in history.

ADDRESS: (Home) Gran Via Corts Catalanes 307-311, Esc. A, 4a. 1a., 08014 Barcelona, Spain. Telephone: 4253741. (Office) Universidad de Barcelona, División de Ciencias de la Educación, Departamento de Didáctica de la Escuela de Ciencias Sociales. Baldiri Reixac s/n, 08028 Barcelona, Spain. Telephone: 4409200, extension 3633.

CAREER: Professor of social sciences at the Universidad de Barcelona.

PROFESSIONALORGANIZATIONS: Colegio de Doctores y Licenciados de Cataluña y Baleares; Sociedad Catalana de Arqueología; Sociedad Catalana de Arqueología Industrial.

WRITINGS: More than twenty books of literature for children and young people, written and illustrated.

SIDELIGHTS: "I have the double vocation of writer and illustrator. Basically, I work with history. I understand that the interpretation of history requires an active imagination and creativity, and this is satisfying. I am 'crazy' about history . . . I love to illustrate books that I have designed and written, as I can depict precisely those scenes that interest me. At times, however, this is not possible and I am left with no recourse other than to work with another illustrator. I love all periods of history; I am a generalist and I think that the option of teachers is to generalize more than to specialize in a specific area of history. Sources of my inspiration are diverse, but without doubt personal experiences are the most important."

CRITICAL SOURCES:
David N. Missoula. *School Library Journal.* October 1990.
Publisher's Weekly. June 29, 1990.

HERRERA GARCÍA, Juan Ignacio (1949-)

PERSONAL DATA: Born February 4, 1949, in Madrid, Spain, the son of Ignacio and Carmen, he is married to Gloria and they have two daughters, Coral and Virginia. *Education:* Graduated with honors in public administration, with special emphasis in tourism.

ADDRESS: (Home) Tembleque, 16, 1° E, 28024 Madrid, Spain. Telephone: 5186025.

CAREER: Administrator in various industries and enterprises. Since 1978 he has devoted himself exclusively to writing.

PROFESSIONAL ORGANIZATIONS: Asociación Colegial de Escritores de España.

AWARDS, HONORS: Third Prize, Gran Angular Award, 1980; First Prize, Gran Angular Award, 1981.

WRITINGS:
19 biografías en la colección vidas ilustres (series). Madrid: Ed. Susaeta, 1979.

Embarque Puerta 9. Madrid: Ediciones SM, 1982.
Aventuras de Marco y Tina. Madrid: Ed. Susaeta, 1982.
Santiago Ramón y Cajal. Leon: Ed. Everest, 1986.
La isla de las ballenas. Gijon: Ed. Júcar, 1988.
El delfín explorador. Leon: Ed. Everest, 1989.
Colo y el mar. Ed. Luis Vives, 1988.
Lope y su amigo indio. Madrid: Ed. Anaya, 1988.
Pedro pone petardos. Ed. Rialp, 1990.
Haced sitio a mi hermano. Barcelona: Ed. Noguer, 1990.

SIDELIGHTS: "I write because I enjoy it and because I want my stories to be enjoyable to my readers. I want to convince young people that reading is as exciting as any game. It brings amusement, puzzles, and adventure. I think this approach is the best way to get children to embrace the contents of a story, as well as to get them to actively integrate ideas and form new ones from what they read. I would much rather teach children *how* to think, than tell them what to think. I want to stimulate the development of their creativity, their imagination, and their inventiveness through the most fantastic channels. My favorite themes are science fiction, adventures in general, humor, and real life together with the analysis of its problems and contradictions. I am inspired by good literature, regardless of its genre, as well as by cinema, the theater, art in general, science, nature, and whatever ideas spring from myself."

CRITICAL SOURCES:
José I. García Noriega. *La Nueva España.*
Rodrigo Sagredo. *Diario 16 de Burgos.*
María Solé. *ABC.* August 28, 1982.
Alfonso García. *Diario de León.* 1982.
El País. March 2, 1982
Pueblo. March 2, 1982.
Sur. June 30, 1990.

HUNNEUS, Esther
See Paz, Marcela

IONESCU, Ángela (1937-)

PERSONAL DATA: Born in Bucharest, Romania. Her father was Spanish and her mother was Romanian. *Education:* Studies in journalism.

CAREER: Journalist.

AWARDS, HONORS: Doncel Award, 1962; Lazarillo Award, 1963; Honors List for the Andersen Prize.

WRITINGS:
De un país lejano. 1963.
Detrás de las nubes. 1963.
Arriba en el monte. 1967.
Vivía en el bosque. 1969.
El país de las cosas perdidas. 1972.
Donde duerme el agua. 1975.
En el fondo de la caverna. 1980.
La misma piedra. 1981.
Así era el perro. 1984.
Se fue por el puente. 1985.

JANER MANILA, Gabriel (1940-)

PERSONAL DATA: Born November 1, 1940 in Algaida, Isla de Mallorca, Spain, the son of Pere and Coloma. His wife is Alicia and they have four children, María de la Pau, María del Mar, Pere, and Bartomeu. *Education:* Ph.D. in educative sciences from the Universidad de Barcelona.

ADDRESS: (Home) Camino Viejo de Bunyola 73, 07009 Palma de Mallorca, Spain. Telephone: 294998. (Office) Universitat de les Illes Ballears, Facultat de Letras, Carretera Valloemossa, Km. 7.5, Palma de Mallorca, Spain. Telephone: 173001.

CAREER: He is the chairperson at the Universitat de les Illes Balears for the departments of critical theory and history of education.

PROFESSIONAL ORGANIZATIONS: Asociación de Amigos de la UNESCO; Asociación de Escritores en Lengua Catalana; Obra Cultural Balear.

AWARDS, HONORS: Josep Ma. Folch i Torres Prize, 1975; Cavall Fort Award for Theater for Children, 1983; National Award for Literature for Children and Young People, 1988; Nominated for the Andersen Prize, 1990.

WRITINGS:
El rey Gaspar. Barcelona: Ed. La Galera, 1976.
La serpentina. Barcelona: Ed. La Galera, 1983.

The work of Gabriel Janer is originally written in Catalan.

SIDELIGHTS: "To write is a game for me, a game with history and with words. I try to recreate life through language. I have written stories for children and young people, exclusively for them. I still think, however, that a good story for children must also be a good story for adults. My themes are the imagination, tyranny, the destruction of the natural world, etc."

CRITICAL SOURCES:
Teresa Durán. *El Parallelepípede Blau: Estudi de L'Obra Narrativa per a Infants i Joves de Gabriel Janer Manila.* Palma de Mallorca: Conselleria de Cultura, 1990.

JÁUREGUI PRIETO, Diego (1955-)

PERSONAL DATA: Born March 16, 1955, in Mexico, D.F., he is the son of Ernesto Jáuregui and Matilde Prieto. Education: Licentiate in Hispanic language and literature.

ADDRESS: (Home) Rivera 26, Las Águilas, Mexico, D.F. Telephone: 5930161.

CAREER: Actor and librarian.

WRITINGS:
La alacena. Mexico: CIDCLI, 1985.
Diego Rivera. Mexico: CIDCLI, 1986.
Saturnino Herrán. Mexico: CIDCLI, 1989.

SIDELIGHTS: "I write because literature asked me to. Mexican painting is my source of inspiration."

KALNITZKY DE BRENER, Fany Eugenia
See Calny, Eugenia

KRAFFT VERA, Federico Gerardo (1952-)

PERSONAL DATA: Born December 17, 1952, in Mexico, D.F., the son of Federico Krafft and Cristina Vera, he is married to Amparo González Huergo and has three children, Natalia, Federico Krafft Juárez, and Guillermo Krafft González. Education: Licentiate en modern letters.

ADDRESS: (Home) Rinconada Chicastitla 3 B-304 Col. Santa Ursula Xitla, 14420 Mexico, D.F. Telephone: 5733726. (Office) Holanda 13, Col. San Diego Churubusco 04120, Mexico, D.F. Telephone: 6887122.

CAREER: Technical subdirector Primera Feria Internacional del Libro, 1979-80; technical secretary Feria Internacional del Libro Infantil y Juvenil, Secretary of Public Education, 1981-83; director general at the Center for the Promotion of Mexican Literature, 1986-92.

PROFESSIONAL ORGANIZATIONS: Club de Editores.

WRITINGS:
El día que los pájaros cayeron del cielo. Mexico SITESA, 1989.
El mejor pícher y la bailarina. Mexico: Ed. Trillas, 1991.

He has also published the *Hemerografía Literaria* (Mexico: Ed. UNAM, published anually from 1976 until 1980, 1983).

SIDELIGHTS: "Everything I write is the product of a personal restlessness that I hope to transmit into my stories. My inspirations come from everyday life and include loneliness, friendship, love, social solidarity, vitality, and the ecology."

KURTZ, Carmen (Carmen de Rafael Mares) (1911-)

PERSONAL DATA: Born September 18, 1911, in Barcelona, Spain, her given name is Carmen de Rafael Mares. She is the daughter of José Manuel de Rafael and Carmen Mares. She is married to Pedro Kurz Klein and has one daughter, Odile Kurz. *Education:* Bachelor's degree.

ADDRESS: (Home) Ciudad de Balaguer 65, 08022 Barcelona, Spain. Telephone: 4178982.

PROFESSIONAL ORGANIZATIONS: Asociación de Escritores Españoles.

AWARDS, HONORS: Award from the City of Barcelona, 1954; Planeta Award, 1956; Finalist for the Leopoldo Alas Prize, 1961; Finalist for the Café Gijon Award, 1963; Award from the city of Barbastro, 1975; Finalist for the Lazarillo Award, 1963; Lazarillo Award, 1964; Honors List for the Hans Christian Andersen Prize, 1964; CCEI Finalist, 1966, 1978; CCEI Award, 1967, 1975, 1981; Award Ministry of Culture, for the Book of Interest to Children, 1975, 1978, 1979.

WRITINGS:
Oscar cosmonauta. 1962.
Oscar espía atómico. 1963.
Oscar y el yeti. 1964.
Color de fuego. 1964.
Oscar y corazón de púrpura. 1965.
Oscar espeleólogo. 1966.
Oscar y los hombres-rana. 1967.
Oscar y los ovni. 1967.
Oscar agente secreto. 1968.
Oscar en el Polo Sur. 1969.
Oscar en el laboratorio. 1970.
Oscar en los Juegos Olímpicos. 1971.
Oscar en África. 1974.
Chepita. 1975.
Oscar en las islas. 1977.
Oscar, Kina y el laser. 1979.
Oscar, Buna y el rajá. 1980.
Veva. 1980.
Veva y el mar. 1981.
Piedras y trompetas. 1981.
La paloma y el cuervo. 1981.
La ballena y el cordero. 1981.
Fanfamús. 1982.
Querido Tim. 1983.
Pepé y Dudú. 1983.

Pitos y flautas. 1983.
Los mochuelos. 1983.
Oscar y la extraña luz. 1984.
Brun. 1985.
Dame la mano, Habacuc. 1989.
¿Habéis visto un huevo? 1990.
Cosas que se pierden—amigos que se encuentran. 1990.
Pachu, perro guapo. 1992.

FILMS:
Marionetas. In collaboration with Arturo Kaps and Herta Frankel.
Violeta en el oeste. 1971.
Violeta y el cuco.
Violeta y los buscadores de oro.
Violeta y el vagabundo.
Oscar, Kina y el laser. Screenplay and direction by José Ma. Blanco, 1978.
Oscar agente secreto. In production.

SIDELIGHTS: "Life itself is an invaluable source of inspiration. My life has been rich with events both happy and painful. I have thought much, read much, and I have worked long without rest. I have reached the conclusion that Virginia Woolf's ideal is also for me: to have a room of one's own and to be economically independent. Fortunately, I have a home of my own. Children are one of the most precious components of life. Thus, to write for them is a pleasure. As to themes, I think that any is good if it interests and entertains. In order to write for children, vanity and pedantry must be abandoned; you must realize that although they are filled with love, they are in need of it too. I have looked for originality among the themes of my writing, but I just can't find it. I put in whatever has been important to me, usually from the classics. I love animals; I have cats, dogs, and horses who think they are people."

CRITICAL SOURCES:
Aurora Díaz Plaja. "Literatura infantil y juvenil." *Solidaridad Nacional.* November 1964.
Ricardo Vázquez. *Región.* January 31, 1965.
María Monserrat Sarto. "La hora de los autores españoles." *YA.* June 1980.
Aurora Díaz Plaja. *Juventud Siglo XX.* 26, August-September 1981.
Angel Dotor. *La Tarde.* September 1981.
IEPS. 16, December 1981.
Tajamar. Madrid: January 1982.

LAIGLESIA (GONZÁLEZ-LABARGA), Juan Antonio de (1917-)

PERSONAL DATA: Born November 6, 1917, in Madrid, Spain, the son of Eduardo de Laiglesia Romea and Rosario González Labarga, he is the widower of Josefina González de Peredo and has five children, Juan Fernando, Juan Pablo, Juan Miguel, Juan Ignacio, and Juan Carlos. *Education:* Law degree; studies in business and journalism.

ADDRESS: (Home) Nervión 11 El Viso, 28002 Madrid, Spain. Telephone: 5610268.

CAREER: Writer; official for the opposition to the Minister of Culture; journalist.

PROFESSIONAL ORGANIZATIONS: Sociedad de Autores Españoles.

AWARDS, HONORS: Calderón de la Barca National Prize for Theater, 1954; Virgen del Carmen Award; May Prize for Journalism; Second Prize, Lope de Vega Awards; Second Prize, Lazarillo Award; Silver Medal, Barco de Vapor Award; National Award for Radio and Television; García Lorca Poetry Prize.

WRITINGS:
Cuentos de la radio. ERSA, 1962.
Cien nuevos cuentos. ERSA, 1963.
El arte de la historieta. Ed. Doncel, 1964.
Mariquilla la pelá. Madrid: Ediciones SM, 15th ed.,1982.
El cabrerillo. Madrid: Ed. Edelvives, 5th ed., 1987.
Yagú, el lobo azul. Madrid: Ed. Edelvives, 6th ed., 1988.
Maricastaña, la heroína desconocida. Madrid: Ed. Edelvives, 1989.
El libro de las vacas gordas. Madrid: Ed. Susaeta, 5th ed., 1987.
Luciano Farol Metropolitano. Madrid: Ed. Miñón-Susaeta, 1981.
La madrastrita. Madrid: Ed. Miñón-Susaeta, 1984.
Chuic, el contador que no sabía contar. Madrid: Ed. Miñón-Susaeta, 1985.

He has also published works for adults.

SIDELIGHTS: "I am the young people's comedian, like a Rey Mago filled with energy and happiness. I am the author of 'myth breakers,' that is to say, stories designed to deconstruct and replace the negative myths for children that we have inherited from antiquity: the works of those villains of children's literature, Grimm and Andersen; the ferocious monsters of Perrault; magic fairies and magic wands; evil witches; stupid brutes; demonic snakes; fools; wily tricksters. I have investigated the 'proverbial' olden times and found that our fantasies about the past's inhabitants are usually much more inventive than reality. I don't think we need to create Gremlins and Smurfs. Our energies are better spent trying to change the image of traditional fantastic characters, such as trolls and goblins."

CRITICAL SOURCES: Aurora Díaz Plaja, Carmen Bravo Villasante, Bettina Hürlimann, Carolina Toral, and Emma Triguzzio have reviewed and critiqued the works of Juan Antonio de Laiglesia.

LALANA, Fernando (1958-)

PERSONAL DATA: Born in 1958, in Zaragoza, Spain, where he still lives, he is married to Marta and has a daughter, María. *Education:* Law degree.

CAREER: Has been a professional sportsman, cook, trainer of elephants, artistic photographer, trainsman, and, since 1985, writer.

AWARDS, HONORS: Gran Angular Award, 1984, 1988, 1991; National Award for Literature for Children and Young People, 1991; Barco de Vapor Award (shared with José María Almárcegui), 1991.

WRITINGS:
El secreto de la arboleda. Madrid: Ediciones SM, 1982.
El Zulo. Madrid: Ediciones SM, 1985.
El viaje de doble-P. Madrid: Ed. Magisterio, 1988.
El genio. Madrid: Ed. Magisterio, 1989.
Mi amigo Fernández. Co-written with José María Almárcegui. Madrid: Ed. Anaya, 1989.
Hubo una vez otra guerra. Co-written with Luis A. Puente. Madrid: Ediciones SM, 1989.
El regreso de la doble-P. Madrid: Ed. Magisterio, 1989.
Un elefante en mi sopa. Madrid: Ed. Paulinas, 1989.
El dragón. Madrid: Ed. Magisterio, 1990.
Morirás en Chafarinas. Madrid: Ediciones SM, 1990.
Edelmiro II y el dragón Gutiérrez. Madrid: Ed. Bruño, 1990.
El truco más difícil. Zaragoza: Ed. Edelvives, 1991.
La bomba. Madrid: Ed. Bruño, 1991.

SIDELIGHTS: "That I write literature for young people should not lead to the classification of my work as 'children's literature.' Moreover, when I speak of young readers, I do not do so to distinguish them from adults, but from children. To write for children seems to me a difficult and demanding task. But after a certain age— some time around ten years of age—readers mature to the point that I can reach them.

I have known ten-year-olds who read Poe and Defoe completely. I have known sixteen-year-olds who finished and understood all of Kafka. Then again, I have known fifteen-year-olds who have difficulty with Joan Manuel Gisbert."

LANUZA (I HURTADO), Empar de (1950-)

PERSONAL DATA: Born September 18, 1950, in Valencia, Spain, the daughter of Adrián and Josefina, she is married to Francesc and has two children, Guillem and Paula. *Education:* Licentiate in educative science, with advanced study.

ADDRESS: (Home) Gran Via Ferran el Catòlic 19, 12, 46008 Valencia, Spain. Telephone: 3847068. (Office) Conselleria de Cultura, Educació i Ciència, Campanar 32, 46008 Valencia, Spain. Telephone: 3863138.

CAREER: Founded and worked for the Centro de Educación Psicomotriz, 1973-81; professor of Valencian, 1974-77; worked in Bibliographic Information Service, Universidad de Valencia, 1989-90; has worked for the Department of Culture, Education, and Science since 1990.

AWARDS, HONORS: Josep Ma. Folch i Torres Prize, 1978; CCEI Award, 1979; Tirant lo Blanc Award, 1986. In 1991 was honored by the creation of an award for literature for children and young people, called the Empar de Lanuza Prize, in Meliana.

WRITINGS:
El sabio rey loco y otros cuentos. Barcelona: Ed. La Galera, 1980.
Buen viaje, petiblanco. Barcelona: Ed. La Galera, 1983.
La luciérnaga Luci. Illust. by Pau Estrada. Barcelona: Ed. La Galera, 6th ed., 1985.
La grieta asesina. Valencia: Ed. Gregal, 3rd ed., 1988.
El largo viaje de los habitantes de Bóbilis-Bóbilis. Illust. by Paco Giménez.
    Barcelona: Ed. Teide, 1988.
La familia feroz. Illust. by Roser Capdevila. Barcelona: Ed. Aliorna, 1988.
Un diente pendiente. Illust. by Marta Balaguer. Barcelona: Ed. Edebé, 1991.

Included in more than seven literary anthologies, the works of Empar Lanuza are written originally in Valencian. The works here cited are translations into Spanish.

SIDELIGHTS: "I write about whatever interests me at any specific moment, usually histories related to communication, friendship, compassion, loneliness, justice, the wish to discover new things, fantasies, mysteries, adventures . . . I use humor in certain dramatic situations and when I want to illustrate the versatility of language to the reader. I have written in several genres: the novel, novella, poetry, theater, and with great abundance in the short story. My characters have been animals, objects, girls and boys, women and men, characters with fantastic forms, and characters who belong only in fantasy, like witches, ghosts, giants, etc. The sources of my inspiration are gestures: fragments of an instance or an attitude. They are all that we can know of others or that they can know of ourselves through conversation, reading, or sifting through memories for a characteristic that can then be extrapolated."

"I enjoy spending time with my readers when they invite me to their schools and libraries. I try to talk to them without reserve. I answer all their questions, I tell them stories, or help them create their own. We usually say goodbye with a smile or an autograph on a book or piece of paper."

CRITICAL SOURCES:
Several critical assessments of her work have appeared in *Serra d'Or*, edited by
    Aurora Díaz Plaja, as well as in *CLIJ* and *Escola Catalana*.
Teresa Durán, *Catalan Writing* 4.

LARA PEINADO, Federico (1940-)

PERSONAL DATA: Born December 9, 1940, in Hornos de Segura, Jaen, Spain, the son of Julián and Sandalia, he is married to María del Pilar and has three children, Federico, Blanca María, and Beatriz. *Education:* Licentiate in philosophy and letters; Ph.D. in history.

ADDRESS: (Home) Ciudad Universitaria, 28040 Madrid, Spain. (Office) Universidad Complutense, Facultad de Geografía e Historia, Edificio B., Madrid, Spain. Telephone: 3945943.

CAREER: Archivist for the Diputación de Lérida, 1973-76; professor at the Universidad Complutense de Madrid, 1976-.

PROFESSIONAL ORGANIZATIONS: Asociación Española de Egiptología.

AWARDS, HONORS: Silver Medal from the Province of Lérida; Antonio Ponz Prize from the CSIC; S.M. King of Spain Award, from the Academia Bibliográfica Mariana.

WRITINGS:
Mitos sumerios y acadios. Ed. Nacional, 1984.
Himnos sumerios. Ed. Tecnos, 1988.
Himnos babilónicos. Ed. Tecnos, 1989.
La civilización sumeria. Ed. Historia 16, 1989.
Libro de los muertos. Ed. Tecnos, 1989.
Así vivían en Babilonia. Madrid: Ed. Anaya, 1989.
Así vivían los fenicios. Madrid: Ed. Anaya, 1990.
El escarabajo verde. Madrid: Ed. Bruño, 1990.
Abisid, el grumete fenicio. Madrid: Ed. Bruño, 1992.
Código de Hammurabí. Ed. Tecnos, 1992.
Poema de Gilgamesh. Ed. Tecnos, 1992.

SIDELIGHTS: His writings are centered on the ancient Middle Eastern world, from which cultures he receives his inspiration. Through his literature he tries to bring to public attention the great literary works of current and past Oriental cultures.

LARREULA (VIDAL), Enric (1941-)

PERSONAL DATA: Born December 2, 1941, in Barcelona, Spain, the son of Manel and Concepción. *Education:* Licentiate in Catalan language and literature.

ADDRESS: (Home) Passeig de la Guineu 81, 08190 Valldoreix, Spain. Telephone: 5892957.

CAREER: Professor of Catalan language and literature at the Universidad Autónoma de Barcelona.

PROFESSIONAL ORGANIZATIONS: Amnesty International, Greenpeace.

AWARDS, HONORS: Víctor Catalá, 1967; Recull Award, 1969; Xarxa d'Assaig Award, 1983; Critics' Award from *Serra d'Or*, 1984; Pere Quart d'Humnor i Satira Award, 1990; Lola Anglada Prize, 1991.

WRITINGS:
El gigante bueno. Barcelona: Condal Editora, 1981.
Barbabum y la cometa. Barcelona: Condal Editora, 1982.
Barbabum y la comida. Barcelona: Condal Editora, 1982.
Barbabum y la granja. Barcelona: Condal Editora, 1982.

El gigante pequeño. Barcelona: Ed. Teide, 1982.

Quino y la mosca. Barcelona: Ed. Teide, 1982.

La familia de setas. Barcelona: Ed. Teide, 1982.

Las dos nubes amigas. Barcelona: Ed. Teide, 1982.

El país de los cinco sentidos. Barcelona: Ed. Teide, 1982.

La escuela pequeña. Barcelona: Ed. Teide, 1982.

La casa grande. Barcelona: Ed. Teide, 1982.

La luna que perdió su camino. Barcelona: Ed. Teide, 1982.

La mona saltarina. Barcelona; Ed. Teide, 1982.

La calle. Barcelona: Ed. Teide, 1982.

El payés y los caracoles. Barcelona: Ed. Teide, 1982.

El sol que no tenía memoria. Barcelona; Ed. Teide, 1982.

Las tres hormigas. Barcelona: Ed. Teide, 1982.

El payaso que no quería hacer reír. Barcelona: Ed. Teide, 1982.

El búho miedoso. Barcelona: Ed. Teide, 1982.

El ciervo que fue a buscar a la primavera. Barcelona: Ed. Argos-Vergara, 1983.

Melisa. Barcelona: Ed. Argos-Vergara, 1983.

El jabalí y el cerdo. Barcelona: Ed. Teide, 1983.

Romero. Barcelona: Ed. Teide, 1984.

Hospital de campaña. Barcelona: Ed. Teide, 1984.

Las dos tribus. Barcelona: Ed. Teide, 1984.

El arca de Noé. Barcelona: Ed. Teide, 1984.

La flor nueva. Barcelona: Ed. Teide, 1984.

Tragantón I. Barcelona: Ed. Teide, 1984.

Rey Nito. Barcelona: Ed. La Galera, 1984.

El paquete. Barcelona: Ed. La Galera, 1984.

Comilona galáctica. Barcelona: Ed. La Galera, 1985.

Sol y luna. Barcelona: Publicaciones de l'Abadía de Montserrat, 1985.

Kanguelo. Barcelona: Ed. La Galera, 1986.

La baronía de Vallehermoso. Barcelona: Ed. La Galera, 1986.

Los colores. Barcelona: Ed. La Galera, 1986.

Los grillos y las cigarras. Barcelona: Ed. La Galera, 1986.

Brillante. Barcelona: Ed. Cruillá, 1986.

Las memorias de la bruja aburrida. Barcelona: Ed. Planeta, 1986.

La bruja aburrida y la mona. Barcelona: Ed. Planeta, 1986.

Los arruganariz. Barcelona: Ed. Teide, 1987.

Los animales vergonzosos. Barcelona: Ed. Aliorna, 1987.

La boda de la bruja aburrida. Barcelona: Ed. Planeta, 1987.

La fiesta mayor de la bruja aburrida. Barcelona: Ed. Planeta,1987.

Las vacaciones de la bruja aburrida. Barcelona: Ed. Planeta, 1988.

La bruja aburrida se va a París. Barcelona: Ed. Planeta, 1989.

La marmota inventora. Barcelona: Ed. La Galera, 1989.

La bruja aburrida va a la Gran Bretaña. Barcelona: Ed. Planeta, 1990.

La bruja aburrida visita Venecia. Barcelona: Ed. Planeta, 1990.
Homénica, Villa Olímpica. Barcelona: Ed. La Galera, 1990.
La bruja aburrida en Nueva York. Barcelona: Ed. Planeta, 1991.
La navidad de la bruja aburrida. Barcelona: Ed. Planeta, 1991.

The works of Enric Larreula are written in Catalan. Nevertheless, his publishers usually translate them immediately, so that they are almost always released in two languages, Spanish and Catalan. Some of his works have also been translated into English, French, Portuguese, Italian, Danish, German, Swedish, Basque, and Gallego.

SIDELIGHTS:
"The marginalization of Catalan language and culture in my country gave me the desire to cultivate and teach them to others. I write for love of my language, love of adventure, nature, animals, liberty, and all the little everyday things. Above all, I write to entertain myself and others. And to contribute, if possible, in making the world a little bit better."

CRITICAL SOURCES:
Véronique Peiffer. *Tesis de licenciatura.* Universidad Católica de Louvain.

LEZAETA CASTILLO, Gabriela (1921-)

PERSONAL DATA: Born December 1, 1921, in Santiago, Chile, the daughter of Alberto and Lavinia, she is married to Robert Holmes Cave and has four children, Robert, Roland, Susan, and Alan. *Education:* Holds a degree from the Escuela de Bellas Artes in sculpture.

ADDRESS: (Home) Hendaya 639, Las Condes, Santiago, Chile. Telephone: 2083524. (Office) Casilla 52134, Santiago, Chile.

PROFESSIONAL ORGANIZATIONS: PEN Club Internacional; IBBY; Sociedad de Escritores de Chile.

AWARDS, HONORS: First Prize, Gabriela Mistral Competition, 1969; First Prize, Pedro de Oña, 1975; First Prize, Jorge Luis Borges International Story Competition, 1976, 1978; Third Prize, Cuarto Certamen de Cuentos from the Universidad del Norte, 1980; Special Mention, Ed. Atlántida Contest, 1982; María Luisa Bombal Prize, 1985; Second Place, Andrés Bello Awards, 1991; Third Prize, Mila Oyarzún Story Competition, 1991.

WRITINGS:
Color hollín. Santiago, Chile: 1970.
La tertulia musical de los Irizarte. Santiago, Chile: Ed. Andrés Bello, 1985.
Lectura complementaria. Santiago, Chile: Ed. Andrés Bello, 1985.
Yo pienso y aprendo. Santiago, Chile: Ed. Andrés Bello.
Cuentos cortos de la tierra larga. Santiago, Chile: Ed. Andrés Bello, 1989.
Cuentos de príncipes, garzas y manzanas. Santiago, Chile: Ediciones SM, 1991.
Nuestros cuentos A. M. Santiago, Chile: Ed. Andrés Bello, 1991.
Leyendas iberoamericanas. Santiago, Chile: Ed. Andrés Bello.

SIDELIGHTS: "For several years I was a writer for adults, and now I am interested in literature for children because of its meticulous distillation of language into concrete, fundamental concepts. Also, I find it easy to communicate with children. For me, inspiration often comes from surprising and varying sources; this is not strange because I find myself interested in everything."

CRITICAL SOURCES:
Colibrí. 10, Year 4.

LLAMAZARES, Julio (1955-)

PERSONAL DATA: Born in Vegamián, Leon, Spain, in 1955. *Education:* Law degree.

ADDRESS: (Home) Gravina 4, 28004 Madrid, Spain. Telephone: 5214242.

CAREER: Journalist; writer for the radio and television.

AWARDS, HONORS: Jorge Guillén Prize, 1982.

WRITINGS:
La lentitud de los bueyes. 1979.
Memoria de la nieve. 1982.
Luna de lobos. Seix Barral, 1985.
La lluvia amarilla. Seix Barral, 1988.
El río del olvido. Seix Barral, 1990.

CRITICAL SOURCES:
César Antonio Molina. La V*oz de Galicia.*

LLORENS LLONCH, Rafael (1935-)

PERSONAL DATA: Born June 3, 1935, in Sabadell, Barcelona, Spain, the son of Mateo and Montserrat, he is married to Ana María and has a daughter, María. *Education:* Master's degree in primary education.

ADDRESS: (Home) Amadeo Vives 6, 08510 Roda de Ter, Spain. Telephone: 8540474. (Office) Escuela Pública "Verge del Sòl del Pont," calle Escuelas s/n., Roda de Ter, Spain. Telephone: 8450955.

CAREER: Professor of E.G.B. since 1958.

PROFESSIONAL ORGANIZATIONS: UEV (Unió Excursionista de Vic).

AWARDS, HONORS: Ajuntament de Calldetenes Award, 1987; Andersen Prize, Twenty-fifth Anniversary.

WRITINGS:
La carretera del Meranjol. Zaragoza: Ed. Edelvives, 1990.
Clara. Zaragoza: Ed. Edelvives, 1992.

SIDELIGHTS: "My favorite theme is nature; I write stories about woodland animals, and I try to make readers aware of technology's growing threat to the natural world (*La carretera de Meranjol*). I write about themes that have special significance to those living in communities, in the countryside, and in rural areas. My source of inspiration is my living contact with nature and with the people of the countryside, and it comes from my awareness of the lives of the animals of the forest. I write about these themes because they are the things that I know best. Also, I write about them because I profoundly love nature and I want to communicate love and respect for nature to my readers."

LOMAS GARZA, Carmen (1948-)

PERSONAL DATA: Born in 1948, in Kingsville, Texas, U.S.A. *Education:* Bachelor of science degree from Texas Arts and Industry in Kingsville, Texas; Texas teacher certification; Master of education from the Juárez-Lincoln/Antioch Graduate School in Austin, Texas; Master of arts, San Francisco State University.

ADDRESS: (*Home*) 342 Prospect Ave., San Francisco, California 94110. Telephone: 2828503.

CAREER: Graphic designer for the National Migrant Information Clearinghouse at Juárez-Lincoln Center, Austin, Texas, 1972-73; teacher of art, Allan Junior High School, Austin, Texas, 1974-75; curator and assistant administrator at the Galería de la Raza/Estudio 24, San Francisco, California, 1974-75 and 1980-81; independent painter since 1982.

AWARDS, HONORS: California Arts Council Artist-in-Residence Grant, sponsored by Galería de la Raza/Studio 24, 1979, 1982; National Endowment for the Arts Fellowship in Printmaking, 1981; California Arts Council Artist in Residence Grant, co-sponsored by the Mexican Museum and Real Alternatives Program, San Francisco, 1984; California Arts Council Artist-in-Residence Grant, sponsored by the Mexican Museum, 1986; National Endowment for the Arts Fellowship in Painting, 1987; California Arts Council Fellowship in Painting, 1990; Illinois State University Visiting Artist for April, 1991; *Cuadros de familia* selected as one of the twenty books nominated for the Texas Bluebonnet Award, 1992.

WRITINGS:
Family Pictures/Cuadros de familia. Co-written with Harriet Rohmer, San Francisco: Children's Book Press, 1990.

LÓPEZ GARCÍA, David (1949-)

PERSONAL DATA: Born May 31, 1949, in Alhama de Murcia, Spain, the son of David López and Purificación García, he is married to Mercedes Sandoval and has two children, David and Antonio. *Education:* Licentiate in philosophy and letters, with emphasis in art.

ADDRESS: (Home) Estación 10, 6° C, Molina de Saguera, Murcia, Spain. (Office) Instituto de Bachillerato Alfonso X el Sabio, Isaac Peral, s/n, Murcia, Spain.

CAREER: Professor of Spanish language and literature at the Instituto Bachillerato de Baena, 1973; he now teaches at the Instituto Alfonso X el Sabio de Murcia.

WRITINGS:
Antonio Dupar y Francisco Salzillo. Murcia: Academia Alfonso el Sabio, 1970.
El arco y la paloma. Murcia: Ed. Regional de Murcia, 1982.
Por casualidad. Embajada de España en Marruecos, 1985.
Antología de la poesía barroca murciana. Murcia: Ed. Regional de Murcia, 1987.
Raisuni. Madrid: Ed. Alfaguara, 1991.

CRITICAL SOURCES:
Ramón Jiménez Madrid. *Narrativa brava de autor murciano*. Murcia: Ed. Regional de Murcia, 1985.
Ramón Jiménez Madrid. *La Opinión*. Murcia: December 18, 1991.

LÓPEZ NARVÁEZ, Concha (Concepción) (1939-)

PERSONAL DATA: Born August 27, 1939, in Seville, Spain, the daughter of Rafael and Concepción, she is married to Carmelo Salmerón and has four children, María, Rafael, Miguel, and Teresa. *Education:* Licentiate in the history of America.

ADDRESS: (Home) Mediterráneo 30, 28007 Madrid, Spain. Telephone: 5506726.

CAREER: Professor of history.

PROFESSIONAL ORGANIZATIONS: Asociación Española de Amigos del Libro (Amigos del IBBY).

AWARDS, HONORS: Lazarillo Award for Literature; CCEI Award, finalist twice, Honors List four times; Honors List for the IBBY, 1986; candidate for the Andersen Prize, 1992; president for three years of the Asociación Española de Amigos del Libro.

WRITINGS:
La tierra del sol y la luna. Madrid: Ed. Espasa-Calpe, 1982.
El amigo oculto y los espíritus de la tarde. Barcelona: Ed. Noguer, 1984.
La cadena de Edeta. Madrid: Ed. Espasa-Calpe, 198-.
El árbol de los pájaros sin vuelo. Madrid: Ed. Anaya, 198-.
Nieve de julio. Barcelona: Ed. Edebé, 198-.
Endrina y el secreto del peregrino. Madrid: Ed. Espasa-Calpe,198-.
Un puñado de miedos. Madrid: Ediciones SM, 198-.
Amigo de palo. Madrid: Ediciones SM, 198-.
Memorias de una gallina. Madrid: Ed. Anaya, 1990.
El tiempo y la promesa. Madrid: Ed. Bruño, 1990.
La sombra del gato. Madrid: Ed. Alfaguara, 1992.

SIDELIGHTS: "For me writing is a form of communicating about myself. I write for children because I want to communicate myself especially to them. Also, to create, to give life to a character or story that otherwise does not exist is a genuine pleasure.

My favorite themes are those that show the customs of people and explore how it feels to be human. It doesn't matter when a story takes place. I frequently write using historical themes, although today's problems are also important to me. Writing for children, I try to leave out fantastic abstractions and instead tell the stories of the things and animals that surround us."

CRITICAL SOURCES: Aurora Díaz Plaja, Severiano Calleja, and Francisco Cubelle have devoted much critical attention to the writings of Concha López Narváez. Reviews of her work have appeared in Spanish and Japanese journals and magazines, as well as in newspapers, including El P*aís, El Nacional, Ya, Diario 16,* and *ABC.*

LUJÁN, Fernando (1912-1967)

PERSONAL DATA: Born in San Jose, Costa Rica in 1912 and died there in 1967. *Education:* Primary and secondary.

WRITINGS:
Tierra marinera. Imprenta Soley y Valverde, 1940.
Poesía infantil. Imprenta Soley y Valverde, 1941.
Oda a las ruinas de Copán. Tegucigalpa: Imprenta La República, 1963.
La flauta de piedra. San José, Costa Rica: Ed. L'Atelier, 1963.
Anochecer de otoño. San José, Costa Rica: Ed. L'Atelier, 1964.
Himno al mediodía. Ed. Costa Rica, 1964.
Musgo en la piedra. San José, Costa Rica: Ed. L'Atelier, 1965.

SIDELIGHTS: Fernando Luján traveled throughout Mexico, Venezuela, and Central America. He lived for some years in Guatemala. The poetry of Rafael Alberti and Juan Ramón Jiménez had an early influence on him, as did the rural environment of his homeland, filled with the games and activities of childhood. His early poetry reflects this upbringing, filled with games of language and rhythm.

MACHADO (MARTINS), Ana María (1941-)

PERSONAL DATA: Born December 24, 1941, in Rio de Janeiro, Brazil, the daughter of Mario Martins and Dinah Almeida Martins, she is married to Lourenzo Baeta

Bastos and has three children, Rodrigo, Pedro Martins Machado, and Luisa Martins Baeta Bastos. *Education:* Master of arts degree in Romance languages from the Universidad Federal de Rio de Janeiro; Doctorate in linguistics from l'Ecole Pratique des Hautes Etudes in Paris.

ADDRESS: (Home) Rua Ingles de Souza 193/302, Jardim Botanico 22460, Rio de Janeiro, Brazil. Telephone: 2946092. (Office) Rua Marqués San Vicente 52/367. Gavea 22451. Rio de Janeiro, Brazil. Telephone: 2395644.

CAREER: Professor of Brazilian literature at the Universidad Federal de Rio de Janeiro and at the University of Paris IV; works for the magazine *Elle* in Paris; also works on consignment for the BBC in London; columnist for various Brazilian magazines; news editor for the Radio Jornal do Brasil; Libreria Malasartes, 1979-; author of stories for children.

PROFESSIONAL ORGANIZATIONS: IBBY; Fundaçao Nacional do Livro Infantil; Sindicato de Escritores de Rio de Janeiro.

AWARDS, HONORS: Selo de Ouro, Melhor Livro Infantil Brasileiro, 1980, 1981, 1982; Casa de las Americas Award, Havana, 1981; Award from the APCA (Paulist Association of Art Critics), 1981, 1982; IBBY Honors List, 1982, 1984; APPLE (Association for the Promotion of Literature for Children), 1988; president of judges for the Hans Christian Andersen Award, 1990.

WRITINGS:
Bisa Bea, Bisa Bel. Madrid: Ed. Noguer, 1985.
Del tamaño justo. Madrid: Ed. Alfaguara, 1985.
Palabras, palabritas y palabrotas. Buenos Aires: Ed. Emecé, 1987.
El perro del cerro y la rana de la sabana. Caracas: Ed. Ekaré, 1988.
Comilón, comilón. Madrid: Ediciones SM, 1989.
Un montón de unicornios. Madrid: Ediciones SM, 1990.

Ana María Machado writes in Portuguese. She has published more than seventy books, with more than 2 million copies sold to children and adults.

SIDELIGHTS: "I love language and stories, and I am enchanted with the possibility of living other lives through my characters. I want to understand and grasp the world inside and out. My themes blend reality with imagination, distinct times, and characters who want to discover who they are and question authority and prejudice."

CRITICAL SOURCES:
Marisa Lajolo. *Ana María Machado*. Sao Paulo: Ed. Abril, 1981.
Regina Zilberman and Ligia Cadermatori. *Literatura Infantil: Autoritarismo e*

emancipacão. Sao Paulo: Ed. Atica, 1982.
Vanda Maria Resende. *I menino na literatura brasileira*. Sao Paulo: Ed. Perspectiva, 1983.

MALINOW, Lydia Inés

PERSONAL DATA: Education: Ph.D. in literature from the Faculty of Philosophy and Letters at the Universidad de Buenos Aires.

CAREER: She has dedicated herself to literature, journalism, diplomacy, and teaching. Since 1949 she has written for several newspapers, Argentinian as well as foreign. From 1984 to 1989 she was cultural adjutant to Belgium. She has also taught literature and grammar.

AWARDS, HONORS: Cámara Argentina Award for the Novel, 1949; Distinction from the Consejo de Escritores, 1962; Fellowship from the National Foundation for the Arts, 1962, 1966; Alfonsina Storni Prize from the Festival Infantil de Necoches, 1964; Distinction from the Argentinian Society for the Protection of Animals, 1977; Honors List for the Sociedad Argentina de Escritores, 1955, 1974, 1985.

WRITINGS:
Canciones para mis nenas llenas de sol. Buenos Aires: Cicordia y Rodríguez, 1958.
Versitos para caramelos. Buenos Aires: Cicordia y Rodríguez, 1961.
El libro de las nenas. Buenos Aires: Ed. Fariña, 1966.
Las aventuras de Pinocho. Buenos Aires: Centro Editor para América Latina, 1968.
Muchas veces cuatro patas. Buenos Aires: Ed. Sigmar, 1976.
Aquíiii Inosito. Buenos Aires: Ed. Plus Ultra, 1976.
¡Buena suerte, Inosito! Buenos Aires: Ed. Plus Ultra, 1977.
Osito Kinkajú. Buenos Aires: Ed. Kapelusz, 1984.
100 cuentos de Inés Malinow. Buenos Aires: Ed. Sigmar, 1988.
Tricota cuenta sus bolsillos. Ed. Sigmar, in print.
Cuaderno de viaje I y II. Ed. Sigmar, in print.

She has also published fiction and poetry for adults.

CRITICAL SOURCES: Her work has received considerable attention in periodicals and literary journals, especially by: Raúl Lagmanovich, Carlos Arcidiácono, Hugo Becacece, Luisa Valenzuela, Alma González Paz, Raúl H. Castagnino, Raúl Gustavo Aguirre, Oscar H. Villordo, María Adela Renard, Emilio J. Corbiere, and Luis Ricardo Furlan.

MANYARI REY DE CÓRDOVA, Olga (1938-)

PERSONAL DATA: Born October 13, 1938, in Lima, Peru, the daughter of Moisés Marino Manyari and Ernestina Rey, she is married to Eusebio Córdova and has a daughter, Karina Olga. *Education:* Ph.D. in education from the Universidad Nacional Mayor de San Marcos.

ADDRESS: (Home) Angamos Este 2600, Lima 34, Surquillo, Peru. Telephone: 484996.

CAREER: Professor of secondary education.

PROFESSIONAL ORGANIZATIONS: Member of the Commission on Lexicography; Member of the Academia Peruana de la Lengua; Catedrática U.P. Inca Garcilaso; Board of Directors of the Asociación Nacional de Escritores y Artistas ANEA; Mesa Redonda Panamericana de Santa Beatriz; Asociación de Profesoras Egresadas de San Marcos.

AWARDS, HONORS: Finalist for the Woman of the Year Award in 1969 from the UMA, Peruvian branch; vocal director for the ANEA; member of the Commission for the Celebration of the One-Hundred-fiftieth Birthdate of Ricardo Palma; investigator for the Seminar on the Peruvian Language, Facultad de Letras, Universidad Nacional Mayor de San Marcos.

WRITINGS:
Poesías excelsas. Ed. Jurídica, 1966.
Sueños infantiles. Ed. Asociación Nacional de Escritores y Artistas, 1978.
Pinceles del tiempo. Ed. Artes Visuales, 1980.

SIDELIGHTS: "I write because I feel a need to express myself to others. I began writing poetry for children after having published *Sueños infantiles*, dedicated to my first daughter and to all the children of the world. I also write idyllic and metaphysical poetry. My source of inspiration is the world around me, the environment, and the way in which my soul is open to the transcendent, the immanent, and the absolute."

CRITICAL SOURCES:
El Comercio. May 1978.
Expreso. June 17, 1978.
Ricardo González Vigil. *El Comercio*. 1980.

MARCUSE, Aída E(imer de) (1934-)

PERSONAL DATA: Born February 12, 1934, in Montevideo, Uruguay, the daughter of Máximo Elmer and Sara Malek de Elmer. She is married to Robert Jacques Marcuse and has three children, Monique Aline, Michel Louis, and Alain Marcel. *Education:* Bachelor's degree in law; four-year study of letters; two years as a professor of literature and history.

ADDRESS: 1541 Brickell Ave., Miami, Florida 33129. Telephone: 8543173.

CAREER: Author of books for children; translator; editor; advisor concerning literature for children; teacher of literary seminars; journalist.

PROFESSIONAL ORGANIZATIONS: SADE; CAPLI (Central Argentina for Literature for Children); AVELIJ (Venezuelan Association for Literature for Children); Centro Lingüístico Ricardo J. Alfaro, Panama; Society of Children's Book Writers, Los Angeles, California.

AWARDS, HONORS: Honorary Member, Centro Lingüístico Ricardo J. Alfaro; her book *Había una vez un cuerpo* was made required reading at the Ministerio de Cultura de Argentina.

WRITINGS:
Había una vez un cuerpo. Buenos Aires: Ed. Paidos y Plus, 1973.
Marcelo Casi-Casi. Buenos Aires: Ed. Paidos, 1976.
Muñeca de trapo. Buenos Aires: Ed. Plus Ultra, 1977.
Un caballo a motor. Buenos Aires: Ed. Plus Ultra, 1982.
"Un vinten pa'l judas." *Cuentos, mitos y leyendas para niños de América Latina.*
     UNESCO/CERLALC, 1983.
Un barrilete para Grompón. Buenos Aires: Ed. Plus Ultra, 1985.
Cuentos de antes de ayer. Buenos Aires: Ed. Plus Ultra, 1987.
La cocina viajera. Buenos Aires: Ed. Plus Ultra, 1987.
Prudencio el prudente. Buenos Aires: Ed. Plus Ultra, 1992.
Caperucita y la luna de papel. California: Laredo Publishing, 1992.
La hormiguita. California: Hampton-Brown Co., 1992.

She has translated from English and French various works of literature for children, as well as literature in general.

SIDELIGHTS: "Probably, one who can choose not to be a writer was never a writer in the first place. It is an impulse that is impossible to repress, a vital need one feels to express oneself. Personally, I think that words are a difficult medium of expression for ideas and feelings. Music is able to be more abstract and is therefore a better medium (or it seems so to me). I write for children to satisfy my own inner child, who is always creating poetry and inventing stories. But the writer transforms them, and they pass beneath the microscope of all that surrounds them. It is as if the writer puts everything beneath the lens of a microscope, including herself. Inspiration comes from every place; nothing is banal or of too little interest. Every experience can be transformed, can germinate into a creative moment. My favorite themes are poems of life, the everyday, the imagination, love, and nature."

MARTÍN (FARRERO), Andreu (1949-)

PERSONAL DATA: Born May 9, 1949, in Barcelona, Spain, he is the son of Inés and Andrés. He is married to Rosa María and has one daughter, Clara. *Education:* Holds a degree in psychology from the School of Philosophy and Letters in Barcelona.

ADDRESS: (Home) Gran Vía de les Corts Catalanes 426, 3a. 1a., 08015 Barcelona, Spain. Telephone: 3259032.

CAREER: He has worked as an editor at several publishing houses and he is the founder of a comics magazine. He has collaborated on several short narratives, articles, and comic strips for Spanish, Catalan, and French magazines.

PROFESSIONAL ORGANIZATIONS: Asociación Colegial de Escritores de Lengua Catalana.

AWARDS, HONORS: Cycle of Crime Award, 1980; Alfa 7 Award; Hammet Award from the International Association of Police Fiction; National Award for Literature for Children, 1989.

WRITINGS:
Aprende y calla. Barcelona: Ed. Plaza & Janés, 1979.
El señor Capone no está en casa. Barcelona: Ed. Plaza & Janés, 1979.
A navajazos. Gijon: Ed. Júcar, 1980.
Prótesis. Madrid: Ed. Planeta, 1980.
La otra gota de agua. Barcelona: Ed. Plaza & Janés, 1981.
Por amor al arte. Barcelona: Ediciones B, 1982.
Si es no es. Barcelona: Ed. Plaza & Janés, 1982.
La camisa del revés. Barcelona: Ed. Salvat, 1983.
Crónica negra. Ed. Alfa 7, 1984.
El caballo y el mono. Ed. Anagrama, 1984.
Amores que matan, ¿y qué? Ed. Alfa 7, 1984.

Momento de difuntos. Ed. Alfa 7, 1984.

El día menos pensado. Ed. Alfa 7, 1986.

Ahogos y palpitaciones. Ed. Salvat, 1987.

No pidas sardina fuera de temporada. Co-written with Jaume Ribera. Madrid: Ed. Alfaguara, 1987.

El pozo de los mil demonios. Madrid: Ed. Alfaguara, 1987.

La Antártida en peligro. Co-written with Juanjo Sarto. Ed. Molino, 1987.

S.O.S. Canguros. Co-written with Juanjo Sarto. Ed. Molino, 1987.

Infierno forestal. Co-written with Juanjo Sarto. Ed. Molino, 1987.

Operación 20 tigres. Co-written with Juanjo Sarto. Ed. Molino, 1987.

Crímenes de aficionado. Barcelona: Ed.Timum Mas, 1987.

Barcelona Connection. Barcelona: Ediciones B, 1988.

A martillazos. Gijon: Ed. Júcar, 1988.

El que persigue al ladrón. Ed. Renfe, 1988.

Mar negro, mar muerto. Co-written with Juanjo Sarto. Ed. Molino, 1988.

Operación "Moby Dick". Co-written with Juanjo Sarto. Ed. Molino, 1989.

Cuidados intensivos. Barcelona: Ed. Plaza & Janés, 1989.

Lo que más quieras. Ed. Cambio 16, 1990.

Jesús en los infiernos. Barcelona: Ed. Plaza & Janés, 1990.

Todos los detectives se llaman Flanagan. Co-written with Jaume Ribera. Madrid: Ed. Anaya, 1991.

Approximately the first half of the works here cited are detective fiction, one of the principal genres in which the author writes; the rest are novels for young people.

SIDELIGHTS: "It has been said that the writer does not choose his themes, but the themes choose the writer. The only answers that occur to me when I am asked why I write are 'I have no idea' and 'because I enjoy it'; but these are a bit too simple. A third answer would derive from the knowledge I have about complicated psychological motivations, problems during childhood, inhibitions, and unconscious exorcisms. I suppose I write for the same reason that everyone else does, to play, to enjoy myself, and to earn a living."

CRITICAL SOURCES:
Patricia Harst. *The Spanish Sleuth: Detectives in Spanish Fiction.* London: Rutherford Madison, Fairleigh Dickinson University Press.

MARTÍN FERNÁNDEZ DE VELASCO, Miguel (1927-)

PERSONAL DATA: Born July 18, 1927, in Valladolid, Spain, the son of José and

Concepción, he is married to María and has six children, Miguel, Carlos, Joaquín, Alfonso, Ignacio, and Juan. *Education:* Law degree.

ADDRESS: (Home) Plaza Spain 14, 47001 Valladolid, Spain. Telephone: 306748.

AWARDS, HONORS: Lazarillo Award, 1983; CCEI Award, 1984; Libélula Award, 1986; Finalist for the Lazarillo Award, 1987; Altea Award, 1987; Centros Castellanos del País Vasco Award, 1988; CCEI Honorable Mention, 1989; White Raven Award from Bologna Children's Book Fair, 1989.

WRITINGS:
Pabluras. Barcelona: Ed. Noguer, 1983.
Grandullón. Barcelona: Ed. Noguer, 1985.
Pabluras y Gris. Barcelona: Ed. Noguer, 1987.
Alifar. Ed. Rialp, 1988.
Dardo y Huracán. Zaragoza: Ed. Edelvives, 1988.
Me regalaron un lobo. Ed. Paulinas, 1989.
Poché. Ed. Rialp, 1989.
Paladín. Zaragoza: Ed. Edelvives, 1989.
La pantera negra. Ed. Rialp, 1991.

SIDELIGHTS: "I usually write about personal experiences in relation to the natural world. Bears, wolves, falcons, and other animals are the heroes of my best pages. In my nonbiographical works, some principal themes are the courage of the individual before a group, a person's sense of responsibility, and the need to persevere in the face of defeat in order to make life worth living."

CRITICAL SOURCES:
Isabel Paraíso. *La literatura en Valladolid en el siglo XX (1939-89)*.
Jesús Castañón. "Tres premios Lazarillo." *Literatura contemporánea en Castilla y León*. 1986.

MARTÍN GAITE, Carmen (1925-)

PERSONAL DATA: Born December 8, 1925, in Salamanca, Spain, the daughter of José and María. *Education:* Ph.D. in philology of Romance languages.

ADDRESS: (Home) Doctor Esquerdo 43, 7° B, Salamanca, Spain. Telephone: 5745644.

AWARDS, HONORS: National Award for Literature; Nadal Award; Prince of Spain Award; Castilla and Leon of Letters Award; Gold Medal of Salamanca.

WRITINGS:
El castillo de las tres murallas. Ed. Lumen, 198-.
El pastel del diablo. Ed. Lumen, 1983.
Caperucita en Manhattan. Ed. Siruela, 1990.

SIDELIGHTS: "I write out of an irresistable urging. I think it needs no explanation; it is like drinking when one is thirsty. One of my favorite themes is the escape: the child who must do the impossible and yet keeps on, nourished only by dreams of freedom."

MARTÍN IGLESIAS, Francisco (1940-)

PERSONAL DATA: Born February 22, 1940, in Lugo, Galicia, Spain. His parents are Francisco and Cándida. He is married to Ángela Franco and has two children, Belén and Francisco. *Education:* Doctorate in primary education.

ADDRESS: (Home) Rúa Ourense 93, 2a. D 27004 Lugo, Spain. Telephone: 218077. (Office) Colegio Público Luis Pimentel, calle Santo Grial s/n, 27004 Lugo, Spain. Telephone: 227058, 212469.

CAREER: Teacher of primary education since 1962; supervisor for the production and service of teaching material in Galician since 1988.

PROFESSIONAL ORGANIZATIONS: AELG. (Asociación de Escritores en Lengua Gallega; GALIX, IBBY of Galicia.

AWARDS, HONORS: National Award for Literature for Children and Young People, 1986; Losada Diéguez Prize, 1985; Barco de Vapor Award, 1984; IBBY Honors List, 1986; Lucense of 1988; elected to the White Ravens, Internationale Jugendbibliothek, 1988, 1990.

WRITINGS:
Cosas de Ramón Lamote. Madrid: Ediciones SM, 1987.
Memoria nueva de antiguos oficios. Madrid: Ediciones SM, 1989.

The work of Francisco Martín is written originally in Galician, his native language, and has been translated into several other languages. The publications cited here are translations into Spanish.

SIDELIGHTS: "I certainly do not know the scientific reasons why I became a writer. Maybe it is from a desire to communicate with others and a desire to be adept at using the words necessary to do so. My source of inspiration is everyday life, the miseries and joys that occur in any situation, on any day, and to any person. These are my favorite themes, blended with a bit of fantastic elaboration. Some critics have said that my work bears resemblance to the literature of magical realism."

CRITICAL SOURCES:
Anxo Tarria. *De letras y de signos, ensayos de semiótica y de crítica literaria.* Ed. Xerais-Vigo. 1987.
Anxo Tarria. *Literatura gallega.* Madrid: Ed. Taurus, 1988.

MARTÍN VIGIL, José Luis (1918-)

PERSONAL DATA: Born October 28, 1918, in Oviedo, Spain, the son of Natalio and Sara. *Education:* University studies in classics, philosophy and letters, and theology.

ADDRESS: (Home) Doctor Castelo 5, 5° A, 28009 Madrid, Spain. Telephone: 5761213.

CAREER: Priest and writer.

PROFESSIONAL ORGANIZATIONS: Club Náutico (Alicante); Asociación de Escritores y Artistas (Madrid): Sociedad General de Autores (Madrid).

AWARDS, HONORS: Award from the city of Oviedo; Pérez Galdós Prize; Award from the Catholic Office of Paris; Gran Angular Award.

WRITINGS:
La vida sale al encuentro. Barcelona: Ed. Juventud, 1955.
Tierra brava. Barcelona: Ed. Juventud, 1959.
Un sexo llamado débil. Barcelona: Ed. Juventud, 1968.
Mi nieto Jaime. Barcelona: Ed. Planeta, 1989.
Iba para figura. Barcelona: Ed. Juventud, 1991.
Porvenir para un hijo. Barcelona: Ed. Planeta.

Habla mi viejo. Madrid: Ediciones SM, 1968.
Los niños bandidos. Barcelona: Ed. Planeta.
Ganímedes en Manhattan. Barcelona: Ed. Planeta, 1990.

SIDELIGHTS: As a teacher, he has dedicated his life to the young; it is because of this that he writes his books, inspired by his work with students.

MARTÍNEZ (DE SOSA), Paulina (Dorlisa) (1932-)

PERSONAL DATA: Born April 24, 1932, in Buenos Aires, Argentina, the daughter of Andrés Sosa and Dorlisa Rodríguez. She is married to Constantino Alfonso Martínez and has two children, Laura Raquel and Gustavo Alfonso. *Education:* Studies in literature, psychology, fiction, literature for children, and theater.

ADDRESS: (Home) Aristóbulo del Valle 2743, 1602 Florida, Provincia de Buenos Aires, Argentina.

PROFESSIONAL ORGANIZATIONS: Secretary for the Comisión Directiva del ALIJA (Asociación de Literatura Infantil y Juvenil de la Argentina), 1979.

AWARDS, HONORS: Second Place for the Leyendas Argentinas Award.

WRITINGS:
"Goyo" and "Nicanor" in *Cuentos para leer y contar.* Ed. by Susana Izcovich. 1972.
A la una, a las dos y a las tres: había una vez... Co-written with Irene Grinberg, Eva
     Rey, and Pirucha Romera. 1975.
El osito y su mamá. Centro Editor de América Latina, 1977.
El gallito. Centro Editor de América Latina, 1977.
¿Dónde estás Carabás? Centro Editor de América Latina, 1977.
Leyendas argentinas. Co-written with Eva Rey and Pirucha Romera. Buenos Aires:
     Ed. Sigmar, 1979.
El patito Nicolás. Co-written with Eva Rey and Pirucha Romera. Buenos Aires: Ed.
     Plus Ultra, 1982.
De ternuras y encuentros. Co-written with Eva Rey and Pirucha Romera. Ed.
     Palermo, 1984.
El cabrito negro. Co-written with Eva Rey. Buenos Aires: Ed. Plus Ultra, 1987.
La sorpresa del abuelo. Buenos Aires: Ed. Plus Ultra, 1987.
Las andanzas de Juancito el zorro. Co-written with Pirucha Romera. Buenos Aires:
     Ed. Plus Ultra, 1988.

Tortitas de manteca. Buenos Aires: Ed. Braga, 1992.
Dicen que... Ed. Paulinas, 1992.

SIDELIGHTS: "I am worried at the lack of folklore for the children of Argentina; it is my country and these are my children, and although they are all part of our culture, they are yet largely unaware of it. I discovered that we have a treasure of stories and legends, compiled by folklorists, but to which only adults had access. Thus I decided to dedicate my work to bring these stories and legends to the attention of children. My work, then, is largely derived from our cultural myths, and it so happens that they are also my source of inspiration."

CRITICAL SOURCES:
La Opinión. June 30, 1976.
La Nación. December 15, 1976.
La Nación. January 21, 1978.
La Opinión. July 1, 1979.
Hispanic Journal. 1981.
Vivir. September 1986.
La Voz del Interior. Cordoba: October 1987.

MARTÍNEZ GIL, Fernando (1956-)

PERSONAL DATA: Born May 23, 1956, in Toledo, Spain, the son of Antonio Martínez Ballesteros and Rosa María Gil, he is married to María de los Ángeles Ferreras and has a son, Fernando. *Education:* Holds a degree in anthropology and ethnology, emphasizing Native-American cultures; doctorate in modern history.

ADDRESS: (Home) Santa Clara 30, Bargas, Toledo, Spain. Telephone: 358865.

CAREER: Professor of modern history at the Facultad de Letras at the Universidad de Castilla-La Mancha, Toledo, 1988-.

PROFESSIONAL ORGANIZATIONS: Greenpeace.

AWARDS, HONORS: National Award for Literature for Children, 1979; Lazarillo Award for Literature for Children and Young People, 1986.

WRITINGS:
El río de los castores. Barcelona: Ed. Noguer, 1980.

El juego del pirata. Barcelona: Ed. Noguer, 1987.
Paparrruchas. Madrid: Ed. Magisterio, 1988.
Amarintia. Madrid: Ed. Susaeta, 1990.
La isla soñada. Madrid: Ed. Alfaguara, 1991.

SIDELIGHTS: "I write about whatever interests me and about those things that I would like to change. It is certain that I try to defend and uphold my ideals. My favorite themes are the ecology, the passing of time, adventure and travel, and the points of contact and confusion between reality and fantasy, friendship, and naturally, love."

MARTÍNEZ (LÓPEZ-HERMOSA), Alicia (1942-)

PERSONAL DATA: Born March 3, 1942, in Ibiza, Islas Baleares, Spain, the daughter of Pedro Martínez and Concepción López-Hermosa. She has two children, Alicia and Jaime. *Education:* Holds a degree in philosophy and letters, with emphasis in modern English philology, from the Universidad de Barcelona.

ADDRESS: (Home) Lucano 7, 1° 1a., 08022 Barcelona, Spain. Telephone: 2115615.

CAREER: Professor of English; writer.

PROFESSIONAL ORGANIZATIONS: Asociación de Cultura Psicológica; Segunda Colegiada en el Colegio Oficial de Doctores y Licenciados en Filosofía y Letras de Cataluña.

AWARDS, HONORS: Selected for the Planeta Award, 1986.

WRITINGS:
Cuentos de Ibiza. Barcelona: Ed. Juventud, 1980.

SIDELIGHTS: "My father was a rural doctor in Ibiza and I would go with him to little towns or to isolated homes to help the sick. In those free times I read Wells, Greek mythology, the Spanish greats, and others. My mother introduced me to the natural world, going with me on long walks along the beach. I fell in love early with life and with the earth. I write for children, for those who have never seen the sunrise over the ocean, or a sky dotted with brilliant stars, or small animals. In my work I also try to send to my readers an educational message, about which they can later reflect as naturally as enjoying a sunny day. In Ibiza, in those times, there was only one school where children from the city, the country, and even fishermen's children, all attended together. In that building I saw an incredible mixture of lifestyles, traditions, ways of thinking, and personalities. My memories of that place have been a great help to me for characters, themes, and plots."

CRITICAL SOURCES:
Cosme Vidal Lláser. *Diario de Ibiza.*
Mara Asunción Guardia. *La Vanguardia.* Barcelona: March 6, 1981.
El País. September 6, 1981.

MARTÍNEZ-MENCHÉN, Antonio (Antonio Martínez Sánchez) (1930-)

PERSONAL DATA: Born March 9, 1930, in Linares, Jaen, Spain. His parents were Antonio and Eladia. He is married to Jesusa Aguirre Benito and has three children, Susana, Marina, and Carlos. *Education:* Law degree.

ADDRESS: (Home) Avenida de Manzanares 68, 7° B., 28019 Madrid, Spain. Telephone: 914697332. (Office) MUFACE (Mutualidad de Funcionarios Civiles del Estado), Plaza Ciudad de Viena 4, 28071 Madrid, Spain. Telephone: 913460875.

CAREER: State administrator, 1961-.

PROFESSIONAL ORGANIZATIONS: Asociación Colegial de Escritores.

AWARDS, HONORS: IBBY Honors List.

WRITINGS:
Fosco. Madrid: Ed. Alfaguara, 1985.
Una historia sin nombre. Madrid: Ed. Anaya, 1987.
La huida. Madrid: Ed. Espasa-Calpe, 1988.
Del seto de oriente. Zaragoza: Ed. Edelvives, 1988.
El despertar de Tina. Madrid: Ed. Alfaguara, 1988.
Fin de trayecto. Madrid: Ed. Alfaguara, 1991.
Mi amigo el unicornio. Madrid: Ed. Anaya, 1992.

SIDELIGHTS: "I enjoy evoking the world of my own childhood. Besides this, my literature is predominantly realistic but with escapades into fantasy, that magical fantasy is another aspect of reality to children."

CRITICAL SOURCES:
Gonzalo Sobejano. *Novela española de nuestro tiempo*. Second. ed.
Ignacio Soldevila Durante. *La novela desde 1956 (Historia de la literatura española actual)*.
Gundel Mattenklott. *Frankfurter Allgemeine Zeitung*. July 13, 1991.

MASGRAU, Fina (1953-)

PERSONAL DATA: Born in Banyoles, Gerona, Spain, in 1953. *Education:* Studied psychology at the Universidad de Valencia.

CAREER: Since 1975 she has been a teacher and has helped organize various seminars on literature for children.

AWARDS, HONORS: Critics' Award from *Serra d'Or*, 1991.

WRITINGS:
La rata Marieta. Valencia: Ed. Tandem, 1990.

Fina Masgrau has published more than ten books in her native language, Valencian. The work cited here is a translation into Spanish.

SIDELIGHTS: "To be able to express ideas, feelings, to describe situations and characters, to imagine . . . It is for me a game, a game at which I have had successes and failures. When they were failures, I returned to teaching. Writing requires a certain emotion. I write because I have friends who encourage me to do so, and because of the Valencian children who should be able to read books in their native language. I think that I write for children because I live with them daily. I am part of their world, and through them, at times, I am able to feel like a girl again, and to remember my own childhood memories."

MATEOS (MARTÍN), Pilar (1942-)

PERSONAL DATA: Born August 30, 1942, in Valladolid, Spain. *Education:* Two years study at the Facultad de Filosofía y Letras, Universidad de Valladolid.

ADDRESS: (Office) Alcalde Sainz de Baranda, 31, 3° D, 28009 Madrid, Spain. Telephone: 5731438.

CAREER: Writer. She has written screenplays for the radio, cinema, and television.

AWARDS, HONORS: Second Place, Barco de Vapor Award, 1980; Barco de Vapor Award, 1981; Second Place, Altea Award, 1981; Lazarillo Award, 1982.

WRITINGS:
Historias de ninguno. Madrid: Ediciones SM, 1980.
Jeruso quiere ser gente. Madrid: Ediciones SM, 1981.
Un pelotón de mentiras. Madrid: Ediciones SM, 1981. Also Brasil: Ed. Paulinas, 1982.
Lucas y Lucas. Madrid: Ediciones SM, 1983.
Capitanes de plástico. Madrid: Ediciones SM, 1983.
La bruja Mon. Madrid: Ediciones SM, 1984.
El cuento interrumpido. Barcelona: Ed. Noguer, 1984.
Molinete. Madrid: Ediciones SM, 1984. Also Dinamarca: Tellerup, 1987. Also Brasil: Ed. Paulinas, 1992.
La isla menguante. Madrid: Ediciones SM, 1987.
El vidente. Zaragoza: Ed. Edelvives, 1987.
Mi tío Teo. Madrid: Ed. Anaya, 1987.
Quisicosas. Ediciones SM, 1988.
Zapatones. Madrid: Ediciones SM, 1988.
Doneco Teleco. Zaragoza: Ed. Edelvives, 1989.
La princesa que perdió su nombre. Zaragoza: Ed. Edelvives, 1991.
Qué desastre de niño. Madrid: Ediciones SM, 1992.
La casa imaginaria. Mexico: Ed. Fondo de Cultura Económica, 1992.

SIDELIGHTS: "I write literature for children because it is the literary exercise that has allowed me to earn a living. I write especially for today's child. I aim for the urban child, between six and twelve years of age, and thus also use children like this for my characters. The most characteristic aspect of my work is the blending of fantasy and the everyday life of the child protagonist. The stories almost always develop in an atmosphere of humor."

CRITICAL SOURCES:
Jesús Zotón. *Nueva España de Oviedo.* May 10, 1957.
La Noticia. October 31, 1984.
María Solé. *ABC.* Madrid: April 9, 1988.
Alfonso García. *Diario de León.*
Julia Arroyo. *Ya.* Madrid.
Noticias del Mundo. New York, 1991.

MATHEWS CARMELINO, Daniel Alfredo (1953-)

PERSONAL DATA: Born September 15, 1953, in Lima, Peru, the son of Alfredo Mathews and Elisa Carmelino. *Education:* Studied literature at the Universidad de San Marcos.

ADDRESS: (Home) Tacna 352, San Miguel, Lima 32, Peru. Telephone: 622485.

CAREER: Writer; writing consultant for publishers and other clients.

PROFESSIONAL ORGANIZATIONS: APLIJ.

WRITINGS:
Viaje a Eutanasia. Ed. Llurca, 1985.
Hombres y fiestos. Ed. Horavi, 1987.
Sobre gustos y colores. 1989.
Juegue con la pala abra. Ed. Tarea, 1991.

SIDELIGHTS: "I write about things that affect me. The basis of my writing is play."

CRITICAL SOURCES:
Rocío Silva Santiesteban. *El Comercio.*
Alfonso la Torre. *La República.*

MATUTE, Ana María (1925-)

PERSONAL DATA: Born in Barcelona, Spain, in 1925.

AWARDS, HONORS: Lazarillo Award, 1965; Honors List for the Andersen Prize, 1970.

WRITINGS:
El país de la pizarra. 1960.
Paulina, el mundo y las estrellas. 1961.
El saltamontes verde. 1961.
Caballito loco. 1965.
El polizón de Ulises. 1965.
Sólo un pie descalzo. 1983.

Her works have been translated into German, French, Russian, Polish, Portuguese, and Japanese.

MÉNDEZ Y MERCADO, Leticia (Irene) (1948-)

PERSONAL DATA: Born October 20, 1948, in Mexico, D.F. the daughter of Eugenio Méndez and Guadalupe Mercado. She has a son, Ricardo. Education: Doctorate in ethnology and ethnolinguistics, earned in Paris, France; master's degree in human development from the Universidad Iberoamericana.

ADDRESS: (Home) Tecoyotitla 262, Col. Florida, San Angel 01030, Mexico, D.F. Telephone: 5247746.

CAREER: University teacher, 1970-75; supervisor on a research project for the Instituto Nacional Indigenista, 1980-82; university professor, 1980-92; researcher for UNAM, 1987-92.

PROFESSIONAL ORGANIZATIONS: Association a la Recherche Scientifique Ecole des Hautes Etudes en Sciences Sociales, Paris.

AWARDS, HONORS: Fellowship from UNICEF, 1973; Grant from the French government, 1975-79; Fellowship from the Cammelia Foundation, 1984-85; Sistema Nacional de Investigadores (SNI), 1988; PREPAC, 1990-92; Honorable Mention in exams for master's and Ph.D. in ethnology.

WRITINGS:
La piñata. Ed. Patria.
El mercado. Ed. Patria.

SIDELIGHTS: "I began in the field of literature for children after I discovered that it was a possible career. I think that science should be made understandable to children and taught to them early because the age from preschool to adolescence is the age when they can learn the most rapidly, and the age during which their interests are formed. I want the reader, the child, to find in my characters similarities underlying any differences. My characters may have different cultural origins and traditions, but I want the reader to see them as human beings, with feelings and interests, similar joys and fears, and not as folk stereotypes, outside the reader's life experience. I want to continue working in this field, although for the moment I find myself at a halt. I want to write a work of theater in which a common ground can be reached, across the differences between the characters and the audience. My inspiration comes from anthropology and human contact."

MENDIOLA (INSAUSTI), José María (1929-)

PERSONAL DATA: Born May 18, 1929, in San Sebastian, Spain, the son of Antolín and Concepción, he is married to María Antonia. *Education:* Attorney and journalist.

ADDRESS: (Home) Pio Baroja 4, 9° B, 20006 San Sebastian, Spain. Telephone: 310227. (Office) Agencia Inmobiliaria, Easo 14, Bajo 20006 San Sebastian, Spain. Telephone: 471617, 471064.

CAREER: Editor of *El Diario Vasco;* real estate agent; legal advisor to the Provincial Board for the Protection of Basque Minors; director of the M-1 operation for metallurgical exportation.

AWARDS, HONORS: Nadal Award for the Novel, 1963; Award from the city of San Sebastian, 1962; Award for the novel *Ciudad de Irun*; Award for the novel *Puente colgante de Bilbao*, 1974; Award for the novel *Café Gijon.*

WRITINGS:
La gaviota de la plaza Guipuzcoa. Madrid: Ed. Alfaguara.
El castillo de Lora. Madrid: Ed. Bruño.
La momia Regina. Madrid: Ed. Anaya.
¿Quién cuida los pajaritos? Madrid: Ed. Susaeta.
Los límites del lobo. Gijon: Ed. Júcar.
Mi prima de Bilbao. Gijon: Ed. Júcar.

In addition to the works cited here, he has written more than seven novels and various essays.

SIDELIGHTS: "I write what I write in an attempt, doomed to dreamy failure, to interpret, or reinterpret, human life through the unique lens of childhood."

MOLINA LLORENTE, Pilar (1948-)

PERSONAL DATA: Born December 11, 1948, in Madrid, Spain, the daughter of

Agustín and Isabel, she is married to Vicente and has three children, David, Fátima, and Flavia. *Education:* Fine arts and philology.

ADDRESS: (Home) Fomento 3, 28013 Madrid, Spain. Telephone: 5424823.

CAREER: Writer.

AWARDS, HONORS: Doncel Award for the Novel; Doncel Award for Biography; Finalist for the Lazarillo Award; CCEI Award; Second Prize, Barco de Vapor Award; CCEI Honors List; two Silver Medals for the Barco de Vapor Collection.

WRITINGS:
Ut y las estrellas. Ed. Doncel, 1964. Also Barcelona: Ed. Noguer, 1980.
Romualdo el grillo. Ed. Cus, 1973.
El terrible Florentino. Ed. Doncel, 1973. Also Barcelona: Ed. Noguer, 1984.
El mensaje del maese Zamaor. Madrid: Ediciones SM, 1981.
Patatita. Madrid: Ediciones SM, 1983.
Primer libro de lecturas. Madrid: Ediciones SM, 1984.
Poemas. Madrid: Ediciones SM, 1985.
La vista de la condesa. Madrid: Ed. Susaeta, 1987.
El largo verano de Eugenia Mestre. Madrid: Ed. Anaya, 1987.
Aura gris. Madrid: Ed. Bruño, 1988.
El aprendiz. Ed. Rialp, 1989.
Lecturas para primer curso. Madrid: Ediciones SM, 1991.
Compañero de sueños. Madrid: Ed. Bruño, 1992.

SIDELIGHTS: "I create characters who become involved in situations in which they must assess and then act in order to reach a solution. This process occurs before the reader, but without moralizing or trying to influence the reader's opinion. I want children and young people to take into account the importance of thinking and feeling, and to value all other human beings as unique and individual. I am interested in all themes related to liberty, responsibility, truth, and love. I situate my characters in times and environments in which the events of the story can be more clearly and conveniently related."

CRITICAL SOURCES:
Jesús Ballaz. *J20.*
Alfonso García. *Diario de León.*
Tomás Martínez. *Radio Popular.*
Sindo Froufe Quintas. *La Noticia de Huelva.*
María Solé. *ABC.*
Rosana Torres. *El País.*
Radio Murcia.
Radio España de Madrid.

MONAY QUIRARTE, David (1941-)

PERSONAL DATA: Born April 14, 1941, in Ameca, Jalisco, Mexico, the son of José María Monay and Trinidad Quirarte. He is married to Lucía Díaz Zuno and has four children, David, Guadalupe, Gerardo, and Iván. *Education:* Licentiate in Spanish language and literature.

ADDRESS: (Home) Gabino Vázquez 2093, 21130 Mexicali, Baja California, Mexico. Telephone: 553334.

CAREER: Professor of primary education.

PROFESSIONAL ORGANIZATIONS: Comisión de los Derechos Humanos en el estado de Baja California; Orden Rosacruz, AMORC.

AWARDS, HONORS: State Award for Literature for Children, 1990-91.

WRITINGS:
Colección de cuentos infantiles. Mexicali: Instituto de Cultura de Baja California, 1991.

CRITICAL SOURCES:
Marcia Coronado. *Zeta.* November 16, 1990.
Dyna Zendejas. *La Crónica.* September 29, 1991.
Carlos Gutiérrez Vidal. *La Crónica.* October 6, 1991.
Carlos Payán Velver. *La Jornada.* January 19, 1992.

MONKMAN, Olga (Gómez de) (1929-)

PERSONAL DATA: Born August 19, 1929, in Buenos Aires, Argentina, the daugther of Rafael Gómez and Olga Spinetto, she is the widow of Roberto Monkman and has three children, Guillermo, Mary Anne, and Nora. *Education:* Master's degree; occupational therapist certification; National Public Translator's certification (English, French).

ADDRESS: (Home) Callao 1253, 8° C, 1023 Buenos Aires, Argentina.

CAREER: Occupational therapist; primary school teacher; writer; independent writing consultant.

PROFESSIONAL ORGANIZATIONS: SADE.

AWARDS, HONORS: Second Prize, Marta Salotti Story Competition, 1985, 1990; Special Mention at the Fiesta Nacional de Letras, 1986; Second Prize, Instituto F. Bernasconi Story Competition, 1986; Special Mention, Biblioteca del Docente Municipal, 1987; First Prize, Asociación Argentina de Lectura, 1989; SADE Honors List, 1989, 1990; Second Prize, Story and Song Competition of the Instituto de Cultura Hispánica, 1990; Special Mention, Manuel Villafañe Competition, 1990; ALIJA Honors List, 1991; Aarón Cupit Prize for Literature for Young People, 1992.

WRITINGS:
"La tristeza de las jirafas." *Billiken.* 1984.
"Cometas." *Antología Piolín de Barrilete.* Ed. La Obra, 1985.
"Aniceto." *Antología del cuento folklórico.* Caja Nacional del Ahorro, 1986.
Detrás de la puerta. Ed. Métodos, 1988.
El diario de Adelina. Ed. Métodos, 1989.
Cuentos de magia y realidad. Buenos Aires: Ed. Guadalupe, 1989.
El regalo del abuelo. Buenos Aires: Ed. Guadalupe, 1989.
"Un sombrero para muchas cabezas." *Los troesmas cuentan.* Ed. Colihue, Buenos Aires:1990.
Dos perros y una abuela. Ed. Guadalupe, 1991.
La venganza del Altillo. Ed. Métodos, 1991.
Historia de amor en miau. Buenos Aires; Ed. Braga; 1991.
La casa del cerdo azul. Co-written with Irma Verolín. Ed. Métodos, 1992.
Con la pluma y la palabra. Ed. Colihue, 1992.
Las locuras de Rufi. Buenos Aires: Ed. Plus Ultra, 1992.
Un rey sin corona no puede ser. Buenos Aires: Ed. Braga, 1992.
Celedonia Bustamante y otros personajes insólitos. Buenos Aires: Ed. Braga, 1992.

SIDELIGHTS: "I am dedicated especially to literature for children and young people. It began when my employment put me in contact with them. A restlessness arose in me and I turned toward children, to whom I wanted to communicate, and to whom I had much to say. I like realistic themes, but I am also attracted to the fantastic. Most of my work is one or the other, and I sometimes mix in aspects of the absurd, humor, and irony. At times it is difficult to discern the origin of my inspiration. Events, memories, imaginations, the experiences gathered through my travels: they all trigger my creativity. And when I write, the real and the imaginary integrate into one inseparable entity."

CRITICAL SOURCES:
Oscar Bosetti. *Tiempo Argentino.* July 7, 1985.
Ruth Mehl. *La Nación.* 1986.
Verónica Podestá. *La Nación.* December 24, 1989.

MONTERDE (HEREDIA), Bernardo (1919-)

PERSONAL DATA: Born March 26, 1919, in Castejon de las Armas, Zaragoza, Spain. He is the son of Bernardino and Pascuala. He is married to Pilar Urbano Marina and has two daughters, María Pilar and Clara Isabel.

ADDRESS: (Home) Barrio Nuevo 6, Castejon de las Armas, Zaragoza, Spain. Telephone: 872101.

CAREER: Shepherd and goatsherd.

WRITINGS:
El gigante de la selva. Spain: Mondadori, 1989.
El delfín de oro. Spain: Mondadori, 1989.
El anillo de Simplicio. Spain: Mondadori, 1989.
La sortija milagrosa. Spain: Mondadori, 1989.
La amazona de los bosques. Spain: Mondadori, 1989.
La hija del minero. Spain: Mondadori, 1989.
La calabaza de la suerte. Spain: Mondadori, 1989.

SIDELIGHTS: "Almost everything I have written has been to satisfy the petitions of my friends and readers. My favorite genres are the story, poetry, and theater. Inspiration comes to me through my themes. I feel what to write, I recognize what is important to me, and I put into the protagonists those qualities that I want to investigate, describe, or question. Other than that, imagination is my guide."

CRITICAL SOURCES:
Magdalena Moreno. *Ya.*

MONTES DE OCA, Marco Antonio (1932-)

PERSONAL DATA: Born August 3, 1932, in Mexico, D.F., the son of David Montes de Oca y Mercedes Fernández, he is married to Ana Luisa Vega and has four daughters, Ana Luisa, Gabriela, Alejandra, and Mercedes. *Education:* Licentiate in philosophy and letters from the Universidad Nacional Autónoma de México.

ADDRESS: (Home) Filosofía y Letras 52, Col. Copilco, Mexico, D.F. Telephone: 6587578.

CAREER: Poet.

PROFESSIONAL ORGANIZATIONS: Asociación de Escritores Mexicanos.

AWARDS, HONORS: Villaurrutia Award; Zacatecas Award; Mazatlán Award; National Award for Literature, 1985.

WRITINGS:
Pedir el fuego (twenty-five books of poetry). Ed. Planeta.
El niño pintor. CIDCLI, 1989.

MORANTE CAMPOS, José Gonzalo (1929-)

PERSONAL DATA: Born September 1, 1929, in Camana, Arequipa, Peru, he is the son of José María and María Candelaria. *Education:* Studies at the Instituto Pedagógico Nacional; holds a degree in literature from the Universidad Nacional de San Marcos.

ADDRESS: Garcilaso de la Vega 1522 304, Lima 1, Peru. Telephone: 231529.

CAREER: Professor of primary education since 1983; department chair at the Universidad Católica, 1987-.

PROFESSIONAL ORGANIZATIONS: APLIJ; Asociación Nacional de Escritores y Artistas; Casa del Poeta Peruano.

WRITINGS:
El mentir de las estrellas. Lima: Ed. Asociación de Escritores.
Para que tú me ames. Lima: author's edition, 1991.
La flor de la higuera. Unpublished.

SIDELIGHTS: "I write poetry, fundamentally love poetry. I have also written political (social) poetry. The source of my inspiration: a love of youth. In my social poems I am inspired by Peruvian reality."

CRITICAL SOURCES:
Willy Pinto Gamboa. *La Crónica.*
Max Dextre. *El Nacional.*

MOREL, Alicia (Chaigneau) (1921-)

PERSONAL DATA: Born July 26, 1921, in Santiago, Chile, the daughter of Eduardo Morel Herrera and Inés Chaigneau, she is married to William Thayer and has six children, Luis Eduardo, Julia M. Inés, William, Laura, Alicia, and Tomás.

ADDRESS: (Home) Arturo Medina 3927, Providencia, Santiago, Chile. Telephone: 2252000. Fax: 462323.

CAREER: Composer of radio opera; composer at the Instituto de Educación Rural; occasional puppeteer; writer.

PROFESSIONAL ORGANIZATIONS: IBBY of Chile .

AWARDS, HONORS: IBBY Honors List, 1978, 1983; Order of Merit, Consejo Mundial de Educación, 1989; People's Choice Award, Municipalidad de Providencia, 1990.

WRITINGS:
En el campo y la ciudad. Published by the author, 1938.
Juanilla, Juanillo y la abuela. Illust. by M. Laura Thayer. Santiago, Chile: Ed. Universitaria, 1940.
La hormiguita cantora y el duende mediodía. Illust. by Elena Poirier. Ed. Zig Zag, 1956.
Cuentos de la pícara Polita. Illust. by Elena Poirier. Ed. Lord Cochrane, 1973.
El increíble mundo de Llanca. Illust. by Laura y Alicia Thayer. Ed. Valparaíso, 1977.
Perico trepa por Chile. Co-written with Marcela Paz, illust. by Marta Carrasco. Santiago, Chile: Ed. Universitaria, 1978.
Nuestros cuentos. Edited by Hilda Morel. Ed. Andrés Bello, 1978.
Cuentos araucanos. Illust. by Andrés Jullien. Santiago, Chile: Ed. Andrés Bello, 1983.
Polita va a la escuela. Illust. by Elena Poirier. Santiago, Chile: Ed. Universitaria, 1985.
La flauta encantada. Illust. by Laura and Alicia Thayer. Santiago, Chile: Ed. Andrés Bello, 1986.
Las manchas de Vinca. Illust. by Carlos Rojas Mafioletti. Santiago, Chile: Ed. Andrés Bello, 1986.
El viaje de los duendes al otro lado del mundo. Illust. by Laura and Alicia Thayer. Santiago, Chile: Ed. Andrés Bello, 1988.
El árbol de los cielos. Illust by Laura Thayer. Ed. Patris, 1990.
Polita aprende el mundo. Illust. by Elena Poirier. Santiago, Chile: Ed. Universitaria, 1991.
La hoja viajera. Ed. Salo Libros, 1991.

Hagamos títeres. Illust. by Laura Thayer. Ed. Patris, 1991.
Cuentos de tesoros y monedas de oro. Santiago, Chile: Ediciones SM, 1991.

She has also published translations and various stories selected for literary anthologies.

SIDELIGHTS: "Since the first publication of *Juanilla, Juanillo y la abuela* in 1940, I have had a natural draw to writing literature for children. My favorite themes are based on nature and fantastic characters. I am also inspired by Native American legends, especially those of the Mapuche cultures, the Onas, the Yaganas, and Mexican and Aimaraen myths that can be found in anthologies or books like *El viaje de los duendes.*"

CRITICAL SOURCES:
Cecilia Beuchat.

MOZO SAN JUAN, Paloma (1964-)

PERSONAL DATA: Born September 19, 1964, in Madrid, Spain, the daughter of Julio Mozo and Pepa San Juan. *Education:* Licentiate in information sciences, with emphasis in journalism.

ADDRESS: (Home) Paseo de las Delicias 29, 7° C, Madrid, Spain. Telephone: 4678725. (Office) Padre Damián 43, Madrid, Spain. Telephone: 3450447, 3450496.

CAREER: Editor for a news agency, 1990-.

AWARDS, HONORS: Finalist for the National Award for Literature for Children, 1992.

WRITINGS:
Me la he cargado. Madrid: Ed. Alfaguara, 1991.

SIDELIGHTS: "I don't know why I write what I write. But, for the moment, my best and biggest source of inspiration is reality itself."

CRITICAL SOURCES:
ABC. Madrid: María Solé, 1991.
El Urogallo. Edition dedicated to literature for children, 1992.
El País. February 8, 1992.

MUÑOZ MARTÍN, Juan (1929-)

PERSONAL DATA:: Born May 13, 1929, in Madrid, Spain, the son of Ovidio and Matilde, he is married to María Sacramento and has four children, Ninfa, Juan, Joaquín, and Matilde. *Education:* Holds a degree in French philosophy.

ADDRESS: (Home) Asunción Castel 5 B, Esc. 2, 28020 Madrid, Spain. Telephone: 5790418. (Office) Juan Montalvo 22, Instituto Jamer, 28020 Madrid, Spain. Telephone: 5332628.

AWARDS, HONORS: Doncel Award, 1966; Barco de Vapor Award, 1979; Third Prize, Gran Angular Award; three Silver Medals for his works of more than 100,000 copies sold; Gold Medal for his works of more than 500,000 copies sold.

WRITINGS:
Las tres piedras. Madrid: Ediciones SM, 1966.
Fray Perico y su borrico. Madrid: Ediciones SM, 1979.
El pirata Garrapata. Madrid: Ediciones SM, 1981.
El libro de los prodigios. Madrid: Ediciones SM, 1983.
Fray Perico y la guerra. Madrid: Ediciones SM.
Fray Perico: nuevas aventuras. Zaragoza: Ed. Edelvives, 198-.
Garrapata en África. Gijon: Ed. Júcar, 1988.
Baldomero, el pistolero. Zaragoza: Ed. Edelvives, 1988.
Las tres piedras y otros cuentos. Madrid: Ed. Bruño, 1988.
El feo, el bobo y el malo. Madrid: Ed. Bruño, 1989.
Garrapata en tierra de Cleopatra. Gijon: Ed. Júcar, 1989.
Garrapata llega a pie al templo de Abbu Simbel. Gijon: Ed. Júcar, 1989.
Las tres carabelas. Zaragoza: Ed. Edelvives, 1990.
Los trece hijos brutos del rey Sisebuto. Madrid: Ediciones SM, 1991.
El pirata Garrapata en China. Gijon: Ed. Júcar, 1991.
El pirata Garrapata en Pekín. Gijon: Ed. Júcar, 1991.
El pirata Garrapata en la ciudad prometida. Gijon: Ed. Júcar, 1992.
El pirata Garrapata en la India. Gijon: Ed. Júcar, 1992.
Ciprianus, Gladiator Romanus. Madrid: Ed. Bruño, 1992.

SIDELIGHTS: "I write about fictional characters who nevertheless have the appearance of being real. Characters who are funny, kind, simple in appearance, but who do the right thing in situations. Characters who develop in groups, religious communities (Fray Perico), large social groups (Fray Garrapata), and crowds (Baldomero el pistolero). Also, I always leave open the possibility of following the stories of people who are strongly characterized (as in the series of Fray Perico, or Baldomero, Ciprianus Gladiator Romanus). I also like popular stories composed of clashing ideals and disparate sequences, like *El feo, el bobo, el malo*, and *Las tres piedras*. I like action, dialogue, dynamics, and nonlinear situations."

MURCIANO, Carlos (1931-)

PERSONAL DATA: Born November 21, 1931, in Arcos de la Frontera, Cadiz, Spain, he is the son of Antonio and María. He is married to Antonia and has six children, María de las Nieves, Antonia María, Carlos María, María Auxiliadora, Luis María, and Jorge Francisco. *Education:* Masters of business administration.

ADDRESS: (Home) Virgen de la Monjia 2, 28027 Madrid, Spain.

CAREER: Vice-president of administration for RCA Victor of Spain, 1956-87. He has been dedicated to literature for children and young people since 1987.

PROFESSIONAL ORGANIZATIONS: Directing member of the Asociación de Escritores y Artistas Españoles; corresponding member of the Academia Venezolana de la Lengua, 1990-; Member of the Academia Nacional de la Historia de Venezuela, 1991-.

AWARDS, HONORS: Award from the city of Barcelona; Boscán Award; González de la Lama Prize; Francisco Quevedo Prize; Leonor Award; Ibn Zaydun Prize; Prometeo de la Poesía Award; Fellowship from the March Foundation, 1965; National Award for Literature, 1970; Guatemala Poetry Award, 1974; Andalucía Poetry Award, 1977; Jorge Manrique Prize, 1981; National Award for Literature for Children, 1982; CCEI Award, 1986; Order of Andrés Bello, awarded by the government of Venezuela, 1986.

WRITINGS:
Las manos en el agua. Barcelona: Ed. Noguer, 1981.
El mar sigue esperando. Barcelona: Ed. Noguer, 1983.
Los libros amigos. Madrid: Fundación Germán Sánchez Ruipérez, 1984.
Tres y otros dos. Madrid: Ed. Escuela Española, 1985.
La bufanda amarilla. Madrid: Ed. Escuela Española, 1985.
Cuento con Tigo. Barcelona: Ed. Noguer, 1986.
Los habitantes de Llano Lejano. Madrid: Ediciones SM, 1987.
Lun. Zaragoza: Ed. Edelvives, 1987.
La niña enlunada. Madrid: Ediciones SM, 1988.
Las sayas en las sayas. Gijon: Ed. Júcar, 1988.
Sor Guitarra. Madrid: Ed. Susaeta, 1988.

La rana mundana. Madrid: Ed. Bruño, 1988.
Lirolos, ciflos y paranganalios. Zaragoza: Ed. Edelvives, 1988.
La niña que aprendía los nombres. Madrid: Ed. Magisterio, 1989.
La niña calendulera. Madrid: Ediciones SM, 1989.
El gigante que perdió una bota. Madrid: Ed. Anaya, 1989.
Duende o cosa. Zaragoza: Ed. Edelvives, 1990.
La bufanda amarilla y dos abecedarios. Madrid: Ediciones SM, 1990.
Niña y Perro. Barcelona: Ed. Noguer, 1990.

SIDELIGHTS: "I write from an irresistable vocation; I have published more than seventy books: poetry, fiction, essay, translation, investigation . . . The themes and sources of inspiration are for me as varied as life itself. In the field of literature for children I prefer the imagination, fantasy, and the invention of new things and settings."

CRITICAL SOURCES: After forty years of publishing books and stories, Carlos Murciano could "fill more than forty files" with critical material assessing his work.

MURILLO, José (1922-)

PERSONAL DATA: Born August 18, 1922, in Ledesma, Jujuy, Argentina, he is the son of José Justino Murillo and Dolores Eulalia Vall. He is married to Regina Leicy Härdelin and has two children, Cristina Leicy, and Eugenio. *Education:* Two years studying philosophy and letters.

ADDRESS: (Home) Castro 845 E. Telephone: 5898.

PROFESSIONAL ORGANIZATIONS: Sociedad Argentina de Escritores.

AWARDS, HONORS: Enrique Banchs Prize; Casa de las Américas Award; First Mention, Robin Hood Competition; Second Prize, Teatro La Máscara Competition.

WRITINGS:
Mi amigo el pespir. Buenos Aires: Ed. Guadalupe.
Cinco patas. Buenos Aires: Ed. Guadalupe.
El tigre de Santa Bárbara. Buenos Aires: Ed. Guadalupe.
Rubio como la miel. Buenos Aires: Ed. Guadalupe.
El último hornero de Cabra Corral. Buenos Aires: Ed. Guadalupe.
Brunita. Buenos Aires: Ed. Guadalupe.

El niño que soñaba el mar. Buenos Aires: Ed. Guadalupe.
Renancó y los últimos huamules. Buenos Aires: Ed. Guadalupe.
Silvestre y el hurón. Buenos Aires: Ed. Guadalupe.
Mi amigo el hombre. Buenos Aires: Ed. Guadalupe.
El perro salvador y otros cuentos. Buenos Aires Ed. Bureau de Promoción.
Aquel caballo bragado. Buenos Aires: Ed. Pedagógicas.
Leyendas para todos. Buenos Aires: Ed. Guadalupe.

SIDELIGHTS: "I write in order to give children my personal experiences in the forests of northwestern Argentina, to introduce them to its wildlife. My themes fit into two categories: those about life and reality, and those about Argentina's wealth of wildlife."

CRITICAL SOURCES:
Alga Marina Elisegaray. *En torno a la literatura infantil* and *Autores, niños y libros*. Pablo Medina. *Folleto de Editorial Guadalupe*.

NANNI DE SMANIA, Estela (1942-)

PERSONAL DATA: Born May 7, 1942, in Parana, Entre Ríos, Argentina, she is the daughter of Carlos Alberto Nanni and Estela Manuela Mayer. She is married to Eduardo Victorio Smania and has three children, Claudia María, Andrea María, and Gisela María. *Education:* Notary public certification from the Universidad Nacional de Córdoba; law degree from the Universidad Nacional de Córdoba; three years' postgraduate study in journalism; doctorate in public speaking and scenic arts from the Instituto Provincial de Bellas Artes at Entre Ríos.

ADDRESS: (Home) Valencia 1439, Barrio Crisol, 5014 Cordoba, Argentina. Telephone: 222456, 244621.

PROFESSIONAL ORGANIZATIONS: Founding member of the Centro de Difusión e Investigación de la Literatura Infantil y Juvenil (CEDILIJ), Cordoba; advising editor of the journal *Piedra Libre*, for CEDILIJ, Cordoba; director of the journal *Notarial*, Cordoba; editorial secretary for the review *Foro*, Cordoba.

AWARDS, HONORS: First and Second Prize, Sebastián Tallón National Competition; First Prize, Second Edition, Sebastián Tallón National Competition; Special Mention, Third Edition, Sebastián Tallón National Competition; Second Prize, Jardín Story Competition; First Prize, Leopoldo Lugones National Award for

Literature; Second Prize, SADE; Special Mention, El Quijote de Plata Competition, Santa Fe; ALIJA Honors List, Buenos Aires.

WRITINGS:
"Jacinto." *Desde Córdoba les contamos.* Buenos Aires: Ed. Plus Ultra.
"Jacinto y la estatua." *Desde Córdoba les contamos.* Buenos Aires: Ed. Plus Ultra.
"La rebelión del lunes." *Entre nubes y huevos fritos.* Buenos Aires: Ed. Plus Ultra.
Día de visitas. Buenos Aires: Ed. Colihue, 1990.
Pic-Nic. Buenos Aires: Ed. Atlántida. Also Cordoba: Ed. La Voz del Interior.
La noche de los ruidos. Buenos Aires: Ed. Latina, 1974. Also Cordoba: Ed. La Voz del Interior.
"Fuga de vocales." *Desde Córdoba les contamos.* Buenos Aires: Ed. Plus Ultra.
Cambalache. Buenos Aires: Ed. El Quirquincho, 1989. Also Cordoba: Ed. La Voz del Interior.
Historia de un girasol inquieto. Cordoba: Ed. Municipalidad de Córdoba, 1983.
Otoño. Cordoba: Ed. Lerner, 1986.
"Un viaje al campo." *Antología.* Ed. Municipalidad de Córdoba, 1989.
"¿Conoces a José?" *Entre nubes y huevos fritos.* Buenos Aires: Ed. Plus Ultra, 1991.
El viejo buscador de sueños. Cordoba: Ed. T.A.P.A.S., 1982.
El doctor Nicomedes y la señorita Gloria. Cordoba: Ed. La Voz del Interior.
Pido gancho. Buenos Aires: Ed. Sudamericana, 1991.
"Pena capital." *Puro cuento.* Buenos Aires: 1992.
Sucedió en la selva y sus alrededores. Cordoba: Ed. La Voz del Interior.
Los huérfanos. Cordoba: Ed. La Voz del Interior.

SIDELIGHTS: "I began to write for children after my studies in journalism and my work as a writer and supervisor of programs for children and adolescents on the National Radio. Since then I have devoted myself to this genre (although I continue to write for adults as well). I find it fascinating when writing is done with a genuine sense of responsibility and respect for young readers and a commitment to their interests. I write from experience, and my sources of inspiration are the readers for whom I write, and the children with whom I stay in contact through schools, libraries, workshops, and correspondence. Without preconceptions, without any motivation other than to promote freedom of the spirit, I put my stories together each day using three fundamental elements: memories, actual occurrences, and imagination. I struggle to attain a better literature for children, one that leaves behind pedantic moralizing and the valorization of facile ideologies."

CRITICAL SOURCES:
Tesis de Licenciatura en Letras Modernas.
Graciela Rosa Gallelli. *Panorama de la literatura infantil y juvenil argentina, guía comentada.* Buenos Aires: Ed. Plus Ultra, 1986.
María Luisa C. de Leguizamón. "Para leer con placer." *Latinoamericana de Lectura.* 1991.

Adriana Vulponi. *El juego en los cuentos infantiles de Estela Nanni de Smania.*

NEUMANN DE REY, Eva (1929-)

PERSONAL DATA: Born September 6, 1929, in Vienna, Austria, the daughter of Leo Neuman and Adela Fischer. She is married to Roberto E.A. Rey and has three children, Daniel Eduardo, Pablo Marcelo, and Ana Silvia. *Education:* Licentiate in philosophy and letters, with emphasis in folklore literature for children.

ADDRESS: (Home) La Pampa 2934, 5° F, 1428 Buenos Aires, Argentina. Telephone: 7847753.

CAREER: Investigator of folklore and legends; writer of literature for children; translator of stories from English and German.

PROFESSIONAL ORGANIZATIONS: SADE; ALIJA; IBBY of Argentina.

AWARDS, HONORS: Second Prize, Award to the Best Edited Stories of 1977, Cámara Argentina de Publicaciones.

WRITINGS:
A la una, a las dos y a las tres: había una vez... Co-written with P. Martínez, P. Romera, and Iregrynberg. Ed. Gránica y Bureau de Promoción, 1975.
"El pajarito remendado." *El molinillo mágico.* Ed. de América Latina, 1977.
Leyendas argentinas. Co-written with P. Martínez and P. Romera. Buenos Aires: Ed. Sigmar, 1977.
Leyendas americanas. Co-written with P. Martínez and P. Romera. Buenos Aires: Ed. Sigmar, 1979.
El patito Nicolás. Co-written with P. Martínez and P. Romera. Buenos Aires: Ed. Plus Ultra, 1982.
La familia Rocamora viaja por la Argentina. Ed. Daly, 1984.
El cabrito negro. Co-written with Paulina Martínez. Buenos Aires: Ed. Plus Ultra, 1987.
Leo con figuras (collection of six books). Buenos Aires: Ed. Sigmar, 1991.

SIDELIGHTS: "Books were invaluable friends when I was growing up. I now want to give my love of books to my children, and thus I feel the need to write stories of my own. My inspirations are life, nature, and fantasy. I want children to share an adventure in my stories and to discover the pleasures of reading. Other interests of mine are myths, legends, and folklore. They provide me with inspiration and ideas; they contain human archetypes as well as plots, customs, and tricks upon which the practice of storytelling is based."

CRITICAL SOURCES:
Rosalía Am-basual. *La Opinión.* June 30, 1976.
Susana Iraola. *La Nación.* December 15, 1976.
César Magrini. *El Cronista Comercial.* January 4, 1978.
Ana María Ramb. *Vivir.* September 1986.
Hispanic Journal. University of Pennsylvania, August 1981.

OBIOLS (Prat), Miguel (1945-)

PERSONAL DATA: Born April 14, 1945, in Roda de Ter, Barcelona, Spain, the son of Josep and Dolores, he is married to Mariona and has two children, Berta and Aina. *Education:* Holds a degree in Hispanic philology from the Universidad de Barcelona.

ADDRESS: (Home) Bruc 28 Quart, 08010 Barcelona, Spain. Telephone: 4125352. (Office) Televisión Española, Cataluña, Apartado Postal 300, 08190 Sant Cugat, Barcelona, Spain. Telephone: 5823664.

CAREER: Professor of Catalan and Castilian; author of books for children and young people; author of screenplays for television; program director.

PROFESSIONAL ORGANIZATIONS: Asociación de Escritores en Lengua Catalana.

AWARDS, HONORS: Critics' Award from *Serra d'Or*, 1978, 1988; Award from the Minister of Culture, Spain, 1980; Josep Ma. Folch i Torres Prize, 1981; Joaquim Ruyra Prize, 1986; People's Choice Award of Catalunya, 1988; Critici in Erba Award, Bologna Children's Book Fair, 1992.

WRITINGS:
Ay, Filomena, Filomena. Barcelona: Ed. Juventud, 1977.
Una de indios y otras historias. Madrid: Ediciones SM, 1988.
Libro de las M/Alicias. Madrid: Ediciones SM, 1990.

The work of Miguel Obiols is originally written in Catalan; he has published more than twelve books. The works cited here are translations into Spanish.

SIDELIGHTS: "I write books and television screenplays because to write is a way of capturing experience in a timeless form. Without writing I would be very unhappy. Moreover, I feel the need to create and recreate imaginary worlds, which are much more stimulating than the mundane world in which we live, because I find reality and people somewhat ungraceful. I like to create a mirror of life in my stories and to risk myself by constantly experimenting with form. I love linguistic games and reading stories against the grain. I am inspired by the cinema, the world of the imagination, and above all, the theater."

CRITICAL SOURCES:
Victoria Fernández. *CLIJ.*
Federico Martín Nebras. *Acción Educativa.*
Felicidad Orquín. *El País.*
Andreu Sotorra. *Avui.*
Nuria Ventura. *Faristol.*

OLAIZOLA (SARRÍA), José Luis (1927-)

PERSONAL DATA: Born December 25, 1927, in San Sebastian, Spain, the son of Bibiano and Juana, he is married to María Luisa Morales and has eight children, María Luisa, José Luis, Carlos, Lourdes, Matilde, Cayetano, Fátima, and Rocío. *Education:* Law degree.

ADDRESS: (Home) De las Lomas 58, Boadilla del Monte, D.P. 28660 Madrid, Spain. Telephone: 6330293.

CAREER: Worked as an attorney before dedicating himself to writing.

PROFESSIONAL ORGANIZATIONS: Asociación Colegial de Escritores de España.

AWARDS, HONORS: Ateneo de Sevilla Award, 1976; Planeta Award, 1983; Barco de Vapor Award, 1982; Grand Prix de la Academie des Lecteurs, Paris.

WRITINGS:
A nivel de presidencia. Madrid: Ed. Magisterio Español, 1974.
El ajuste. Ed. Sedmay, 1975.
Lolo. Barcelona: Ed. Planeta, 1976.
Planicio. Barcelona: Ed. Planeta, 1976.

La tarde de la víspera. Barcelona: Ed. Planeta, 1978.
El señor del huerto. Madrid: Ed. Magisterio Español, 1980.
El hijo del quincallero. Madrid: Ediciones SM, 1981.
Cucho. Madrid: Ediciones SM, 1983.
La guerra del general Escobar. Barcelona: Ed. Planeta, 1983.
Bibiana y su mundo. Madrid: Ediciones SM, 1985.
Ciudadana mínima. Barcelona: Ed. Planeta, 1985.
El adolescente indómito. Barcelona: Ed. Planeta, 1986.
Senen. Madrid: Ediciones SM, 1986.
Micaela no sabe jugar. Valladolid: Ed. Miñón, 1986.
El cazador urbano. Valladolid: Ed. Miñón, 1987.
La paloma azul. Madrid: Ed. Susaeta, 1987.
El gato chino. Ed. Luis Vives, 1987.
La leyenda de Boni Martín. Madrid: Ed. Anaya, 1987.
Mi hermana Gabriela. Madrid: Ed. Anaya.
Cómo se hace una película. Madrid: Ediciones SM.
El secreto de Gabriela. Madrid: Ed. Anaya.
De Vietnam a Extremadura. Ed. Clip.
El Cid, el último héroe. Barcelona: Ed. Planeta.
Hernán Cortés, crónica de un imposible. Barcelona: Ed. Planeta.
La China se va a Bolivia. Ed. Roble Centenario.
La puerta de la esperanza. Barcelona: Ed. Planeta/Rialp.
Bartolomé de las Casas, crónica de un sueño. Barcelona: Ed. Planeta, 1991.
Viaje al fondo de la esperanza. Ed. Rialp, 1991.

SIDELIGHTS: "I write as much for adults as for children and young people. I write about characters that inspire me, and about historical figures."

ORTIZ MONASTERIO GARZA, Valentina (1973-)

PERSONAL DATA: Born November 30, 1973, in Mexico, D.F., the daughter of Fernando Ortiz Monasterio Prieto and Rosalba Garza Hernández. Education: Student.

ADDRESS: Fernández Leal 128, Coyoacan, Mexico, D.F. 6581174.

WRITINGS:
Mariposa monarca. CIDCLI, 1987.

ORTIZ MONASTERIO PRIETO, Fernando (1949-)

PERSONAL DATA: Born October 15, 1949, in Mexico, D.F., the son of Fernando Ortiz Monasterio and Leonor Prieto. He has three children, Valentina, Tatiana, and Fernando. Education: Licentiate in engineering from the Universidad Iberoamericana; postgraduate studies in planning and development from the University of London.

ADDRESS: (Home) Parque 22, Mexico, D.F. (Office) Mazatlan 96, Col. Condesa, Mexico, D.F. Telephone: 2864625, 2864626.

*CAREER: Environmental engin*eer; professor at the Universidad Autónoma Metropolitana; director of the ERM, Mexico.

PROFESSIONAL ORGANIZATIONS: Asociación de Energía Solar; Amnesty International.

AWARDS, HONORS: Amnesty International Collective Nobel Prize.

WRITINGS:
Historia ambiental de México. Mexico: Secretaría de Educación Pública, 1988.
Manejo de recibos industriales peligrosos en México. 1986.
Mariposa monarca vuelo de papel. Mexico: CIDCLI, 1987.

SIDELIGHTS: "My source of inspiration is nature. I write for the development of an ecological culture."

PACHECO, Miguel Ángel (1944-)

PERSONAL DATA: Born in 1944, in Spain. *Education:* Holds a degree in fine arts.

CAREER: Works for the television show *Un globo, dos globos, tres globos*; writer and illustrator.

ILLUSTRATED WORKS:
Bravo-Villasante, Carmen. *Antología de la literatura infantil universal.* 1971.
Ionescu, A. *Maestros de la fantasía.* 1972.
Bravo-Villasante, Carmen. *Vida y muerte del Doncel.* 1973.
Pacheco, M.A., and J.L. García Sánchez. *Soy un árbol, soy una roca.* 1974.
Rico de Alba, L. *Llorón, hijo de dragón.* 1975.

Grimm. *Madre nieve*. 1975.
Pacheco M.A., and J.L. García Sánchez. *El último lobo y Caperucita*. 1975.
Bravo-Villasante, Carmen. *Una, dola, tele, catola*. 1976.
Hoffmann, E.T.A. *El niño extraño*. 1976.
Wilde, O. *El ruiseñor y la rosa*. 1976.
Fuentes, Gloria. *La oca loca*. 1977.
Bravo-Villasante, Carmen. *Adivina, adivinanza*. 1978.

WRITTEN AND ILLUSTRATED WORKS:
Gracias al agua, gracias a la madera. Co-written with J.L. García Sánchez. 1975.

SIDELIGHTS: In his illustrations Miguel Ángel Pacheco introduced the artistic trend of *The Yellow Submarine*, by Heinz Edelmann, and helped rejuvenate modernism in illustration.

PÁEZ, Enrique (1955-)

PERSONAL DATA: Born in Madrid, Spain, in 1955. He has a son, Elías. *Education:* Holds a degree in Hispanic literature.

CAREER: Teacher in public colleges in Madrid, New York, and Algeciras. For two years he wrote for free radio. Currently works as an editor.

AWARDS, HONORS: Lazarillo Award for Literary Creation, 1991.

WRITINGS:
Siete por siete, antología. Bilbao: C.L.A., 1975.
Acércate al rincón de la tiniebla. Madrid: 1982.
Julia. Segovia: La Granja de San Ildefonso, 1988.
Devuélveme el anillo, pelo cepillo. Madrid: Ed. Bruño, 1992.

SIDELIGHTS: "Writing is my way of traveling through time and space. When I write I take the place of my characters and live through all of their thoughts and actions. I write so that I can experience lives that would otherwise remain out of my reach. I create different worlds. I become more than what I am when I write; I surpass myself and everything else. I suppose that for me writing is a way of making the monotony of everyday life more bearable."

PANAIFO TEIXEIRA, Arnaldo (1948-)

PERSONAL DATA: Born July 12, 1948, in Iquites, Peru, the son of Arnoldo and Luisa, he is married to Neri Alicia Rojas Morote. *Education:* Instituto Superior de Periodismo and Universidad Nacional de la Amazonia Peruana.

ADDRESS: Apartado Postal 03-5022, Salamanca, Lima 03, Peru. Telephone: (Office) 49318.

CAREER: Journalist; administrator for radio and television for the town of Huamanaga from 1976 to 1979; director of programs for radio and television, 1979.

PROFESSIONAL ORGANIZATIONS: Asociación Nacional de Escritores y Artistas; APLIJ; Federación de Periodistas del Perú; Colegio de Periodistas del Perú.

AWARDS, HONORS: Second Prize, Fourth Biennial Awards for Stories, 1985; First Prize, Bodas de Plata de la UNAP National Story Competition; Honorable Mention, José María Arguedas International Story Competition, France; Alfonsina Storni Award, 1978; Alberada Amaze Award, 1986.

WRITINGS:
Cuentos y algo más. 1981.
El pescador de sueños. Ed. Campa, 1982.
El ocaso de Ulderico el multiforme. Talleres Gráficos de JC Editores, 1986.
Julia Zumba, la nodriza reina. Lluvia Editores, 1993.
El parpadeo insomne. Lluvia Editores, 1987.
Piñón a babor. Lluvia Editores, 1993.
Los jóvenes de la serial. Shamiro Editores, 1992.
El río encantado. Ironyodla, 1992.
Mericha. Ironyodly, 1993

SIDELIGHTS: "The Amazons have always been one of the most exploited and marginalized cultures of my country. When I was in high school, we were given national anthologies of literature, but we still did not have access to authors from our region. The rest of the country was simply ignorant of us. This drove me to try to bring the works of Amazonian authors to national and international attention. I discovered my vocation early and have cherished it to today. My themes: the world of magic, my life, and the societies of the native, rural, and urban peoples of the Amazon. My sources of inspiration are social criticism, and the defense of the natural world and the ecological system."

CRITICAL SOURCES:
Marcos Yauri Montero. Prologue to *Cuentos y algo más.* 1981.

Humberto Morey Alejo. Prologue to *El pescador de sueños*. 1982.
Germán Lequerica Perea. Prologue to *El ocaso de Ulderico el multiforme*. 1987.
Roger Rumrill García. Prologue to *Julia Zumba la nodriza reina*. 1987.
Jaime Vásquez Izquierdo. Prologue to *El parpadeo insomne*. 1987.

PANTIGOSO PECERO, Manuel Trinidad (1936-)

PERSONAL DATA: Born August 27, 1936, in Lima, Peru, the son of Manuel Domingo and María Antonia, he is married to Lucía and has four children, Francisco, Flavio, Leonil, and Paulo. *Education:* Doctorate in literature and philology; doctorate in education from the Universidad Mayor de San Marcos; postdoctorate studies in Italy, Brasil, and Spain.

ADDRESS: (Home) Paseo de la República 6151, 7° San Antonio Miraflores, Lima, Peru. Telephone: 453602. (Office) Sor Tita 306, Depto. 301, Surco, Lima, Peru.

CAREER: Department chair at the Universidad San Marcos (professor emeritus); supervisor of public relations at the same university; writer.

PROFESSIONAL ORGANIZATIONS: Academia Peruana de la Lengua; founder and president of the Sociedad Peruana de Educación por el Arte; co-founder of the Asociación Peruana de Literatura Infantil y Juvenil del Perú; corresponding member of the Brazilian Academy of Letters.

AWARDS, HONORS: National Award for Literature, 1970; National Award for Theater, 1980, 1982; Honorary Professor, Universidad Nacional San Luis Gonzaga, ICA, Peru.

WRITINGS:
Contrapunto de la mitomanía. Ed. Universitaria, 1970.
Sydal. Author's edition, 1972.
Didáctica de la interpretación de textos literarios. Ed. Universo, 1975.
Salamandra de hojalata. Ed. Universitaria, 1977.
Didáctica creativa. Intihuatana, 1980.
Proposición de una metodología para conducir un taller de teatro y educación. Peru: Universidad de San Marcos, 1983.
Retablo de la naturaleza. Unpublished.
Los días de la palabra. Intihuatana, 1988.
Reloj de flora. Author's edition, 1980.

Nazea. Author's edition, 1986.
Amaromar. Buenos Aires: Ed. Proa, 1992.

He has also been published in various anthologies in Peru and Brazil.

SIDELIGHTS: "Writing is a way of using the word to sound the human soul in nature."

CRITICAL SOURCES:
Luis Hernán Ramírez. *Boletín de la Academia Peruana de la Lengua.*

PASTOR, Rodolfo (Sigfredo) (1940-)

PERSONAL DATA: Born January 13, 1940, in Trenel, La Pampa, Argentina. His parents are Sigfredo Ricardo Pastor and Dora Armisén. He is married to Petra Adriana Steinmayer and has two children, Ernesto Sigfredo and Emiliano Pablo. *Education:* Studied cinematography at the Escuela de Bellas Artes at the Universidad de La Plata.

ADDRESS: (Home) Marqués de Barberá 1, Principal Primera, 08001 Barcelona, Spain. Telephone: 3180314.

CAREER: Journalist of politics and culture from 1960 to 1968; designer, constructor, and owner of a two-story merry-go-round that paid his way through film school, 1970-72; founder and director of the group CINE (Children's Educative Cinema) for the creation of short animated features, 1972-76; moved to Mexico then Germany, and finally became a professor of film in Barcelona, 1976-78; since then he has made numerous animated films for children for Spanish television.

AWARDS, HONORS: Judge for the Festival of Fantastic Cinema at Sitges, Spain.

WRITINGS:
La sombra asombrosa. Madrid: Ed. De la Torre.
El espanto y los pájaros. Madrid: Ed. De la Torre.
El hombre gris. Madrid: Ed. De la Torre.
En un oscuro rincón del Far-West. Madrid: Ed. De la Torre.

SIDELIGHTS: "I used to read books for children and try to imitate my heroes. My familiar environment and the friends of my parents inspired me, and the idea to write has always boiled in my head. Sometimes the steam comes out of my ears so powerfully that I don't have to wash them. Maybe it's because of this that I write. I don't need a source of inspiration, just a couch. I lie back and let my little ideas simmer and grow. I go from idea to idea, jotting down what I like, until a story is finished. When I am a quarter asleep and three-quarters awake, I am best able to think. When this proportion is inverted, I use what little of my brain is left to think about what the rest of me is dreaming. My favorite themes are the vitality and the joy of life."

PAZ, Marcela (Esther Hunneus Salas) (1902-1985)

PERSONAL DATA: Born February 28, 1902, in Santiago de Chile, Chile. She died there June 12, 1985. She wrote under a variety of pseudonyms: Marcela Paz, Paula de la Sierra, Luki, Retse, P. Neka, Juanita Godoy, and Picadilly.

CAREER: Founder and editor of the journal *Pandilla*, published by Zig-Zag, 1959; editor of the children's section of *La Nación*, 1959; president of the IBBY, 1964-67.

AWARDS, HONORS: Health Award, 1927; Club Hípico Award, 1934; Rapa Nui Award of Honor, 1947; Honors List for the Andersen Prize, IBBY, Switzerland, 1968; Gold Medal from the Cultural Institute of Providence, 1979; Selection des Treize FOCS-OCL selected as one of the thirty best books published in France, Bordas Editions, 1980; Diploma of Honor from the Ilustre Municipalidad de Santiago, 1981; National Award for Literature, 1982; Andrés Bello Prize from the Minister of Education, 1983.

WRITINGS:
Pancho en la luna. Lectura Selecta, 1927.
Tiempo, papel y lápiz. Sociedad Impresora y Litografía Universo, 1933.
Soy Colorina. Ed. Ercilla, 1935.
Papelucho. Ed. Rapa Nui, 1947.
La vuelta de Sebastián. Ed. Ercilla, 1950.
Papelucho casi huérfano. Ed. Ercilla, 22nd ed., 1952.
Papelucho historiador. Ed. del Pacífico, 1954.
Caramelos de luz. Ed. del Pacífico, 1954.
Papelucho detective. Ed. del Pacífico, 1956.
Papelucho en la clínica. Ed. del Pacífico, 1958.
A pesar de mi tía. Ed. del Pacífico, 1958.
Papelucho perdido. Ed. Pomaire, 1960.

Papelucho: Mi hermana Ji. Ed. Pomaire, 1964.
Papelucho misionero. Ed. Pomaire, 1966.
Papelucho y el marciano. Ed. Pomaire, 1968.
Papelucho: Mi hermano hippie. Ed. Pomaire, 1971.
Papelucho en vacaciones. Ed. Pomaire, 15th ed.,1972.
Papelucho: ¿Soy dixleso? Santiago, Chile: Ed. Universitaria, 12th ed., 1974.
Muselina Pérez Soto. Ed. Lord Cochrane, 1974.
Cuentos para cantar. Ed. Lord Cochrane, 1974.
Los pecosos. Ed. Universitarias de Valparaíso, 7th ed.,1976.
Perico trepa por Chile. Co-written with Alicia Morel. Santiago, Chile: Ed. Universitaria, 10th ed.,1978.
El soldadito rojo. Santiago, Chile: Ed. Universitaria, 1981.
Los secretos de Catita. Santiago, Chile: Ed. Universitaria, 1981.

She also collaborated on the most important journals and newspapers in Chile.

CRITICAL SOURCES:
Virginia Cruzat. *Marcela Paz. Un mundo incógnito.* Santiago, Chile: Ed. Universitaria, 1992.

PELLICER LÓPEZ, Carlos (1948-)

PERSONAL DATA: Born March 26, 1948, in Mexico, D.F., the son of Juan Pellicer Cámara and Blanca López, he is married to Julia Yuste López and has two children, María and Carlos. Education: Studied painting at the Escuela Nacional de Artes Plásticas.

ADDRESS: (Home) Sierra Vertientes 693, Lomas de Chapultepec, 11000, Mexico, D.F. Telephone: 5961172.

*CAREER: Paint*er.

PROFESSIONAL ORGANIZATIONS: IBBY of Mexico.

AWARDS, HONORS: Promexa Award, 1982; Antoniorrobles Award, 1983; Placa de la Bienal Bratislava, 1985; IBBY Honors List, 1985; Bronze Medal, Jack Ezra Keats Awards, 1986.

ILLUSTRATED WORKS:
Las tres manzanas de naranja. Mexico: Ed. CIDCLI, 1982.

Una indita en su chinampa. Mexico: Ed. El Ermitaño, 1984.
Poetas tabasqueños. Mexico: Instituto de Cultura de Tabasco, 1987.

WRITTEN AND ILLUSTRATED WORKS:
Juan y sus zapatos. Mexico: Ed. Promexa, 1982.
Julieta y su caja de colores. Mexico: Ed. Patria, 1984.

SIDELIGHTS: "I write because I like to imagine stories and histories for my two children. Along with my wife they are, of course, my inspiration. My favorite theme... no, I don't have a favorite theme. More important than theme is mode, the form of what is said, the way of telling what is told."

PERERA, Hilda (1926-)

PERSONAL DATA: Born September 11, 1926, in Havana, Cuba, the daughter of José Francisco Perera and Hilda R. Soto, she is married to Juan Aguirre and has two children, Saúl and Hilda. *Education:* Doctorate in philosophy and letters from the Universidad de La Habana, 1951; master of arts from the University of Miami, Coral Gables, 1970.

ADDRESS: (Home) 8371 S.W. 5th St., Miami, Florida 33144. Telephone: 553-2482, 559-4576.

CAREER: Director of the Spanish Department, Academia Ruston, Havana, Cuba, 1948-60; administrator of educational matters and academic activities at the Biblioteca José Martí, 1960-62; associate editor of *Buenhogar*, 1965-66; editor of *Romances*, 1966-67; editor for *Las Américas*, 1985-.

PROFESSIONAL ORGANIZATIONS: Coalition of Hispanic-American Women; Cuban Women's Club; Honor affiliate to the Phi Sigma Iota, Society of Foreign Languages; Instituto Cultural Iberoamericano; Instituto de Cultura Panamericano; Sociedad de Hispanistas.

AWARDS, HONORS: First Prize in Literature, Universidad de La Habana; Second Prize, Hernández Catá International Story Competition, Havana; First Prize for the Best Journalistic Article; Award at the Story Competition for the Club de Mujeres Profesionales de Cuba; Fellowship, Instituto Cultural Cubano-Norteamericano; First Place, First Competition of Literature for Children, Consejo Nacional de Cultura de Cuba; First Finalist for the Planeta Awards, 1972; Lazarillo Award, 1975,

1978; Finalist for the Nadal Award, 1975; Award from the Cuban Women's Club; Honors List for the Comisión Nacional Católica de Literatura Infantil for published books, 1980; Finalist for the Novedades-Diana Award, Mexico; Special Prize, Art Critics Association of Florida; Dynamic Woman Award, American Cancer Society, 1989; Silver Medal from Ediciones SM; Honors List, Comisión Católica de la Infancia.

WRITINGS:

Cuentos de Apolo. Havana: Ed. Lex, 1947. Also Miami: Ed. Franhil Enterprises, 1975. Also Leon: Ed. Everest, 1983.

Cuentos de Adli y Luas. Havana: Ed. Lex, 1960.

Mañana es 26. Havana: Imprenta Lázaro y Hno, 1960.

Una niña bajo tres banderas. Havana: Editora Nacional de Cuba, 1963.

Cuentos para chicos y grandes. 1975.

Kike. Madrid: Ediciones SM, 1984.

Mai. Madrid: Ediciones SM, 1983.

Podría ser que una vez. Leon: Ed. Everest, 1981.

Pericopín. Leon: Ed. Everest, 1981.

Rana ranita. Leon: Ed. Everest, 1981.

Pepín y el abuelo. Leon: Ed. Everest, 1982.

La fuga de los juguetes. Leon: Ed. Everest, 1986.

La pata Pita. Co-written with Mana Fraga. New York: Ed. Minerva Books, 1984.

La pata Pita vuelve. Co-written with Mana Fraga. New York: Ed. Minerva Books, 1984.

Mamú. Madrid: Ed. Bruño, 1990.

La jaula del unicornio. Barcelona: Ed. Noguer, 1991.

Javi. Leon: Ed. Everest, 1991.

El burrito que quería ser azul. Leon: Ed. Everest, 1992.

Tomasín y el periquito. Leon: Ed. Everest, 1992.

She has also published specialized works, grammar books, and novels for adults.

SIDELIGHTS: "For me, writing is a difficult pleasure, almost a burden: like a craziness or an invincible stubbornness. It is involuntary, like breathing or blood running through the veins. When I first started, I was not able to put down my pen. Every fleeting emotion would cause me to pick it up again and continue my scribblings, though deeply felt ones. There was in me a kind of drum roll that said 'write, only write.' Ah, but this drive, this vocation of clenched teeth, was difficult for those around me to bear. They, of good faith and devotion, yet wearied of seeing me do nothing but write."

CRITICAL SOURCES: Her work has been reviewed and critiqued in various newspapers and journals by Celedonio González, Anita Arroyo, Waldo Medina,

María Elena Saavedra, Juana de Ibarbourou, Eugenio Florit, Germán Arciniegas, José Antonio Portuondo, Lydia Cabrera, Carlos Murciano, Enrique Labrador, Carlos Alberto Montaner, Manuel Barbadillo, Rafael Esténger, Gastón Baquero, Rosario Hiriart, Alicia Aldaya, and Daniel Alcoba.

Ya.
Excélsior. Mexico.
Vogue. Mexico.
Las Américas. April 22, 1982.
El Observador. Barcelona: July 27, 1991.
La Vanguardia. Barcelona: September 1991.
Francisco Cubells Salas. *Comunidad Educativa.* 191, November 1991.
White Ravens. 1992.

PÉREZ AVELLO, Carmen (1908-)

PERSONAL DATA: Born April 13, 1908, in Cadavedo, Asturias, Spain, the daughter of Leandro and Carmen. *Education:* Doctorate in primary education, with emphasis in Spanish.

ADDRESS: (Home) Casa de Ejercicios, Latores, 33193 Oviedo, Spain. Telephone: 5254763.

AWARDS, HONORS: Doncel Award, 1965, 1967; Chest of Silver Award, 1968, 1969.

WRITINGS:
Un muchacho sefardí. Madrid: 1965. Also Leon: Ed. Everest, 1990.
Vikingos al remo. Barcelona: Ed. Noguer, 1981.
Sueño de un gato negro. Barcelona: Ed. Noguer, 1983.
Unos zuecos para mí. Madrid: Ed. Anaya, 1988.

SIDELIGHTS: "Sensitive to beauty, I was attracted to the fine arts. I wanted to create beauty with the word and chose literature for children and young people. I especially wanted to direct my energies toward children, to enrich their vocabularies, and to give them a love of reading."

CRITICAL SOURCES:
Carmen Bravo-Villasante. *Antología.*

Mercedes Gómez del Manzano. *Literatura infantil*. Madrid: Ed. Narcea, 1987.
María Elvira Muñiz. *El Comercio*. April 24, 1992.

PÉREZ-LUCAS (ALBA), María Dolores (1925-)

PERSONAL DATA: Born September 22, 1925, in Salamanca, Spain, the daughter of Ignacio and Catalina, she is married to José María Vargas Zúñiga.

ADDRESS: (Home) Plaza de los Basilios 7, 3° 37001 Salamanca, Spain. Telephone: 265509.

PROFESSIONAL ORGANIZATIONS: Asociación Cultural Alfonso X el Sabio, Salamanca; Amigos del Museo del Prado, Madrid; Asociación de Escritores Españoles, Madrid.

AWARDS, HONORS: Extraordinary Doncel Award, 1964; Second Prize, CCEI, 1969; Chest of Silver Award, 1969, 1973, 1983; Second Prize, New Future Award, 1974; Pluma de Oro de Santa Teresa, 1975; Aller, 1979.

WRITINGS:
La Cucaña. Madrid: Ed. Doncel, 1964.
La pequeña gota de agua que quiso ver el mundo. 1967.
Cuatro cuentos para ti. Ed. Marfil, 1968.
La pajarita sabia. Ed. Marfil, 1969.
Un concurso en televisión. Ed. Marfil, 1971.
El trasplante. Ed. Marfil, 1972.
El misterio de los diamantes. Ed. Marfil, 1974.
Secuestro aéreo. Ed. Marfil, 1974.
La mar, los peces y su amigo José. Ed. Marfil, 1979.
Teresa de Jesús cuenta su vida a los niños de hoy. 1981.
Francisco de Asís cuenta su vida a los niños de hoy. 1982.
Seis eran seis. Leon: Ed. Everest, 1983.
El juego de las gafas. Valladolid: Ed. Miñón, 1983.
Leyendas de Salamanca. Instituto de Ciencias de la Educación y Universidad de Salamanca, 1985.
Europa cuenta su vida a los niños de hoy. Salamanca: Ed. Diputación de Salamanca, 1986.
Don inventos. Madrid: Ed. Anaya, 1989.
Doña Nube. Leon: Ed. Everest, 1990.

Don Río. Leon: Ed. Everest, 1990.
Doña Montaña. Leon: Ed. Everest, 1990.
Don Bosque. Leon: Ed. Everest, 1990.
Don Árbol. Leon: Ed. Everest, 1990.
Doña Pradera. Leon: Ed. Everest, 1990.
Juan de la Cruz cuenta su vida a los chicos de hoy. Ed. Sígueme, 1990.
¡Paso a la Reina Isabel! Madrid: Ed. Susaeta, 1990.
Fray Luis de León os habla de tú a tú. Ed. Sígueme, 1991.

SIDELIGHTS: "Writing for children gives me great enjoyment. They have so much to discover! Helping them to learn is invigorating. I think that reading is fundamental for children, and even more so in our age of television. A child in front of the TV is a passive subject, bombarded by images from a screen, as opposed to a child who is reading, transformed by the process of reading into an active, dynamic subject. The reader thinks, recreates the characters that have been designed by the author, but in a wholly original way. Imagination and fantasy are other qualities that reading stimulates; but they are sadly undiscovered by the majority of today's children, who suffer from our society's inactive rationalism."

CRITICAL SOURCES:
Emilio Salcedo. *El Norte de Castilla*. Valladolid.
Montserrat Sarto. *La literatura infantil*.
Jesús Ventosa. *El Adelantado*. Salamanca, 1983.

PÉREZ VALERO, Rodolfo (1947-)

PERSONAL DATA: Born in 1947, in Guanabacoa, Havana, Cuba. *Education:* Holds a degree in philology from the Universidad de La Habana; also studied dramatic art at the Escuela Nacional de Arte de Cuba.

ADDRESS: (Home) Calle E 664, entre 27 y 29, Apto. 15, Vedado, Havana, Cuba. Telephone: 323065, 321410.

CAREER: Actor and assistant director of theater; director of the journal *Enigma*, by the Spanish branch of the AIEP (Asociación Internacional de Escritores Policiacos).

PROFESSIONAL ORGANIZATIONS: Vice-president, AIEP; president, Sección de Escritores Policiacos, UNEAC.

AWARDS, HONORS: National Award for Detective Fiction, 1974, 1976, 1981; *La Edad de Oro* Award for Theater for Children, 1978; Mention at the UNEAC Awards; Second Prize at the National Awards for Detective Fiction, 1983.

WRITINGS:
Las siete puntas de la corona del rey Tragamás. Havana: Ed. Gente Nueva, 1979.
Los apuros de Popito. Ed. Letras Cubanas, 1981.
El misterio de las cuevas del pirata. Havana: Ed. Gente Nueva, 1980.

Detective Fiction:
No es tiempo de ceremonias. 1974.
Para vivir más de una vida. 1976.
Crimen en noche de máscaras. 1981.
Confrontación. 1983.

SIDELIGHTS: "The first thing that I wrote, in 1972, was for theater and was in fact my first work in the theater. Then I wrote *No es tiempo de ceremonias*, a detective fiction. That same year (1974) I got work as an actor for the Teatro Nacional de Guiñol, and my direct contact with child spectators impressed me so much that I immediately began to write for them. I wrote *Los apuros de Popito* soon after. A difference between writing and the theater is that the actor can immediately see how the audience reacts to his work. I enjoy thinking about how children will react to this or that scene in my writings, and this is a great motivation."

PERIS LOZANO, Carme (1941-)

PERSONAL DATA: Born November 30, 1941, in Barcelona, Spain, the daughter of Antonio and Paquita, she is married to José and has four children, Roser, Oriol, Arnau, and Daniel. *Education:* Holds a bachelor's degree with studies at the Escuela Superior Artes Suntuarias Massana, the Escuela de Artes y Oficios Artísticos, and Bellas Artes de San Jordi.

ADDRESS: (Home) Rector Ubach 6 SA, Barcelona, Spain. 2090774.

CAREER: Graphics and advertising work at Seix y Barral Artes Gráficas, 1956-64; painter and illustrator,1980-.

PROFESSIONAL ORGANIZATIONS: Asociación Profesional de Ilustradores de Catalunya.

AWARDS, HONORS: Finalist for the Apelles Mestres Award; People's Choice Award from Catalunya; CCIA Award; president for six years of the Catalan Council of Books for Children; president for three years of the Spanish Organization of Books for Children.

ILLUSTRATED WORKS AND PUBLICATIONS:
El caracol volador. Japan: Gakken, 1983.
La tanca mágica. Abadía de Montserrat, 1985.
Bela-Bela. Japan: Gakken, 1989.
La luna y yo. Ediciones B, 1991.
La caperucita roja. Hymsal, 1986.
Robinson Crusoe. Edad Antigua, Edad Contemporánea.
Mis deportes. Ed. Parramón, 1989.
La naturaleza. Ed. Parramón, 1989.

Her works have been translated into English, French, Japanese, and German.

SIDELIGHTS: "Basically, I illustrate books, but I have also written seven of my own. My favorite themes are nature and anecdotes about my family, and there are many, since I have four children. Animals are also a source of inspiration, but not always common animals; rather, I write about ravens, dinosaurs, silkworms, and hamsters. I also like to write about memories of fragrances."

CRITICAL SOURCES:
Andrew Soterra. *Avui.*
Cesar Vázquez. *Avui.*

PETTERSSON, Aline (1938-)

PERSONAL DATA: Born May 11, 1938, in Mexico, D.F., the daughter of Gustavo Pettersson and Aurelia Ferrel. She has three children, María Aline, Axel, and Constanza. *Education:* Licentiate in Hispanic letters from the Universidad Nacional Autónoma de México; postgraduate studies in Hispanic letters and English.

ADDRESS: (Home) Mercaderes 127, 1002 San Jose Insurgentes, Mexico, D.F. Telephone: 6801167.

CAREER: Editor, translator, conductor of creative writing workshops, and reading director.

PROFESSIONAL ORGANIZATIONS: PEN Club and SOGEM.

AWARDS, HONORS: Fellowship from the Centro de Escritores; Invited to the Iowa Writers' Program; Finalist for the Villaurrutia Award.

WRITINGS:
El papalote y el nopal. Mexico: Ed. CIDCLI, 1985.
Clara y el cangrejo. Mexico: Secretaría de Educación Pública, 1990.

Most of Aline Pettersson's work is for adult readers.

CRITICAL SOURCES:
Gonzalo Veldes Mendellín. *Unomasuno.* Mexico.
Miriam Moscona. *La Jornada Semanal.* Mexico.
Ramón Xirau. *Diálogos.* Mexico.

PIÉROLA, Mabel (1953-)

PERSONAL DATA: Born November 30, 1953, in Madrid, Spain, the daughter of Alberto and María Dolores, she is married to Luis Maniagua and has three children, Alberto, Isabel, and Pablo. *Education:* Fine arts degree from the Universities of San Fernando, Madrid, and Sant Jordi in Barcelona.

ADDRESS: (Home) Plaza de la Villa 7 D., 08192 Sant Quirze del Valles, Barcelona, Spain. 7109699.

CAREER: Painter; illustrator; sculptor; writer.

PROFESSIONAL ORGANIZATIONS: Asociación Profesional de Ilustradores de Cataluña.

AWARDS, HONORS: First Prize for Illustrated Stories from the city of Olot, 1987; Selected by Catalonia for the Ezra Jack Keats Competition, 1987; First Prize, Tarjetas de Navidad, UNICEF, 1990; First Prize, Caterina Albert Poetry Awards, 1990; Apelles Mestres Award, 1991.

WRITINGS:
Santa Engracia número dos o tres. Madrid: Ed. Anaya, 1989.
El palacio de cristal. Barcelona: Ed. Aliorna, 1989.

La perla verde. Zaragoza: Ed. Edelvives, 1990.
El asunto de mis papás. Madrid: Ed. Destino, 1991.
Los ríos de la luna. Zaragoza: Ed. Edelvives, 1991.
El rey y el país con granos. Ed. Lumen, 1991.
El libro del buen amor. Ed. Lumen, 1991.
Muchas cosas. Madrid: Ed. Anaya, 1992.
Don Miedo, Doña Oscura y la maga Sombra. Madrid: Ed. Anaya, 1992.

The other works of Mabel Piérola are published in Catalan.

SIDELIGHTS: "Writing is one of the advantages of being an adult. I love answering the questions that I asked as a girl and was unable to grasp at the time. I play with fantasy and reality. I combine the transcendent with the absurd. I don't think about children when I write, who all know that I think I am one of them. Maybe I am! I try in life to shout 'I am!' rather than waste time around those who don't like me; and I believe that anything is possible. I love to laugh and do so until my stomach hurts; I shout no from down in my stomach, and I think that everything that happens is better off that way. Also, I love. I love very much."

CRITICAL SOURCES:
Faristol.

PINTO CAÑÓN, Ramiro (1961-)

PERSONAL DATA: Born September 1, 1961, in Madrid, Spain, the son of Ramiro and María Dolores, he is married to Yolanda and has two children, Rayo and Omar.

ADDRESS: (Home) Mariano D. Berrueta 4, 2° 24003 Leon, Spain. Telephone: 7256239.

CAREER: Professor of theater; teacher of adults in disadvantaged environments (single working mothers, criminals).

PROFESSIONAL ORGANIZATIONS: Survival, Los Verdes, Projuventud.

AWARDS, HONORS: Finalist for the XIII Certamen de la Sonrisa Vertical.

WRITINGS:
El circo de la fantasía. Co-written with María Yolanda Prieto. Madrid: Ed. Escuela

Española, 1990.
El espantapájaros amigo de los pájaros. Co-written with María Yolanda Prieto. Madrid: Ed. Escuela Española, 1990.

SIDELIGHTS: For Ramiro Pinto, writing is "a way of experimenting in our thoughts with the world in which we live." His themes include "man's struggle to be himself" and "the defense of the authenticity of dreams." "Everyday life" and "conversations with friends" inspire his work.

CRITICAL SOURCES:
Félix C. Fernández López. *Diario de León.*

PLA, Imma (1964-)

PERSONAL DATA: Born in Barcelona, Spain, in 1964. *Education:* Designer at the Escuela Elisava.

CAREER: In addition to illustrating books for children, she works on projects and collaborations related to design.

AWARDS, HONORS: Special Mention, Lazarillo Award, 1990; Apelles Mestres Award, shared with Montserrat Ganges, for *Zip y la oveja del sueño,* 1991; Mention at the Graphic Awards of the Bologna Children's Book Fair for *Zip y el dragón fanfarrón,* 1992.

ILLUSTRATED WORKS:
Montserrat Ganges. *Una mosca en la sopa.* Barcelona: Ed. Publicaciones de l'Abadía de Montserrat, 1989.
Montserrat Ganges. *Zip y el dragón fanfarrón.* Barcelona: Ed. Destino, 1991.
Montserrat Ganges. *Zip y la oveja del sueño.* Barcelona: Ed. Destino, 1992.

She has published three other works in Catalan.

SIDELIGHTS: "I dedicated myself to illustration very recently. I began working in graphic design until little by little I began to focus my time on illustration. I thought, illustration for children? But then, why not? It provides a lot of artistic freedom and is generous. I think that the writer and the illustrator need to understand each other's role and importance. I think that Montse [Montserrat Ganges] and I have followed this understanding and even expanded upon it. I think that it is important to start with a text that you like and to invite the ideas of your partner (for this reason, I said that this type of illustration is free and generous). I also think that, and to me this is essential, the central part of a scene, comprised of text and illustration is the graphic part. These relations are important because a book is a broad and complex set of concepts, whether contemplated by an audience or not."

PONCE DE LEÓN PATIÑO, Soledad (1903-)

PERSONAL DATA: Born in Huetamo de Nuñez, Michoacan, Mexico. Her parents were Ramón Ponce de León and Juana Patiño. *Education:* Master's degree in primary education, with emphasis in literature and linguistics; studies in theater and mime.

ADDRESS: (Home) Alcerreca 2058-B, Col. Orizaba, Mexicali, Baja California, Mexico.

CAREER: Primary school teacher since 1931; secondary school teacher since 1975.

PROFESSIONAL ORGANIZATIONS: Orden Rosacruz, AMORC.

AWARDS, HONORS: First Place, Awards to Teachers and National Culture, 1986; Recognized by SEP for the Education Movement in Baja California, 1990.

WRITINGS:
El teatro en el primer ciclo. Thesis, 1963.
Estrellitas de la infancia 1. Author's edition, 1972.
Estrellitas de la infancia 2. Author's edition, 1990.

SIDELIGHTS: "I write as a contribution to education in general. My favorite themes are those that support teaching and give enjoyment to children. Childhood is my source of inspiration."

CRITICAL SOURCES:
Armando Aguirre. *La Voz de la Frontera.*
Antonio Ortega. *Excélsior.* December 10, 1986.
Alejandro Becerra Quiroz. *Voz-a-nova.* October 7, 1990.

POSADAS (MAÑÉ), Carmen de (1953-)

PERSONAL DATA: Born August 13, 1953, in Montevideo, Uruguay. Her parents are Luis and Sara. She is married to Mariano Rubio and has two children, Sofía and Jimena Ruiz del Cueto.

ADDRESS: (Home) Jovellanos 5, 28014 Madrid, Spain. Telephone: 5213860.

CAREER: Writer.

WRITINGS:
Ángel de esperanza. Buenos Aires: Ed. Juárez, 1984.
Historias Biblias. Madrid: Ediciones SM, 1980.
Kiwi. Madrid: Ediciones SM, 1984.
El Sr. Viento Norte. Madrid: Ediciones SM, 1987.
El mercader de sueños. Madrid: Ed. Alfaguara, 1990.

SIDELIGHTS: "I began writing for children and continue doing so although I also write for adults. For me writing for children is a challenge. My favorite theme is fantasy because it presents more possibilities than reality and, one can address real problems in an indirect manner. Many of my books (almost all of them) have animals as protagonists."

PRIETO MARTÍNEZ, María Yolanda (1962-)

PERSONAL DATA: Born April 17, 1962, in Santibáñez de la Isla, Leon, Spain, she is the daughter of Félix Prieto and María Ascención Martínez. She is married to Ramiro Pinto and has two children, Rayo and Omar. *Education:* Licentiate in biology.

ADDRESS: (Home) Mariano D. Berrueta 4, 2° 24003 Leon, Spain. Telephone: 256239.

CAREER: Director of a theater group for children, 1989-92.

PROFESSIONAL ORGANIZATIONS: Centro Estable de Animación Teatral (CEAT); Asociación Cultural Grupo de Teatro "Los Pequeños Teatristas"; Asociación Deportivo Cultural "Río Tuerto".

AWARDS, HONORS: Finalist for the Third Literary Debate Theater Contest.

WRITINGS:
El circo de fantasía. Co-written with Ramiro Pinto. 1990.
El espantapájaros amigo de los pájaros. Co-written with Ramiro Pinto. 1990.

SIDELIGHTS: "I write because of my classes and courses of theater for children."

CRITICAL SOURCES:
Félix C. Fernández López. *Diario de León.*

PUNCEL (REPARAZ), María (1927-)

PERSONAL DATA: Born May 3, 1927, in Madrid, Spain, the daughter of Luis Puncel Bosch and Dolores Reparaz Linazasoro.

ADDRESS: (Home) Paseo del Pintor Rosales 22, 29008 Madrid, Spain. Telephone: 5481782. (Office) Elfo 32, 28027 Madrid, Spain. Telephone: 3265400.

CAREER: Editor since 1969.

PROFESSIONAL ORGANIZATIONS: Asociación Colegial de Escritores; OEPLI; IBBY of Spain.

AWARDS, HONORS: AETIJ, 1971; Lazarillo Award, 1971, 1981; Aro de Plata, 1972; AMADE Award, 1977; Second Prize, Lazarillo Award, 1980; Barco de Vapor Award, 1981.

WRITINGS:
Isabel de Hungría. Illust. by Margarita Puncel. Ed. Cantábrica, 1967.
Clara de Asís. Illust. by Margarita Puncel. Ed. Cantábrica, 1968.
Francisco de Asís. Illust. by Margarita Puncel. Ed. Cantábrica, 1969.
Operación Pata de Oso. Illust. by Ulises Wensell. Madrid: Ed. Doncel, 1971.
Juegos para una tarde de lluvia. Ed. Sarpe, 1973.
Chiquito. Illust. by Wilhelm Bush. Ed. Marpol, 1977.
Cuando sea mayor seré enfermera. Illust. by Ulises Wensell. Madrid: Ed. Altea, 1979.
Cuando sea mayor construiré casas. Illust. by Gerardo R. Amechazurra. Madrid: Ed. Altea, 1979.

Cuando sea mayor seré marino. Illust. by Ulises Wensell. Madrid: Ed. Altea, 1979.

Cuando sea mayor seré piloto. Illust. by J. Antonio Alcázar. Madrid: Ed. Altea, 1979.

Cuando sea mayor seré comerciante. Illust. by María Rius. Madrid: Ed. Altea, 1979.

Cuando sea mayor trabajaré en una granja. Illust. by Letizia Galli. Madrid: Ed. Altea, 1979.

Cuando sea mayor seré mecánico. Illust. by Francisco Delicado. Madrid: Ed. Altea, 1979.

Cuando sea mayor haré cine. Illust. by Arcadio Lobato. Madrid: Ed. Altea, 1979.

Cuando sea mayor seré músico. Illust. by Letizia Galli. Madrid: Ed. Altea, 1980.

Cuando sea mayor seré periodista. Illust. by Alexandra Hellwagner. Madrid: Ed. Altea, 1980.

Dos cuentos de duendes. Illust. by Karin Schuber. Madrid: Ed. Altea, 1980.

Dos cuentos de princesas. Illust. by Viví Escrivá. Madrid: Ed. Altea, 1980.

Dos cuentos de dragones. Illust. by Miguel A. Pacheco. Madrid: Ed. Altea, 1981.

Dos cuentos de encantamientos. Illust. by Carme Peris. Madrid: Ed. Altea, 1981.

Dos cuentos de brujas. Illust. by María Manhes. Madrid: Ed. Altea, 1981.

Dos cuentos de príncipes. Madrid: Ed. Altea, 1981.

Dos cuentos de ogros. Illust. by Letizia Galli. Madrid: Ed. Altea, 1981.

Dos cuentos de gnomos. Madrid: Ed. Altea, 1981.

Dos cuentos de sirenas. Illust. by Asun Balzola. Madrid: Ed. Altea, 1981.

Dos cuentos de gigantes. Madrid: Ed. Altea, 1981.

Abuelita Opalina. Illust. by Margarita Puncel. Madrid: Ediciones SM, 1981.

Los caramelos mágicos. Illust. by Adan Ferrer. Ed. Santillana, 1981.

El hombre de la lluvia. Madrid: Ed. Altea, 1981.

Un duende a rayas. Illust. by Margarita Puncel. Madrid: Ediciones SM, 1982.

Clara y el caimán. Illust. by Margarita Puncel. Madrid: Ed. Altea, 1983.

El prado del tío Pedro. Madrid: Ediciones SM, 1983.

Un hatillo de cerezas. Illust. by Viví Escrivá, 1984

La isla de la bruma. Madrid: Ed. Altea, 1985.

Juana de Lestonnac. Illust. by Karin Schuber. Ed. Lestonnac, 1989.

SIDELIGHTS: "I write because after I discovered that I had the ability and the inclination to tell stories, I liked the idea of dedicating myself to the world of children, to educating them with fun and interesting stories. My sources of inspiration are my own life, my experiences, and my continual contact with children and adolescents. Also literature, of course. My favorite themes are those relating to knowledge, respect and appreciation of others, being good to others. I also find inspiration in animals, things, reality, nature."

RAMB, Ana María (1936–)

PERSONAL DATA: Born July 29, 1936, in Cordoba, Argentina, the daughter of José Alberto Ramb and Margarita Hughes, she is married to Joaquín Carmona and has a son, Federico. *Education:* Technical education in publication.

ADDRESS: (Home) Carlos Calvo 2067, 4° E, 1230 Buenos Aires, Argentina. Telephone: 9416769. (Office) Uruguay 1371, 1001 Buenos Aires, Argentina. Telephone: 13520.

CAREER: Teacher and editor.

PROFESSIONAL ORGANIZATIONS: Sociedad Argentina de Escritores; ALIJA; IBBY of Argentina; (UTBA) Workers' Press Union of Buenos Aires.

AWARDS, HONORS: Casa de las Américas Award for the Novel, 1975; Second Prize from CERLAL, 1979; Honors List, Sociedad Argentina de Escritores, 1981.

WRITINGS:
Renancó y los últimos huemules. 1975.
Un zapato con ceniza y lluvia. Buenos Aires: Ed. Plus Ultra, 1981.
Canelo el aventurero. 1985.
Patio abierto. 1987.
Milonga de Malena. 1987.
Pandurito. 1989.

SIDELIGHTS: "Works of fiction, in whichever genre, should try to attain a certain level of artistic achievement. Writers should not subordinate literary standards to the diffusion of facile morality, protected under the guise of literature for children. The intention of the writer should always be to construct a work of art. All other objectives should be subordinate to this. Literature for children is, moreover, not the enemy of television, nor vice versa. On the contrary, writers could and should better use television's widespread accessibility to bring their works to children."

CRITICAL SOURCES:
Rosemarie G. de Armando. *Pájaro de fuego.*
Río Negro. May 25, 1982.
El Litoral. Santa Fe: February 14, 1983.
Clarín. April 11, 1985; April 18, 1985; August 5, 1988.
Vida Silvestre. June 1985.
María Adelia Díaz Ronner. *La Capital.* October 27, 1985.
La Voz del Interior. August 3, 1986

RAMON I BOFARULL, Elisa (1957-)

PERSONAL DATA: Born February 6, 1957, in Barcelona, Spain, the daughter of Bartolomé and María del Carmen, she is married to Ramón Suris and has two children, Alex and Oscar. *Education:* Three years of law school at the Facultad de Derecho in Barcelona.

ADDRESS: Vallmajor 35, 3° 2a., 08021 Barcelona, Spain. Telephone: 2097161.

CAREER: Administrative positions in a psychology practice and a construction firm.

WRITINGS:
El deseo de Sofía. Illust. by José María Lavarello. Madrid: Ed. Espasa-Calpe, 1986.
Aventura en Australia. Illust. by Gemma Sales. Barcelona: Ed. Timun Mas, 1987.
La desaparición de la doctora Rinner. Illust. by Gemma Sales. Barcelona: Ed. Timun Mas, 1987.
El aullido de los lobos. Illust. by Gemma Sales. Barcelona: Ed. Timun Mas, 1988.
El fantasma del capitán Ahab. Illust. by Gemma Sales. Barcelona: Ed. Timun Mas, 1988.
La cigarra holgazana. Illust. by Gustí Asensio. Ed. Ángulo, 1988.
La derrota de Gustavo. Illust. by Roser Capdevila. Ed. Ángulo, 1988.
El ingenioso ratón y el cascabel de latón. Illust. by Mercè Aránega. Ed. Ángulo, 1988.
El ratón explorador. Illust. by Grancesc Rovira. Ed. Ángulo, 1988.
Donde las dan, las toman. Illust. by Montse Tobella. Ed. Ángulo, 1988.
La rana envidiosa. Illust. by José María Lavarello. Ed. Ángulo, 1988.
Federica, la liebre asustadiza. Illust. by Horacio Elena. Ed. Ángulo, 1989.
¡Todos a la guerra! Illust. by Valentina Cruz. Ed. Ángulo, 1989.
Florencio, Fulgencio y tres sustos de muerte. Illust. by Gustí. Ed. Ángulo, 1989.
Arístides se pasa de listo. Illust. by Mabel Piérola. Ed. Ángulo, 1989.
El secreto del abuelo lobón. Illust. by Francesc Infante. Ed. Ángulo, 1989.
Corre, corre que te pillo. Illust. by Gemma Sales. Ed. Ángulo, 1989.

SIDELIGHTS: "I write about whatever occurs to me, inspired by everyday things in life: the anecdotes that arise from day to day; the contact I have with children, adults, and elders; from my insatiable curiosity; and from the relationships I have with my children and friends, who are of course my best critics."

RAMOS DE LA TORRE, Luis (1956-)

PERSONAL DATA: Born June 1, 1956, in Zamora, Spain, the son of Luis Ramos Campesino and Inocencia de La Torre Alonso, he is married to Vicenta Picazo Pino and has one child, Lara Ramos Picazo. *Education:* Master's degree in education.

ADDRESS: (Office) Centro de Profesores, Avenida Requejo s/n, 490013 Zamora, Spain. Telephone: 988514398. (Home) Plaza Goleta N13D, Zamora, Spain (winter); C/ Zamora n17, Bamba del Vino, Zamora, Spain. Telephone: 988515769 or 988571070.

CAREER: Professor; director of the Centro de Profesores in Zamora.

WRITINGS:
Guía de lectura de Claudio Rodríguez. Madrid: Ediciones de la Torre, 1989.
Claudio Rodríguez para niños. Madrid: Ediciones de la Torre, 1988.

SIDELIGHTS: "I write about poetry and themes referring to poetry and to music and about the relations that exist between them. I am concerned about the loss, or rather, the erosion of musicality in people and children. In a society with noise but no rhythm, music and poetry have much to say that is fundamental to the recovery and reeducation of our culture. I am interested and inspired by oral narrative, humor, silence, color, songs, the body, and everything else that complements life."

CRITICAL SOURCES:
Educación y Biblioteca. 2, July-August 1989.
Jesús Hernández. *El Correo de Zamora.* August 8, 1989.

RAYÓ FERRER, Eusebia (1951-)

PERSONAL DATA: Born August 13, 1951, in Palma de Mallorca, Islas Baleares, Spain. Her parents are Juan and Micaela. She has two daughters, Inés and Ángela. *Education:* Holds a degree in history and geography.

ADDRESS: (Home) Rector Llompart 25, Bajos, 07141 Sa Cabneta (Marratxi), Baleares, Spain. Telephone: 971602176. (Office) Conselleria Comerc I Industria, Gran Via Asima 4, Bajos, 07071 Palma de Mallorca, Baleares, Spain. Telephone: 971726047.

CAREER: Executive for the public administration, 1975.

PROFESSIONAL ORGANIZATIONS: Asociación de Escritores en Lengua Catalana (AELC).

AWARDS, HONORS: Honorable Mention for "The Woman of the Hour," 1980; Finalist for the Guillem Cifre de Colònya Award, 1985, 1986; CCEI Honors List, 1988; Vocal de la Junta for the AELC.

WRITINGS:
La alquimia del corazón. Barcelona: Ed. La Galera, 1987.
Jaque a la princesa. Barcelona: Ed. La Galera, 1989.
Una voz del pasado. In print.
El ejército de los inocentes. In print.

The works cited here are translations into Spanish. Her works are originally written in Catalan.

SIDELIGHTS: "My favorite themes are magic, adventure, and the historical world. I suppose that writing is for me a way of escaping from the real world, which I don't entirely enjoy. It is also, however, a way of confronting my problems, resolving them, and leaving them behind. Writing has helped my to understand myself better and to accept myself as I am. At times I use personal experiences in my works, and at others (in my historical novels) I use incidents, experiences, and environments that have impressed me."

CRITICAL SOURCES:
Foc Nou. 158, June 1987.
Francisco Cubells Salas. *Comunidad Educativa*. April 1988.
Cavall Fort. 647, July 1989.
El Temps. 270, August 1989.

RAYÓ FERRER, Miguel (1952-)

PERSONAL DATA: Born September 21, 1952, in Palma de Mallorca, Spain, the son of Joan and Miquela. He is married to Assumpció and has two children, María del Mar and Joan. *Education:* Holds a degree in educational science.

ADDRESS: (Home) Arxiduc Luis Salvador 90, 5 15, 07004 Palma de Mallorca, Spain. Telephone: 756673. (Office) Instituto Francesc de B Moll, Palma de Mallorca, Spain.

CAREER: High school teacher.

PROFESSIONAL ORGANIZATIONS: Asociación de Escritores en Lengua Catalana;

Grupo Balear de Ornitología y Defensa de la Naturaleza.

AWARDS, HONORS: Guillem Cifre de Colònya Award, 1982; People's Choice Award of Catalonia, 1986; Joseph Ma. Folch i Torres Prize, 1987; Second Prize, Barco de Vapor Award, 1987.

WRITINGS:
Las uvas del sol y de la luna. Trans. by Jaume Vidal Alcover. Barcelona: Ed. La Galera, 1983.
El secreto de la hoja de encina. Trans. by Jaume Vidal Alcover. Barcelona: Ed. La Galera, 1985.
La bella ventura. Trans. by Jaume Vidal Alcover. Barcelona: Ed. La Galera, 1986.
Las alas rojas. Barcelona: Ed. La Galera, 1988.
El viejecito de la barba verde. Trans. by Ricardo Alcántara. Barcelona: Ed. Teide, 1988.
Un ermitaño y un gigante. Barcelona: Ediciones B, 1989.

The work of Miguel Rayó Ferrer is originally written in Catalan.

SIDELIGHTS: "I write because to do so is a pleasure, a challenge, a passion, a necessity, and a commitment to my language, to my country, and to myself. My favorite themes are adventure, the fantastic and the imaginary, enchantments, fabulous animals, and nature with its problems and its conservation. Ultimately, I am concerned with the relationships among human beings. I am also interested in human intimacy. My sources of inspiration are books and stories, traditional cultures, nature, and my experiences as a conservationist and ornithologist. I am also inspired by children and the stories that other people tell me."

RIBAS PUIG-AGUT, Teresa (1947-)

PERSONAL DATA: Born February 24, 1947, in Barcelona, Spain, the daughter of Jesús and Pilar, she is married to Antoni and has a son, Joan. *Education:* Teacher's certification.

ADDRESS: (Home) Escornalbou 26, 1a., 08026 Barcelona, Spain. Telephone: 2368943.

CAREER: Preschool teacher from 1965 to 1990.

PROFESSIONAL ORGANIZATIONS: Asociación de Maestros Rosa Sensat.

WRITINGS:
Mirem (6 books). 1984.
La bombolla (6 books). 1989.

SIDELIGHTS: "I design books of images without text because I think that the basis of thought is imagination and that children should begin the learning process by becoming aware of what they already know. It is this that stimulates the acquisition of language."

RICO, Lolo (Dolores Rico Oliver) (1935-)

PERSONAL DATA: Born March 21, 1935, in Madrid, Spain, the daughter of Juan and Isabel. She has seven children, Isabel, Santiago, Camino, Nicolás, Dolores, Miguel, and Alejandra. *Education:* Holds a degree in journalism from the Universidad Ciencias de la Información; two years' study of philosophy; several years in the fine arts (drawing and painting).

ADDRESS: (Home) Costanilla de San Pedro 2, 2° C, 28005 Madrid, Spain. Telephone: 3666176.

CAREER: RTVE, 1970-89; program director for children and young people at RNE, 1975-80; director of collections of literature for children and young people for Editorial Bruguera, 1980-83; program director of television shows for children and young people, 1983-.

AWARDS, HONORS: Prensa Femenina y Familiar Award; Radiowaves Award, 1977; Second Place National Award for Literature, 1983; Radiowaves Award for Television, 1986; nominated for the Andersen Prize; CCEI Honors List.

WRITINGS:
Cómo leer un libro. Barcelona: Ed. Planeta-T.V.E., 1970.
Josefa, su mundo y la oscuridad. Barcelona: Ed. La Galera, 1972.
El mausito. Madrid: Ed. Susaeta, 1975.
Angelita la ballena pequeñita. Madrid: Ed. Susaeta, 1975.
Castillo de arena. Madrid: Ed. Alhambra, 1986.
Ramón Ge Te. Barcelona: Ed. Noguer, 1982.
La niña del tintero. In preparation.

SIDELIGHTS: "I write because I am interested in the world of children; among other reasons, because a search for identity is best accomplished through maturity. My principal themes are nature and the things that seem small or insignificant, but that affect the lives of children. I widely use the field of imagination because when problems or conflicts are cast within fantastic realms, it is easier to see your way to resolving them; moreover, they lose some of their dramatic charge. My source of inspiration is my memories of childhood. My characters are based on them."

RIUS, María (1938-)

PERSONAL DATA: Born March 27, 1938, in Barcelona, Spain, the daughter of Adolf and Angels, she is married to Alfred Pérez-Bastardas and has two children, Eulalia and Miguel. *Education:* Licentiate from the Escuela Superior de Bellas Artes at the Universidad de Barcelona; graphic arts studies at Kunstwerkschule in Munster, Germany; design studies at Kunstgewerberschule in Berne, Switzerland.

ADDRESS: (Home) Mallorca 316, Pral. 2a., 08037 Barcelona, Spain. Telephone: 2074583.

CAREER: Illustrator; professor of drawing, painting, and illustration since 1960 at the Escuela Profesional de la Diputación in Barcelona.

PROFESSIONAL ORGANIZATIONS: IBBY of Catalonia; OEPLI; Asociación Profesional de Ilustradores de Cataluña.

AWARDS, HONORS:
Lazarillo Award, 1968; CCEI Award, 1971, 1974; Critics' Award from *Serra d'Or*, 1979, 1981; People's Choice Award of Catalonia, 1983.

ILLUSTRATED WORKS:
Guaracú. Barcelona: Ed. La Galera, 1979.
Kalyndi. Ed. Hogar y Moda, 1982.
Macbeth. Ed. Proa, 1987.
El elefante azul. Tokyo: Ed. Gakken, 1988.
El taxi de mi mamá. Houghton Mifflin, 1992.

She has published more than 200 books; the above citations are examples of her most popular works.

SIDELIGHTS: "Since I was very young, I have felt the need to communicate, and the most personal form of communication I have found is illustration. Because of this, I am an illustrator."

CRITICAL SOURCES:
Faristol. Barcelona, 1986.
Barcelona Divina. 1991.

RIVAS MENDO, Felipe (1940-)

PERSONAL DATA: Born February 13, 1940, in Chiclayo, Peru, the son of Alfonso and Elena, he is married to Teresa and has two children, Jairo and Sergio. Education: Holds a degree from the Escuela Nacional de Arte Dramático, Universidad de Lima.

ADDRESS: (Home) Grau 516-K, Barranco, Lima, Peru. Telephone: 772823. (Office) Teatro Sebastián Salazar Bondy, Paseo de la República s/n, Lima, Peru. Telephone: 240151.

CAREER: Puppeteer; screenwriter for television series for the minister of education, 1972-77; director of national theater at the Instituto Nacional de Cultura since 1991.

PROFESSIONAL ORGANIZATIONS: APLIJ; Asociación Peruana de Educación por el Arte (SUPERARTE); director and founder of the Instituto Peruano de Teatro de Títeres.

AWARDS, HONORS: Palmas Artísticas Award; Distinction upon receiving master's degree; Honors List for the Minister of Education; Silver Medal from the municipality of Barranco; Congratulations from the Council of Lima; Regional Theater Award.

WRITINGS:
Juguemos a los títeres. Lima: Ed. Pinocho, 1965.
Títeres en el aula. Lima: Ed. Pinocho, 1965.
Mi amigo el títere. Bogota: Ed. Pombocandia, 1966.
Cuatro obras para el retablillo. Lima: Ed. Pinocho, 1970.
Los títeres, un medio de comunicación para el Perú. Lima: Ministerio de Educación, 1972.
Un esposo para una ratoncita. Lima: Instituto del Títere, 1980.
La casa de cartón. Lima: Ministerio de Educación, 1972.
Títere tambo. Lima: Ministerio de Educación, 1971.

SIDELIGHTS: "I write in order to teach children and adults the magic of puppets, and in order to give life to the characters that I have sculpted. My favorite themes are revalorization of work and the ecology, valorization of death, analysis of the messages of the communication media, and the upholding of morals and ethics."

CRITICAL SOURCES:
Sonia Luz Carrillo. *Diario Expreso.*
Manuel Velázquez Rojas. *Hojas de Venado.*

ROBLEDA MOGUEL, (Nidia) Margarita (1950-)

PERSONAL DATA: Born April 25, 1950, in Merida, Yucatan, Mexico, the daughter of José Luis Robleda and Nidia Moguel.

ADDRESS: (Home) Unión 27-804, Col. Escandón, 11800 Mexico, D.F. Telephone: 2777540. (Office) Secretaría de Turismo. Masarik 172, 6° Col. Polanco, Mexico, D.F. Telephone: 2540872.

CAREER: Composer; writer; singer; actor; screenwriter; cultural advisor to the Ministry of Tourism.

AWARDS, HONORS: Juan de la Cabada National Award for Stories for Children, 1991; texts selected for a book being prepared by Houghton Mifflin to be released in 1993.

WRITINGS:
De que se puede se puede. 1983.
623 adivinanzas populares y un pilón de M.R.M. Ed. Sitesa, 1988.
Cosquillas de curiosidad. Ed. Amaquemecan, 1988.
Trabalenguas, colmos, tantanes y refranes y un pilón . . . Ed. Sitesa, 1989.
Y va de nuez. Ed. Sitesa, 1990.
Los sueños del caracol. Ed. Amaquemecan, 1990.
Cuentos para pulguitas. Ed. Sitesa, 1990.
Aventuras en la ciudad. Ed. Amaquemecan, 1992.

SIDELIGHTS: "I began as a singer for children. I have two records of my songs, and making them entailed traveling across Mexico. I first wrote stories to go with the music, and then began leaving out the music. I omitted from my stories ghosts, witches, blue princes; I was left with a blank page and so wrote 'Inquietudes de una raya.' Usually in my stories there does not exist magical help; characters obtain their objectives only after struggling with and surmounting internal obstacles. I am worried that we don't realize the importance of many things, things we need. I think we need to champion simplicity, a love for planet Earth, and values like community, friendship, working together, compassion, and solidarity. When we understand what to see, beginning with ourselves, we will discover the immense power that we have, we will become in essence better human beings. In the last few years, I have taught nearly sixty courses to teachers, parents, and children because I am convinced that we have stories to tell."

RODRÍGUEZ ALMODÓVAR, Antonio (1941-)

PERSONAL DATA: Born in Alcala de Guadaira, Seville, Spain, in 1941. *Education:* Doctorate in modern philology.

CAREER: Has been department chair for literature (1975) and lecturing professor at the Universidad de Sevilla; has worked at the Romance Institute of the University of Copenhagen; additionally, directed the Pavillion of Andalucia at the Exposición Universal 1992 in Seville.

PROFESSIONAL ORGANIZATIONS: Society for Folk Narrative Research.

AWARDS, HONORS: Fellowship from the March Foundation, 1977; National Award for Literature for Children, 1984; Elena International Prize, 1991.

WRITINGS:
La estructura de la novela burguesa. Madrid: Ed. Taller JB, 1975.
Cuentos maravillosos españoles. Barcelona: Ed. Crítica, 1982.
Cuentos al amor de la lumbre. Madrid: Ed. Anaya, 1983.
Cuentos de la media lunita. Sevilla: Ed. Algaida, 1986.
Los cuentos populares, o la tentativa de un texto infinito. Murcia: Universidad de Murcia, 1989.
El libro de la risa carnal. Sevilla: Ed. Arquetipo, 1989.
Un lugar parecido al paraíso. Barcelona: Ed. Labor, 1991.

SIDELIGHTS: "I write for children because it is my consolation for the pains of life. Because I become a child. Because I construct a world, like young people, and try to comprehend it. Because I am drawn there and because there, the act of sleep is done with the eyes open, as Machado says. At best, my stories make children happy, and at worst, they occupy them for a time. Respecting my audience, all I would like to do for them is leave a tiny thread, by which I can help guide them along until the hour when they leave for paradise, the most difficult hour a human being faces."

RODRÍGUEZ BONACHEA, Juan Vicente (1957-)

PERSONAL DATA: Born March 8, 1957, in Havana, Cuba, the son of Vicente and Justa, he is married to Milagros Chiroldi and has a son, Gabriel.

ADDRESS: (Home) Línea 1206, entre 18 y 20, Apto. 4, Vedado, Havana, Cuba.

CAREER: In 1984 he dedicated himself to graphic design; professor of drawing at the Instituto Politécnico de Diseño Industrial, 1986-89; professor of painting at the Escuela Vocacional de Arte, 1989-90.

PROFESSIONAL ORGANIZATIONS: UNEAC.

AWARDS, HONORS: Award for Drawing, Salón de la Ciudad, Cuba, 1984; Mention, Noma Competition, Japan, 1986; Third Prize, Noma Competition, Japan, 1988, 1990; Third Prize, Salón Nacional de Ilustraciones, 1991.

ILLUSTRATED WORKS:
Ana María Machado. *De olho nas penas*. Havana: Ed. Casa de las Américas, 1982.
De los lejanos tiempos la lechuza me contó. Ed. Oriente, 1983.
Omar Felipe Mauri. *Lunar*. Havana: Ed. Universidad de La Habana, 1986.
Letras cubanas. Ed. Letras Cubanas, 1988.
Antonio Orlando Rodríguez. *Straf*. Ed. Abril, 1989.
Antonio Orlando Rodríguez. *El sueño*. Ed. José Martí, 1990.
Ivette Vian. *El kilo*. Ed. Unión, 1992.
José Martí. *La edad de oro*. In progress.

RODRÍGUEZ CHÁVEZ, Iván (1941-)

PERSONAL DATA: Born January 26, 1941, in Cajamarca, Peru, the son of Leopoldo and Juana, he is married to María Yadrosich and has four children, Cecilia, Iván,

Adriana, and Mildred. *Education:* Law degree; studies in language and literature; doctorate in education from the Universidad de San Marcos.

ADDRESS: (Home) Enrique Pastor 144, San Borja, Lima 41, Peru. Telephone: 366250. (Office) Prolongación Benavides cuadra 54, Surco, Lima, Peru.

CAREER: Professor at the universities of Ricardo Palma and San Martín de Porres, Lima.

PROFESSIONAL ORGANIZATIONS: Asociación Peruana de Educación por el Arte; Asociación Nacional de Escritores y Artistas; APLIJ.

AWARDS, HONORS: Award for the Essay from the Universidad de San Marcos; Universidad de Lima; Universidad Inca Garcilaso de la Vega; Manuel J. Bustamante Foundation, Arequipa.

WRITINGS:
La ortografía poética de Vallejo. Lima: CIP, 1974.
Manuel Gonzánez Prada en el debate de la educación nacional. Lima: Imprenta Yauyos, 1977.
El derecho en "El mundo es ancho y ajeno". Lima: Imprenta Yauyos, 1982.
Literatura peruana: teoría, historia, pedagogía. Lima: Ed. Seglusa, 1991.

ROJAS MAFFIOLETTI, Carlos (1947-)

PERSONAL DATA: Born July 24, 1947, in Santiago, Chile, the son of Carlos Rojas and Bertina Maffioletti, he is married to Juani and has two children, Tatiana and Carlos Felipe. *Education:* Holds a degree in art, with a major in painting, from the Facultad de Bellas Artes, Universidad de Chile.

ADDRESS: (Home) Erasmo Escala 2405, Santiago, Chile. Telephone: 6815024. (Office) Marcoleta 250, Facultad de Arquitectura y Urbanismo, Universidad de Chile, Santiago, Chile. Telephone: 2226501.

CAREER: University professor of fine arts, architecture, and graphic design since 1972; illustrator.

PROFESSIONAL ORGANIZATIONS: Colegio de Diseñadores Profesionales de Chile; Asociación de Académicos de la Universidad de Chile.

AWARDS, HONORS: IBBY Honors List, 1988; local awards for painting and graphic art.

IN-HOUSE ILLUSTRATION FOR PUBLISHERS:
Editorial Andrés Bello, 1982-92.
Editorial Arrayán, 1989-90.
Editorial Santillana.
Editorial Rayuela (Argentina).
Coedición Latinoamericana. CERLALC-UNESCO, 1986.
Colección Discurso-Orígenes. Memphis State University, 1985.
Colección Discurso-Orígenes. John Gabriele, editor. Ohio, 1987.

CRITICAL SOURCES:
Novum Gebrauchsgraphik. Munich: October 10, 1988.
La Tercera Hora. Santiago, Chile: November 1989.

ROJAS MOROTE, Nori (Alicia) (1945-)

PERSONAL DATA: Born July 17, 1945, in Huanta, Ayacucho, Peru, she is the daughter of Jesús Hernán Rojas and Laura Morote. She has two children, Walter and Gisell. *Education:* Doctorate in education from the Universidad Inca Garcilaso de la Vega.

ADDRESS: (Home) Las Madreselvas 106, Lima 03, Peru. Telephone: 494318. (Office) Facultad de Educación Inicial, Universidad Nacional de Educación, Chosica, Peru.

CAREER: Director of a kindergarten; professor at the Universidad Inca Garcilaso de la Vega, 1983-86; coordinator of primary-level applications for the UNE, 1986-88; supervisor for the Unity of Academic Services for the UNE, 1989-90.

PROFESSIONAL ORGANIZATIONS: APLIJ; Grupo Literario Perú; Asociación Nacional de Escritores y Artistas (ANEA); SUPERARTE; president of the APLIJ Lima.

AWARDS, HONORS: First Prize for the Story, Dirección de Educación de Lima Metropolitana, 1982; Second Prize for Children's Rhyme, Dirección de Educación de Lima Metropolitana, 1982; Diploma of Honor, Literatura Infantil, Oruro, Bolivia, 1990.

WRITINGS:
Antología para el aprestamiento. Peru: Talleres Gráficos UNE, 1985.
Cartitas a mamita y papito. Peru: Ed. Facultad de Pedagogía UNE, 1987.
Rhymes and Poems. Peru: Ed. Facultad Humanidades y Arte UNE, 1987.
Poemario infantil. Lima: Ed. San Marcos, 1988.
Un día de compañía. Lima: Ed. San Marcos, 1991.
Pinceladas de colores. Lima: Ed. San Marcos, 1991.
Isla de luz. Lima: Ed. San Marcos, 1992.
La lectura y su comprensión. Lima: Ed. San Marcos, 1992.

SIDELIGHTS: "I write because I truly love childhood and want to help children develop with a greater sense of self-esteem; because I am very communicative; and because I want to promote the values of truth and justice, and love. In this way, also, I want to inspire a love of nature and an appreciation of beauty (these especially when I write for children). I write about what I have observed of life in my country, compiled through the different travels I have made through it (they serve as inspirations for the poems I have written about love and social problems)."

CRITICAL SOURCES:
Maynor Freyre. Prologue to *Poemario infantil.* 1988.
Alfonso La Torre. *La República.* Lima, 1989.
Patria. Bolivia: March 1990.
Max Dextre. *Nacional.* Lima: August 1, 1991; August 15, 1991.
Nixa. *La Industria.* Chiclayo, Peru: November 30, 1991.
José Vargas. *Olandina.* Lima: 1992.
César Reyes Campos. *Nacional.* Lima: March 16, 1992.
Luis Hernán Ramírez. Prologue to *Isla de luz.* April 15, 1992.

ROMERO SERRANO, Marina (1908-)

PERSONAL DATA: Born February 5, 1908, in Madrid, Spain, the daughter of Federico and Felipa. *Education:* Master's degree in secondary education, Guadalajara; licentiate from Mills College, Oakland, California; studies toward Ph.D. at Rutgers University, New Brunswick, New Jersey.

ADDRESS: (Home) Paseo de La Habana 134 C, 28036 Madrid, Spain. Telephone: 4574385.

CAREER: Professor of Spanish language and literature at various institutions in the

United States, including Mills College, Oakland, California; Middlebury College, Vermont; and Douglass College, New Brunswick, New Jersey.

PROFESSIONAL ORGANIZATIONS: Honorary Member of Sigma Delta Pi, a society for Spanish studies; Asociación de Escritores y Artistas Españoles; Asociación Colegial de Escritores; Sociedad General de Autores de España; Asociación Española de Mujeres Universitarias.

AWARDS, HONORS: Medal of Honor, Universidad Complutense de Madrid; President of Honor, Spanish League for Human Rights; First Prize in photography; INLE Award, selected for *Landscape and Literature of Spain*, an anthology.

WRITINGS:
Alegrías. Madrid: Ed. Anaya, 1973.
Campanillas del aire. Madrid: Ed. Escuela Española, 1984.
Churrupete va a la luna en busca de la fortuna. Madrid: Ed. Escuela Española, 1985.
Disparatillos con Masacha. Madrid: Ed. Escuela Española, 1986.
Poemas a Doña Chavala y Don Chaval. Madrid: Ed. Luis Vives, 1987.
Cuentos rompecabezas. Madrid: Ed. Escuela Española, 1988.
Poemas rompecabezas. Madrid: Ed. Luis Vives, 1989.

She has also published books of poetry for adults.

SIDELIGHTS: "It is difficult to say why I write what I write. I have never given it much thought. Maybe because I feel a need to express myself, and I flatter myself that as a teacher I know a child's character, likes, desires, loves. Also, since I am in love with animals and wildlife, many of my poems are inspired by nature. My *Poemas rompecabezas, Poemas a Doña Chavala y Don Chaval*, and *Cuentos de rompecabezas* are almost entirely about animals. I apply my imagination to different situations that need to be written about, trying to use tenderness, cleverness, color, music, rythme, joy, and at times a moral or lesson that underlies the events. What I write, although intended for the child's mind, is not filled with foolishness. The child's mind is earnest, and it tries with a certain seriousness to apprehend a story; it is therefore inappropriate to play jokes on it or treat it without respect. Taken as a whole, and in contrast with this, my poetry for adults may seem more nihilistic and sad. Sources of inspiration? Life."

CRITICAL SOURCES: Her work has been reviewed since 1935 in several journals and newspapers, among them *ABC* (Madrid), *Diario de Madrid, La Vanguardia* (Barcelona), and *Sunday Times* (New Brunswick, N.J.).

ROSEMFFET, Gustavo Ariel
See GUSTI (Gustavo Ariel Rosemffet)

ROTH, Kornelia

PERSONAL DATA: Born in Innsbruck, Austria. *Education:* Holds a degree from the Escuela de Bellas Artes, Santiago, Chile; School of Arts of Zurich, Switzerland. She resides in Lucca, Italy.

WRITINGS:
El globo de María. Mexico: Ed. Amaquemecan.
Tiquitaco, aventuras de un gato. Mexico: Ed. Celta-Amaquemecan.

RUBIO (PUERTAS), Rodrigo (1931-)

PERSONAL DATA: Born March 13, 1931, in Montalvos, Spain, the son of Buenaventura and Dolores. He is married to Rosa and has two children, Marcos and Germán.

ADDRESS: (Home) Angel Ganivet 28, 28007 Madrid, Spain. Telephone: 4338231.

CAREER: Writer and journalist; supervising editor of the journal *Minusval*, published by the Ministry of Social Programs, 1974-91.

PROFESSIONAL ORGANIZATIONS: Asociación Colegial de Escritores de España (ACE).

AWARDS, HONORS: Gabriel Miró Prize; Planeta Award; Ateneo de Valladolid Award; Guipúzcoa Award; Award for Novels and Stories, Ed. Magisterio; Casa Castilla La Mancha Award; La Estafeta Literaria Award; La Felguera Award; Jauja Award; Alvarez Quintero Prize; Chest of Silver Award; Chest of Gold Award.

WRITINGS:
Tallo de sangre. Madrid: Ed. Anaya, 1989.
La puerta. Madrid: Ediciones SM, 1990.
Los sueños de Bruno. Madrid: Ediciones SM, 1990.

El amigo de Dwnga. Madrid: Ediciones SM, 1992.

Rodrigo Rubio Puertas has published more than thirty novels, short stories, and essays for adults.

SIDELIGHTS: "I write because that is my vocation. As to literature in general, that is, literature usually intended for adults, I am driven by social, political, and religious questions. In literature for children, without abandoning my attention to the social matters of our time (as are addressed in works like *La puerta, Los sueños de Bruno,* and *El amigo Dwnga*), I try to use language that is very clear and comprehensible for younger readers."

CRITICAL SOURCES:
María Solé. *ABC.* Madrid.

SAN MIGUEL, Juan M. (1930-)

PERSONAL DATA: Born February 25, 1930, in San Sebastian, Spain, the son of Ignacio San Miguel and Carmen Querejeta, he is married to Ángela C. Ionescu. *Education:* Journalism.

ADDRESS: (Home) Fermín Caballero 58, 28034 Madrid, Spain. Telephone: 2019032.

CAREER: Journalist and writer; supervisor for the international section of the magazine *Informaciones* from 1959-79.

PROFESSIONAL ORGANIZATIONS: Asociación de la Prensa, Madrid.

WRITINGS:
El nombre en la orilla. Barcelona: Ed. Plaza & Janes, 1976.
Morada y nombre. Barcelona: Ed. Plaza & Janes, 1982.
Alejo. Madrid: Ediciones SM, 1988.
Cerco de fuego. Madrid: Ediciones SM, 1991.

SIDELIGHTS: Juan San Miguel usually writes about persons who are situated in restricted environments or about the impossibility of knowing the interior of the mind.

SANTIRSO (MARTÍNEZ), Liliana

PERSONAL DATA: Education: Licentiate in educational psychology.

ADDRESS: (Home) Galeana 111, Tlalpan, Mexico, D. F. Telephone: 5737900, 5737025.

CAREER: Educational investigator and literary advisor for the Department of Public Education, Mexico; professor at the Universidad Veracruzana; Coordinator of programs for the promotion of reading; creator of books for physically and mentally challenged children; editor of literature for children; advisor to national magazines and journals.

AWARDS, HONORS: Juror for the Juan de la Cabada National Award for Literature for Children; Award from the IBBY of Mexico, 1982; selected for the *White Ravens*, by the Jugendbibliothek, Munich.

WRITINGS:
Cuando el desierto canta. 1982.
El sol es un techo altísimo. 1990.

She has also published literature for children in the United States and Argentina.

SANZ MARTÍN, Ignacio (1953-)

PERSONAL DATA: Born February 24, 1953, in Lastras de Cuellar, Segovia, Spain, he is the son of Mariano and Felicitas. He is married to Claudia and has two children, Mateo and Adrián. *Education:* Holds a degree in sociology.

ADDRESS: (Home) El Socorro, No. 8, 50001 Segovia, Spain. Telephone: 1441487.

CAREER: Ceramist and writer.

AWARDS, HONORS: Emiliano Barral Prize for the Story; Isabel Corral Prize for Travel Stories.

WRITINGS:
Agapito, Pito, Pito. Ediciones de la Torre, 1984.
Noche de enemigas. Zaragoza: Ed. Edelvives, 1990.
El coche de línea. Escuela Española, 1987.

Zaraguel. Trujal, 1991.
Un trabajo de campo. Libertarias, 1990.

SIDELIGHTS: "I write to create a world that is distinct from the real world from which we all try to flee constantly. Imagination alone is potent and beautiful but atrophied. I am interested in transforming the everyday world with surrealistic elements, creating a new reality. My sources of inspiration are oral traditions and certain writers like Borges, Calvino, and Rulfo, as well as the traditional stories of Europe."

CRITICAL SOURCES:
Miguel del Augua. *El País.*
Ramón García Domínguez. *El Norte de Castillano.*
Angélica Tanarro. *El Adelantado de Segovia.*

SASTRÍAS DE PORCEL, Martha (1938-)

PERSONAL DATA: Born November 9, 1938, in Mexico, D.F., the daughter of Fernando and Elena Sastrías, she is married to Jaime Porcel and has five children, Fernando, Jaime, Eduardo, Martha, and Carlos. *Education:* Ph.D. in teaching English as a second language.

ADDRESS: (Home) Camelia 72, Col. Florida, 01030 Mexico, D.F. Telephone: 5249641.

CAREER: Teacher and promoter of literature for children.

PROFESSIONAL ORGANIZATIONS: Cultura Infantil como Alternativa (CUICA); Programa de Acercamiento a la Literatura Infantil.

AWARDS, HONORS: Celestino Gorostiza National Award for Theater for Children, Second Place, 1984; First Place, 1985; Children's Time National Story Award, Third Place, 1985; Antoniorrobles Award, 1991.

WRITINGS:
Periquito verde esmeralda. Mexico: Ed. Amaquemecan, 1985.
"Naranjas y limones." *Antología triunfadores.* Mexico: Editores Mexicanos Unidos, 1985.
Akukúm. Mexico: Editores Mexicanos Unidos, 1986.

Punto de sol. Mexico: Ed. Nugali, 1986.
Cuentos de un martín pescador y su viaje por México. Mexico: Ed. Sitesa, 1987.
El mundo de los peces y los lagos (Los purépechas). Mexico: Ed. Quinto Sol, 1987.
Encuentra la respuesta. Mexico: Ed. Selector, 1990.
El ingeniero electrónico. Mexico: Ed. Amaquemecan-CONACULTA, in print.
Como motivar a los niños a leer. Mexico: Ed. Pax, in print.

Works Published in Collaboration:
Mi libro de navidad. Group CUICA. Mexico: Ed. Sitesa, 1987.
Juegos y diversiones mexicanos. Group CIUCA. Mexico: Ed. Sitesa, 1987.
Día de muertos. Group CUICA. Mexico: Ed. Sitesa, 1988.

SIDELIGHTS: "One of my principal and favorite themes is the recovery of Mexican traditions, with the intent to recreate them in a manner appropriate to the child of today, in a manner that can relate to the child's life. Sources of inspiration: my environment and works needing investigation. Moreover, I enjoy writing whatever springs spontaneously from my own restlessness, as well as literature I hope children will enjoy and will find useful to their everyday lives."

CRITICAL SOURCES:
Rafael Solana.
Siempre 1864. March 15, 1989.

SCHON, Isabel (1940-)

PERSONAL DATA: Born January 19, 1940, in Mexico, D. F., the daughter of Oswaldo Schon and Ana Schon, she is married to Richard R. Chalquest and has a daughter, Vera. *Education:* Doctorate in education from the University of Colorado, 1974.

ADDRESS: (Home) 7597 Eads Avenue C, La Jolla, California 92037. Telephone: 454-0025. (Office) Center for the Study of Books in Spanish for Children and Adolescents, California State University San Marcos, San Marcos, California 92096-0001. Telephone: 7524070.

CAREER: Professor at Arizona State University, 1974-89; founding professor at California State University, San Marcos, 1989-; director of the Center for the Study of Books in Spanish for Children and Adolescents at that university, 1989-.

PROFESSIONAL ORGANIZATIONS: American Library Association; California

Library Association; National Association for Bilingual Education.

AWARDS, HONORS: Herbert W. Putnam Honor Award, American Library Association, 1979; Grolier Foundation Award, American Library Association, 1986; Women's National Book Award, Women's National Book Association, 1987; Denali Press Award, Reference and Adult Services Division, American Library Association, 1992; U.S. Role Model in Education Award, U.S.-Mexico Foundation, 1992.

WRITINGS:
Doña Blanca y otras rimas y juegos de España y Latinoamérica (bilingual edition). T.S. Denison & Co., 1983.

Isabel Schon has published numerous reference works about books for children and adolescents.

SIDELIGHTS: "I write because for me reading is one of the greatest pleasures in life. I read for entertainment and to inform myself. I write so that young people will have the same enjoyments that I had as a child and that I continue to have. I write to encourage the love of reading among young people."

CRITICAL SOURCES:
School Library Media Quarterly. Autumn 1990.
British Bulletin of Publications. October 1990.
Booklist. December 1991; January 1992.
Journal of Reading 35. May 8, 1992.
Reference & Research Book News. April 1992.

SCHUSSHEIM, Victoria (1944-)

PERSONAL DATA: Born September 2, 1944, in Buenos Aires, Argentina, the daughter of Isaac Schussheim and Iuba Basewicz, she is married to Pedro F. Miret and has two children, Maia and Kiren F. Miret. *Education:* Master's degree in anthropology.

ADDRESS: (Home) Av. Toluca, no. 811-21, 01780 Mexico, D.F. Telephone: 5952448. (Office) Periferico Sur 2453-601, Col. San Jeronimo Lidice, 10200, Mexico, D.F. Telephone: 6813035.

*CAREER: Editorial directo*r at CIESAS, 1973-81; editorial director at Folios

Ediciones, 1981-84; director general at Gatopardo Editores, 1983-86; director general at Pangea Editores since 1986; director general at Schussheim y Asociados since 1989.

PROFESSIONAL ORGANIZATIONS: Colegio de Etnólogos, Antropólogos Sociales; Sociedad Mexicana para la Divulgación de la Ciencia y la Técnica.

WRITINGS:
El guardián de los herbarios del rey. Co-written with Eloy Salas and J.B. Lamarck. Ed. Gatopardo, 1985.
El viajero incomparable, Charles Darwin. Pangea, 1986.
Dinosaurios y otros bichos. Secretaría de Educación Pública, 1988.

SIDELIGHTS: "At the moment (after various jobs concerning anthropology) I write—and only occasionally—works of educational material for children and young people. I put more time in as an editor than an author, and in general I only write what the author leaves out so that it will be prepared for publication. My true interest is in educational literature concerning science and technology, as is produced by Pangea Editores. I sometimes write other kinds of works, in other genres and for adults, but they are not worth mentioning here."

SERRANO, Javier (1946-)

PERSONAL DATA: Born in Valladolid, Spain, in 1946.

CAREER: Painter and animator; many Spanish cities have paintings by Javier Serrano; his paintings have been in expositions throughout the world. Since 1983 he has illustrated books for children; has also worked in-house for publishers and advertisers.

AWARDS, HONORS: National Award for Illustration, 1991.

ILLUSTRATED WORKS:
Amadís de Gaula. Madrid: Ed. Palabra, 1982.
José Antonio del Cañizo. *Oposiciones a bruja y otros cuentos.* Madrid: Ed. Anaya, 1987.
Pilar Mateos. *Mi tío Teo.* Madrid: Ed. Anaya, 1987.
Félix Lope de Vega. *Fuenteovejuna.* Madrid: Ed. Anaya, 1987.
Miguel de Cervantes. *Don Quijote de la Mancha.* Madrid: Ed. Anaya, 1987.
Consuelo Armijo. *En Viriviví.* Madrid: Ed. Anaya, 1988.

El Lazarillo de Tormes. Madrid: Ed. Anaya, 1989.
Joaquín Aguirre Bellver. *El robo del caballo de madera.* Madrid: Ed. Anaya, 1989.
Joaquín Aguirre Bellver. *El lago de plata.* Madrid: Ed. Anaya, 1990.
Miguel Fernández Pacheco. *Oriente de perla.* Madrid: Ed. Anaya, 1991.

SIDELIGHTS: "To illustrate books is, for me, to animate books. Consequently, it is a form, among others, of personal expression, of projecting structure onto concept. It is a pleasure, among others, and a form of apprenticeship. It is also, at times and by force of circumstance, a bit of a pest."

SERRANO DÍAZ, Francisco (1949-)

PERSONAL DATA: Born June 27, 1949, in Mexico, D.F., the son of Francisco Serrano and María Luisa Díaz Salas, he is married to Patricia Van Rhijn and has two children, Pablo and Diego. *Education:* Studied political science and cinema in the Universidad Nacional Autónoma in Mexico.

ADDRESS: (Home) Presidente Carranza 237, Col. Coyoacan, 04000 Mexico, D.F. (Office) Cracovia, Col. San Angel, Mexico, D.F. Telephone: 5487329, 5547983.

CAREER: Professor of cinematography and literature for UAP and UAM; subdirector of Editorial programs for the DGPB in the SEP; director of international relations for the INBA; director of *México en el Arte,* 1986.

AWARDS, HONORS: Fellowship from the Centro Mexicano de Escritores, 1973-74; Fellowship to complete cinematography studies at the Museum of Modern Art in New York, 1977.

WRITINGS:
Cinco poetas jóvenes. Mexico: Secretaría de Educación Pública, 1977.
Canciones egipcias. 1979.
Poema del fino amor. Mexico: Universidad Autónoma de México, 1981.
El cubo de los cambios. 1982.
El libro de los hexaedros. 1982.
La luciérnaga. Mexico: CIDCLI, 1983.
No es sino el azar. Premia Editora, 1984.
Los vampiritos y el profesor. Mexico: CIDCLI, 1986.

SHUA, Ana María (1951-)

PERSONAL DATA: Born April 22, 1951, in Buenos Aires, Argentina, the daughter of Guillermo Daniel Schua and Josefina Szmulewicz, she is married to Silvio Fabrykant and has three children, Gabriela, Paloma, and Vera. *Education:* Doctorate in letters from the Universidad Nacional de Buenos Aires.

ADDRESS: (Home) Santa Fe 2306, 13° B. 1123 Buenos Aires, Argentina. Telephone: 838848. (Office) Pueyrredon 1655, 6o. D. Telephone: 8265643.

CAREER: Advertising editor from 1970 to 1985; journalist and a screenwriter for the cinema.

PROFESSIONAL ORGANIZATIONS: SADE.

AWARDS, HONORS: Award from the Estímulo Fondo de las Artes; SADE Honors List; First Prize, Losada International Narrative Competition; Honorable Mention, International Competition of Stories of the People, Mexico; ALIJA Honors List (IBBY).

WRITINGS:
La batalla entre los elefantes y los cocodrilos. Buenos Aires: Ed. Sudamericana, 1988.
Expedición al Amazonas. Buenos Aires: Ed. Sudamericana, 1988.
La fábrica del terror. Buenos Aires: Ed. Sudamericana, 1990.
La puerta para salir del mundo. Buenos Aires: Ed. Sudamericana, 1992.

CRITICAL SOURCES:
Babel.
Clarín.
El Cronista Comercial.
La Nación.

SIERRA I FABRA, Jordi (1947-)

PERSONAL DATA: Born July 26, 1947, in Barcelona, Spain, the son of Valeriano Sierra Vilá and María Fabra Muntané, he is married to Antonia Cortijos Sánchez and has two children, Georgina and Daniel. *Education:* Bachelor's studies in technical architecture (incomplete).

ADDRESS: (Home) Juan Sebastián Bach 3, 3° 1a., 08021 Barcelona, Spain. Telephone: 2014364.

CAREER: Journalist and director of the principal magazines of rock music in Spain; radio program director since 1970: *El musical* (1969-70), *Disco Expres* (1970-78), *Popular 1* (1973-76), *Super Pop* (1977 to present); writer.

AWARDS, HONORS: Top Magazine Award, 1973; Award to the Best Musical Commentator, 1974; Villa de Bilbao Award for the Novel, 1975; Finalist for the Planeta Award, 1978; Ateneo de Sevilla Award for the Novel, 1979; Gran Angular Award for Literature for Young People, 1980, 1982, 1990; Barco de Vapor Award, 1990.

WRITINGS:
¡Sorpresas! Madrid: Ediciones SM, 1982.
Nuevas sorpresas. Madrid: Ediciones SM, 1985.
¡¡¡ Lamberto!!! Madrid: Ed. Anaya, 1985.
La asombrosa expedición. Gijon: Ed. Júcar, 1988.
Peluconas. Madrid: Ediciones SM, 1988.
Raskundanpelkuf. Barcelona: Ediciones B, 1988.
El largo camino. Leon: Ed. Everest, 1989.
La nave fantástica. Madrid: Ed. Anaya, 1989.
Benezén el pescador. Madrid: Ediciones SM, 1989.
Historias asombrosas. Zaragoza: Ed. Edelvives, 1989.
Mirpeace. Barcelona: Ed. Plaza & Janes, 1989.
La leyenda de Patrácoras. Madrid: Ed. Susaeta, 1989.
Víctor: ¡Hola! ¿puedo ayudar? Barcelona: Ed. Plaza & Janes, 1990.
Víctor: Dando la nota. Barcelona: Ed. Plaza & Janes, 1990.
Víctor: Un día en casa. Barcelona: Ed. Plaza & Janes, 1990.
El gran dragón. Madrid: Ed. Anaya, 1990.
El planeta blanco. Zaragoza: Ed. Edelvives, 1990.
Relatos galácticos. Madrid: Ed. Anaya, 1990.
Víctor: El rockero. Barcelona: Ed. Plaza & Janes, 1991.
Víctor: Los mayores están locos, locos, locos. Barcelona: Ed. Plaza & Janes, 1991.
La fábrica de nubes. Madrid: Ediciones SM, 1991.
Víctor: Tres días salvajes. Barcelona: Ed. Plaza & Janes, 1991.
Víctor: Una boda desmadrada. Barcelona: Ed. Plaza & Janes, 1991.
El hombre que perdió su imagen. Madrid: Ed. Anaya, 1992.
El espejo del futuro. Barcelona: Ed. Edebé, 1992.
Víctor: Sálvese quien pueda. Barcelona: Ed. Plaza & Janes, 1992.

He has also published more than thirty-six works for young people and adults and two books of poetry; he has published three essays and more than eight books about the history of rock music, as well as numerous biographies about rock stars. Some of his works have been translated into French, German, Italian, Greek, and Bulgarian.

SIDELIGHTS: "I have written since age eight, from a vital drive inside me, and at the age of twelve I decided to be a writer. Music has served to make me known and to make me a historian, as well as the primary authority on rock music in Spain. My works take part in all genres: science fiction, fantasy, poetry, history, biography, etc. I am inspired by whatever passes through my head, my experiences, my constant travels, and anything that I can contribute to the real world."

CRITICAL SOURCES:
CLIJ. Barcelona.
El País. Madrid.

SILVA BAFALLUY, María Luisa (1942-)

PERSONAL DATA: Born August 5, 1942, in Santiago, Chile, the daughter of Ernesto Silva Imperiali and Adriana Bafalluy Vásquez, she is married to Sebastián Ortúzar Montalva and has three children, María Luisa, Juan Sebastián, and Ignacio. *Education:* Doctorate in primary education from the Universidad de Chile.

ADDRESS: (Home) Presidente Errazuriz 3575, Depto. 10, Las Condes, Santiago, Chile. Telephone: 2080295.

CAREER: Professor of primary education and editorial advisor to a journal for children.

PROFESSIONAL ORGANIZATIONS: IBBY of Chile; Asociación Chilena de Lectura (ACHIL); Fundación Denpaz.

AWARDS, HONORS: First Mention, National Competition for Poetry and Stories for Children, 1988; Second Place, Gabriela Mistral Competition of Poetry for Children, 1990.

WRITINGS:
Versos para soñar y jugar, vol. 1. Chile: Ed. Pechuen, 1989.
Versos para soñar y jugar, vol. 2. Chile: Ed. Pechuen, 1990.
El cumpleaños del señor Pulpo (y otros cuentiversos). Chile: Ed. Pechuen, 1991.
"Historia de amor de un manzano." *Cuentos de princesas y manzanas*. Madrid: Ediciones SM, 1992.

SIDELIGHTS: "I want to deliver emotion and games to children; I have fun with the sounds of words and am delighted with personification, exaggeration, and rhyme. I write and I enjoy it, perhaps because of the girl in me. Themes: many, especially the sea, everyday things, and nature. Sources of inspiration: everything, life, nature."

SOLÁ LLOPIS, María Lluisa (1918-)

PERSONAL DATA: Born in 1918 in Barcelona, Spain, the daughter of Francesc and María Loreto. She is married to Pedro Ventura and has two children, Xavier and María Clara. *Education:* Studies at the Escuela de Bibliotecarios, Barcelona, Escuela de Artes y Oficios Superiores, and Escuela Municipal de Música de Barcelona.

ADDRESS: (Home) Valencia 51, 3a., 08015 Barcelona, Spain. Telephone: 2261505.

CAREER: Director of the Public Library of Ulldecona; director of the Public Library of Sallent; director of the Library of Catalonia in Barcelona.

PROFESSIONAL ORGANIZATIONS: Asociación de Escritores en Lengua Catalana; Omnium Cultural de Barcelona.

AWARDS, HONORS: Joseph Ma. Folch i Torres Prize, 1972; CCEI Honors List, 1974.

WRITINGS:
Ana. Barcelona: Ed. La Galera, 1973.

The work of María Solé is originally written in Catalan.

SIDELIGHTS:
"I write for children, perhaps because I identify with them more than with adults. I like group adventures and works of the imagination: sirens, witches, ghosts, always with a sense of humor. Inspiration? Myself, my children, memories of when I was young (at least not as old as now), and my grandchildren. I put myself in place of my characters and . . . go!"

CRITICAL SOURCES:
Aurora Díaz Plaja. *Serra d'Or.*
Andreu Sotorras. *Avui.*

SOLER GARIJO, Aranzazu (1968-)

PERSONAL DATA: Born June 18, 1968, in Valencia, Spain, the daughter of Rafael and Araceli, she is married to Pedro Eugenio Delgado Cavilla. *Education:* Law degree.

ADDRESS: (Home) Avenida de la Coruña 2, 4° A, San Fernando de Henares, Madrid, Spain. Telephone: 6737667.

CAREER: Legal advisor for questions of artistic property for the publisher Casset.

PROFESSIONAL ORGANIZATIONS: Unión de Consumidores de España.

WRITINGS:
Los buenos modales o cómo impresionar a los demás. Madrid: Ed. Destino, 1989.

SIDELIGHTS: "I write what I would like to read. I prefer humor and irony. I also try to reflect the simple feelings and sensations of everyday life that deserve to be captured and preserved in order to recreate the magic of each passing moment."

CRITICAL SOURCES:
C. Albert. *Telva.*
C. Palacios. *El País.*
CLIJ.
Ya.

SOLÍS, Valerie Ann (1952-)

PERSONAL DATA: Born May 14, 1952, in Edinburg, Scotland, the daughter of John Oglive Hastie and Sheila Gordon Hastie, she is married to José Luis Solís Ruiz.

ADDRESS: c/o Beldowski, 56 Hunt Rd., Poole, Dorset, BH15 3QF, England. Telephone: 685306.

CAREER: Secretary; teacher of English; illustrator; writer; assistant animator for cartoons since 1986.

WRITINGS AND ILLUSTRATIONS:
Barnaby, la aventura de un ratón. Ed. Juventud, 1986.
Barnaby y los fantasmas. Ed. Juventud, 1988.

Montse Sant. *El libro mágico.* Illust. by Valerie Solís. Ed. Juventud, 1987.
Kiwi. Ed. Juventud, 1992.

SIDELIGHTS: "Books for children are fun, and I hope that my books help make children (or adults) happier. This would satisfy me. I am inspired at times by memories of childhood, by the things that I used to enjoy doing: for example, going to birthday parties, playing, eating, etc. Often I think about ecological themes, and so they find their way into my stories."

SOLÍS RUIZ, José Luis (1947-)

PERSONAL DATA: Born June 19, 1947, in Barcelona, Spain, the son of Francisco Modesto Solís and Elisa Ruiz, he is married to Valerie Anne Hastie.

ADDRESS: (Home) 3, Mount Stuart Square, Cardiff, Wales, United Kingdom. (Office) Sirios Productions. Telephone: 488400.

CAREER: Sound and control technician for the National Radio of Spain in Barcelona, 1967-74; illustrator and creator of animated films, 1974-.

AWARDS, HONORS: Third Place, Honors List of Books for Children.

WRITINGS:
Pepón. Barcelona: Ed. Juventud, 1987.
Baile de luna. Barcelona: Ed. Juventud, 1991.
Ñam, ñam, el comelunas. Barcelona: Ed. Juventud, in print.

SIDELIGHTS: "I enjoy reading works of fiction (as well as science fiction) founded on philosophical or religious premises, although they are not my sources of inspiration. I am inspired basically by what we believe is unattainable, because I often find that it is only impossible because we believe that it is."

SOLOGUREN MORENO, Javier (1921-)

PERSONAL DATA: Born January 19, 1921, in Lima, Peru, the son of Javier Sologuren Peña and Rosa Mercedes Moreno Román. *Education:* Doctorate in

Hispanic literature from El Colegio de México; undergraduate degree in social communication from the University of Lovaina in Belgium.

ADDRESS: (Home) Mance II, 2137, Lima 14, Peru. Telephone: 711789.

CAREER: Has been department chair at the Universidad Nacional Mayor de San Marcos, Pontificia Universidad Católica, Universidad Nacional de Educación, and Universidad Nacional Agraria La Molina.

PROFESSIONAL ORGANIZATIONS: Academia Peruana de la Lengua.

AWARDS, HONORS: National Award for Poetry; Rafael Heliodoro Valle International Poetry Award, Mexico; Palmas Magisteriales for the grade of Comendador; Civic Medal from the city of Lima; Order of Sacred Treasure from the Japanese government.

WRITINGS:
Cuentos y leyendas infantiles. Ed. de la Rama Florida, 1964.
Paseo de lecturas e imágenes. INIDE, 1973.
Retórnelo. Ed. Colmillo Blanco, 1986.

He has also published various books of poetry and translations in Peru and Mexico.

SIDELIGHTS: "The first of my 'educational verses,' which are verses written in order to make better readers of children, occurred by happenstance. Some time ago, when I was entrusted to prepare a book for children who were in the second year of primary school, it was my job to select verses from Peruvian authors and foreigners appropriate for teaching to a young audience. In the course of this pleasant activity I found myself, almost without trying, beginning to write poetry for my future readers. Some of the verses I wrote were included in *Paseo de lecturas e imágenes*, and the others appeared later in magazines and journals."

CRITICAL SOURCES:
Roberto Paoli. *Estudios sobre literatura peruana contemporánea.*
José Miguel Oviedo. *El Comercio.* Lima: June 12, 1966.
Abelardo Oquendo. *Amaru.* 5, Lima: 1968.
Ricardo González Vigil. *El Comercio.* Lima: August 21, 1988.

SOTO, Gary (1952-)

PERSONAL DATA: Born December 14, 1952, in Fresno, California, he is the son of

Manuel Soto and Ángela Trevino. He is married to Carolyn and has a daughter, Mariko. *Education:* Licentiate in English, California State University, 1974; M.F.A. in creative writing, University of California, 1976.

ADDRESS: (Home) 43 The Crescent, Berkeley, California 94708. Telephone: 8454718.

CAREER: Poet; producer of cinema for children; professor of literature.

AWARDS, HONORS: Bess Hokin Prize; Levinson Award; Academy of American Poets Award; Discovery, The Nation Prize; U.S. Award of the International Poetry Forum; California Library Association's John and Patricia Beatty Award; has received fellowships from the Guggenheim Foundation and the National Endowment for the Arts.

WRITINGS: Gary Soto has published ten books of poetry from 1977 to 1992. He is also the author of more than eight works of prose, published in various editions.

Baseball in April. Mexico: Fondo de Cultura Económica, to be published in Spanish in 1993.

STEINER DE WEISS, Susan Emily (1952-)

PERSONAL DATA: Born July 31, 1952, in Mexico, D.F., the daughter of Ricardo Pick and Lore Steiner de Pick. She is married to Jaime Weiss and has three children, Daniel, Arturo, and Sonia. *Education:* Licentiate in social psychology from the Universidad Iberoamericana, Mexico; doctorate in social psychology from the University of London, England.

ADDRESS: (Home) Bosques de Avellanos 156, 11700 Mexico, D.F. Telephone: 5964460. (Office) Malaga Norte 25, Col. Insurgentes Mixcoac, 03920 Mexico, D. F. Telephone: 5985673, 6828031.

CAREER: Department chair at the Facultad de Psicología of the UNAM; president of the Mexican Institute for the Investigation of the Family and Population, A.C.

PROFESSIONAL ORGANIZATIONS: American Psychological Association; American Public Health Association; founding member of the Instituto Mexicano de Familia y Población; Sociedad Interamericana de Psicología; president of the

Asociación Mexicana de Psicología Social; Proprietary member, Consejo Interno de la División de Estudios de Posgrado, Facultad de Psicología, UNAM, 1991.

AWARDS, HONORS: Award of Distinction, Universidad Nacional para Jóvenes Académicos for Investigation in the Social Sciences, 1984.

WRITINGS:
Planeando tu vida: nuevo programa de educación sexual para adolescentes.
    Mexico: Ed. Limusa, 1988.
Yo adolescente: respuestas claras a mis grandes dudas. Mexico: Ed. Limusa, 1990.
Planeando tu vida. Mexico: Ed. Limusa, 1991.

For readers from one to six years of age:
Nuestro cuerpo.
Cuando voy al doctor.
Me baño, me lavo y me peino.
Adiós al pañal.
Aprendiendo a cuidarme.
Lugares a donde voy.
En qué trabaja la gente.
Para estar sano como yo.
Tengo diarrea.
Amar al mundo.
Todos tenemos tareas.
Digo lo que siento.

For readers four and older:
Zonia aprende la importancia de las reglas.
Cuídate de los extraños.
Jugamos, trabajamos y descansamos.
De visita al dentista.
Tú y las medicinas.
¿A cuál vagón te pareces? (Nuestras cualidades y defectos).
Te respeto y me respetas.
El hermano bebé.
Soy importante.
El primer día de escuela.
Aprendiendo sobre el embarazo.
Daniel aprende a organizarse.
Arturo aprende a reconocer sus errores,
Chocolatín aprende a cooperar.
Jumijo se alimenta bien.

For readers seven and older:
Como ayudo en el hogar.
Tú y la televisión.
Por qué se divorcia la gente.
Tú y el dinero.

SIDELIGHTS: "One of the best forms of spreading recent findings in the field of public health, family, and population is the creation of educational programs and materials for children. It is because of this that I have an eagerness to write educational books. The investigations themselves are very inspirational, and the themes are ambitious. Among them are the expression of emotion; family communication; self-reliance; nutrition; sexuality; the prevention of accidents; fear of the unknown; general development; personal development; prevention of alcohol, tobacco, and drug abuse; prevention of sexual abuse; how babies are born; avoiding lies; responsibility; and how we make investigations in the social sciences."

TAMAYO ROSAS, Loreto Ramón (1958-)

PERSONAL DATA: Born July 8, 1958, in Ensenada, Baja California, Mexico, he is the son of Plutarco Tamayo and Ángela Guadalupe Rosas. He is married to Leticia Burgos Mexía and has three children, Miguel Ramón, Gabriel, and Diego. *Education:* Studied veterinary medicine, zoology, plastic arts, and the theater at the Universidad Autónoma de Baja California.

ADDRESS: (Home) Real de Minas Norte 1775, Fracc. Residencial Real del Castillo, Mexicali, Baja California, Mexico. Telephone: 538408. (Office) Departamento de Difusión Cultural, Unidad Universitaria UABC, Boulevard Benito Juárez, Mexicali, Baja California, Mexico. Telephone: 664276.

CAREER: Plastic artist; director and performer for theater; writer.

PROFESSIONAL ORGANIZATIONS: Cooperativa de Artistas Plásticos José G. Arroyo; Grupo Lindero Norte; member of "The Bicycle" theater group.

AWARDS, HONORS: Honorable Mention, November Revolutionary Competition; Third Place, Sixth Biennial State of Plastic Arts Awards; Second Place in Painting and Sculpture, at the Seventh Biennial State of Plastic Arts Awards; Second Place in Sculpture, Eighth Biennial State of Plastic Arts Awards.

WRITINGS:

Versos para bajitos de Baja y otros. Mexicali: Universidad Autónoma de Baja California, 1990.

Dos osos rumorosos y lo que pasó un verano. Mexicali: Universidad Autónoma de Baja California, 1991.

Pinta tu raya de colores. Mexicali: Universidad Autónoma de Baja California, 1991.

Baja cantando y sigue riendo. Mexicali: Universidad Autónoma de Baja California, 1992.

Vida de cuadritos. Mexicali: Universidad Autónoma de Baja California, 1992.

SIDELIGHTS: "I write because there are too few books for children referring to our region (the frontier, the state of Baja California, and the northwest part of Mexico). Above all, I write and work for children because I was a child and it is a way of reviving and conserving and teaching children. I prefer regional themes, themes about the ecology, and educational themes. My sources of inspiration are children, my children, my friends, my environment, and Cri-Cri."

TARANILLA DE LA VARGA, Carlos Javier (1956-)

PERSONAL DATA: Born September 20, 1956, in Leon, Spain, the son of Gregorio Taranilla and Aquilina de la Varga, he is married to Leonía Santos and has a daughter, Leonía María. *Education:* Holds a degree in the history of art from the Universidad de Oviedo.

ADDRESS: (Office) Colegio de Bachiller San Juan de la Cruz, Daoíz y Velarde s/n, Leon, Spain. Centro de Enseñanza Virgen Blanca, San Juan 7, Leon, Spain. Telephone: 259451.

CAREER: Art director for the publisher Everest from 1978 to 1986; since then, has been a teacher; writer.

AWARDS, HONORS: His books have been included in a bibliographic catalogue published by the Ministry of Culture.

WRITINGS:
Viaje a los orígenes de Egipto. Leon: Ed. Everest, 1979.
Simón Bolívar. Leon: Ed. Everest, 1979.
Viaje a los orígenes de Grecia. Leon: Ed. Everest, 1980.
Diccionario de historia del arte. Leon: Ed. Everest, 1982.

Viaje a los orígenes de Roma. Leon: Ed. Everest, 1984.

SIDELIGHTS: "I have had great love since childhood of literature and art. I love sifting through the richness of words and the nuances of language, and also of people. Nevertheless, this is in regard to the great writers; the others we must let time bring to light."

TEIXIDOR (VILADECÁS), Emili (1933-)

PERSONAL DATA: Born December 22, 1933, in Roda de Ter, Barcelona, Spain. His parents were Jaime and Filomena. *Education:* Advanced studies in philosophy and letters, law, and journalism.

ADDRESS: (Home) Instituto Químico de Sarriá 2, 4° 2a., 08017 Barcelona, Spain. Telephone: 2045932.

CAREER: Editor for Editorial Salvat; journalist; columnist for *Avui* and *Diario de Barcelona*; director of the Escuela Betània Patmos, 1958-75.

PROFESSIONAL ORGANIZATIONS: Club Natación Barcelona; PEN Club Catalán; Asociación de Escritores.

AWARDS, HONORS: Critics' Award from *Serra d'Or*, 1979; J. Ruyra Award for Literature for Children, 1976; People's Choice Award of Catalonia, 1983; Honors List for the University of Padova, Italy; P.P. Vergerio Prize; Finalist for the Europa-Poitiers Award, France; Cross of Saint Jordi, 1992.

WRITINGS:
Diego, Berta y la máquina de rizar niebla. Barcelona: Ed. La Galera, 1969.
No me llames Pedro. Barcelona: Ed. La Galera, 1977.
Marcabrú y la hoguera de hielo. Madrid: Ed. Espasa-Calpe, 1985.
Renco y el tesoro. Madrid: Ediciones SM, 1986.
Cada tigre en su jungla. Madrid: Ediciones SM, 1987.
Renco y sus amigos. Madrid: Ediciones SM, 1988.
Las alas de la noche. Madrid: Ediciones SM, 1988.
El soldado de hielo. Madrid: Ediciones SM, 1990.
Federico, Federico, Federico. Madrid: Ed. Espasa-Calpe, 1990.
El príncipe Alí. Barcelona: Ed. Plaza & Janes, 1990.
Un aire que mata. Madrid: Ediciones SM, 1991.

El crimen de la hipotenusa. Madrid: Ediciones SM, 1992.

The work of Emili Teixidor has been translated into French and Portuguese.

SIDELIGHTS: "I write because I like it when I become interested in a theme. My favorite themes are those that mix the unusual with elements of the fantastic or imaginary. My sources of inspiration are observations of reality around me, things I learn through the press and television, and my imagination, which works with these others as raw materials. I enjoy reading my works to students and young people so that I can get their opinions before I go to press."

CRITICAL SOURCES:
Isidor Cónsol and Agustí Pons. *Avui*.
J. Grau. "Los libros de E. Teixidor".
J. Orja. *La Vanguardia*.
María Solé. *ABC*.
Alex Susanna. *El Urogallo*.
Diario de Barcelona.
Serra d'Or.
El País. 1990.

TERZI HUGUET, Marinella (1958-)

PERSONAL DATA: Born September 22, 1958, in Barcelona, Spain, the daughter of Guido and Rosa. *Education:* Holds a degree in information sciences, emphasizing journalism.

ADDRESS: (Home) Segre 20, 2° B, 28002 Madrid, Spain. Telephone: 5647759. (Office) Ediciones SM, Joaquín Turina 39, 28044 Madrid, Spain. Telephone: 2585145.

CAREER: Editor; director of the *Barco de Vapor* collection for Ediciones SM.

AWARDS, HONORS: CCEI Honors List, 1990.

WRITINGS:
La huella árabe en España. Madrid: Ediciones SM/INCAFO, 1989.
Apoteosis del gótico europeo. Madrid: Ediciones SM/INCAFO, 1989.
El imperio de los faraones. Madrid: Ediciones SM/INCAFO.
El imperio chino. Madrid: Ediciones SM/INCAFO, 1989.

La antigua Grecia. Madrid: Ediciones SM/INCAFO, 1989.
Un problema con patas. Zaragoza: Ed. Edelvives, 1989.
El arte rupestre prehistórico. Madrid: Ediciones SM/INCAFO, 1990.
Estornudos con sorpresas. Zaragoza: Ed. Edelvives, 1991.
Rodando, rodando. Zaragoza: Ed. Edelvives, 1992.

SIDELIGHTS: "In regard to my popular works, I write using my memories of life as a reporter. I like to look for documentation about concrete actions after I have created the general structure of my work. In reference to books for children, I like to make stories about themes that concern today's children, putting myself into each one of my books."

CRITICAL SOURCES:
Rodrigo Rubio. *Ya.* June 3, 1989.
Carlos Villades. *Correo de América.* Summer 1989.
Norma Sturniolo. *El Urogallo.* April 1990.
Juan Clemente. *Información Alicante.* May 29, 1991.

TORRENTS (PUIG), Jacint (1949-)

PERSONAL DATA: Born March 7, 1949, in Santa Coloma de Gramenet, Barcelona, Spain, he is the son of Isidre and Ángela. He is married to María Dolors. *Education:* Studied Catalan philology at the Universidad de Barcelona.

ADDRESS: (Home) Ángel Guimerà 38, 08211 Castellar del Vallès, Barcelona, Spain. Telephone: 7143071. (Office) Plaza Catalunya 6, 08208 Sabadell, Barcelona, Spain. Telephone: 7168497.

CAREER: Professor of Catalan, 1970-73; worked at a bank in Santander 1973-74; was a professor of Catalan language and literature at the Instituto de Bachillerato, 1982-83, has worked at the Caja de Ahorros de Sabadell since 1974.

AWARDS, HONORS: Outstanding Distinction upon receiving licentiate degree, Universidad de Barcelona, 1981; Cavall Fort Award, 1975.

WRITINGS:
El gran dragón. Trans. by Lola Poveda. Barcelona: Ed. La Galera, 1976.

He has also published stories and articles in Catalan anthologies and journals, including *Cavall Fort* and *Forja*. The literary work of Jacint Torrents is originally written in Catalan.

SIDELIGHTS: "I began publishing in a journal for children and joined their editing staff soon afterward. I specialized in this type of literature, and it requires a certain set of sensibilities. Now, however, I feel I write more in the essay form than in narrative for children. I used candor and humor, and the positive aspects of life, like friendship, descriptions of beautiful places, and the defense of peace, nature, and culture."

CRITICAL SOURCES:
Aurora Díaz Plaja. *Serra d'Or.* July 1974; June 1976.
Trezevents. April 1976.
Riquer, Comas, Molas. *Historia de la literatura catalana, vol. 10.* 1987.
Vicenz Llorca. *Avui.* September 20, 1990.
Teresa Durán. *El Periódico de Catalunya.* February 19, 1992.

TORRES OLIVER, Francisco (1935-)

PERSONAL DATA: Born in Alicante, Spain. *Education:* Holds a degree in philosophy.

CAREER: Was a professor of secondary education; since 1968 he has been a translator. Translates from English and French.

AWARDS, HONORS: National Award for Translation, 1991.

SPANISH TRANSLATIONS:
Daniel Defoe. *Historias de piratas.* Madrid: Ed. Alfaguara, 1978.
Isak Dinesen. *Anécdotas del destino.* Madrid: Ed. Alfaguara, 1986.
Bram Stoker. *Drácula.* Barcelona: Ed. Montesinos, 1989.
Mary Shelley. *Frankenstein o el moderno Prometeo.* Madrid: Ed. Anaya, 1989.

SIDELIGHTS: "The work of a translator consists of transforming a text from one language to another, and the result is never one of total equivalency. But the translator does help to overcome the barrier of language, to penetrate the book, to make possible the understanding and enjoyment of its spirit."

TURIN, Adela (1929-)

PERSONAL DATA: Born September 28, 1929, in Milan, Italy, the daughter of Gaetano and Margarita Mandele. She is married to Alfredo Turin and has a child, Luca Turin. *Education:* Holds degrees in the history of art and aesthetics.

ADDRESS: 233 Faubourg Saint Honoré, 75008 Paris, France. Telephone: 47632795.

CAREER: Designer and writer. Founded a journal, *Dalla Parte Delle Bambine,* and created a series of feminist books edited in Spain, "En Favor de las Niñas."

AWARDS, HONORS: First Prize, Bologna Children's Book Fair Awards, 1978, 1979, 1981; Citta di San Remo Award, 1980; Europa Award for Literature for Children, 1979; Second Place, Cassa di Rispar Mio Awards for Literature for Children, 1981.

WRITINGS: Between 1975 and 1981 she published more than forty books for children and young people, as well as others in collaboration with other authors. Her journal, *Dalla Parte Delle Bambine,* has been translated into nine languages.

CRITICAL SOURCES: Throughout the 1970s and 1980s there was enormous critical attention given to feminist literature for children. The works of Adela Turin were a subject of principal interest at this time and as such there is a wealth of critical information available concerning her works.

URIBE (ARCE), María de la Luz (1936-)

PERSONAL DATA: Born March 27, 1936, in Santiago, Chile, the daughter of Armando Uribe and Emelina Arce, she is married to Fernando Krahn and has three children, Fernanda, Santiago, and Matías. *Education:* Studied literature at the Universidad de Chile.

ADDRESS: (Home) San Gaudencio 25, Sitges, 08870 Barcelona, Spain. Telephone: 8943940.

CAREER: Was a Montesori teacher from 1960 to 1963, and then a researcher for the Centro de Literatura Comparada of the Universidad de Chile from 1963 to 1966. Writer, 1965-.

PROFESSIONAL ORGANIZATIONS: IBBY of Spain.

AWARDS, HONORS: Apelles Mestres Award, 1982; Clara Campoamor Prize, 1984; juror for the Apelles Mestres since 1984; Austral Award for Literature for Children, 1986.

WRITINGS:
El pequeño monstruo de las casas. Madrid: Ed. Alfaguara, 1979.
Cuenta que te cuento. Barcelona: Ed. Juventud, 1979.
Quien lo diría Carlota María. Madrid: Ed. Alfaguara, 1981.
Doña Piñones. Caracas: Ed. Ekaré, 1982.
El Cururía. Caracas: Ed. Ekaré, 1982.
La señorita Amelia. Barcelona: Ed. Destino, 1983.
El vuelo de Inés. Barcelona: Ed. Argos-Vergara, 1984.
Pero-Pero. Barcelona: Ed. Argos-Vergara, 1984.
Nomo Nemi. Barcelona: Ed. Juventud, 1984.
Cosas y cositas. Madrid: Ed. Espasa-Calpe,.
Quita y Pon. Barcelona: Ed. Destino, 1986.
El primer pájaro de Piko Niko. Barcelona: Ed. Juventud, 1987.
El fiero Ugaldo. Barcelona: Ediciones B, 1989.
Por la vía iba un tren. Madrid: Ediciones SM, 1990.
Los príncipes de piedra. Madrid: Ediciones SM, 1991.

SIDELIGHTS: "After writing essays about literature, I decided to dedicate myself to literature for children. I was aware of its transcendence. I believe that the life of an adult can be changed by what he or she reads, and by what he or she read while growing up. I principally write in verse because the rhythm and rhyme of poetry are indisputably successful ways of reaching the minds and sensibilities of children."

CRITICAL SOURCES:
Victoria Fernández. *El País.*
Federico Martín. *Cuadernos de pedagogía.*
Nuria Ventura. *La Vanguardia.*
CLIJ. Edition dedicated to the author.

URTEAGA CABRERA, Luis Antonio (1940-)

PERSONAL DATA: Born June 1, 1940, in Cajamarca, Peru, the son of Miguel Antonio and Clara Luz, he is married to Hedy Villanueva Dávila and has two children, Katia and Julián.

ADDRESS: (Home) Robert Kennedy 280, Lima 21, Peru. Telephone: 626005. (Office) Julio C. Tello 64511, Lima 14, Peru. Telephone: 702588.

CAREER: Author and screenwriter for the cinema.

AWARDS, HONORS: National Award for Stories, "Visión del Perú"; National Award for the Novel, "Primera Plana Sudamericana"; National Award for Theater; National Award for the Novel, "José María Arguedas."

WRITINGS:
Los hijos del orden. Ed. Mosca Azul, 1973.
La danza de las ataduras. Ed. Textual, 1975.
Carretera de penetración. Ed. Ecoma, 1971.
Una voz en el viento. Ed. Textual, 1969.
Noticias del agua. Ed. Crisis, 1978.
Verdes se agitan las hojas al viento. Ed. Cieloabierto, 1985.
El universo sagrado. Ed. Peisa, 1991.
El otorongo y el oso hormiguero. Ed. Peisa, 1991.

SIDELIGHTS: "I write in search of the identities of myself and my people, our social and cultural fingerprints; and I want to recover from silence many of the aspects of our being and our reality. I tell the stories of marginalized groups of people, events, characters, and conduct, with the intent to investigate who Peruvians are, and with which of our races and histories we should identify."

UZCANGA LAVALLE, Alicia María (1946-)

PERSONAL DATA: Born March 31, 1946, in Veracruz, Mexico, the daughter of Leonardo Uzcanga and Manuela Lavalle, she is the mother of María Leticia. *Education:* Licentiate and master's degree in Spanish letters.

ADDRESS: (Home) Río Bravo 5927, Col. San Manuel, 72570 Puebla, Mexico. Telephone: 450235.

CAREER: Writer; teacher of Spanish as a second language; teacher of theater; literary advisor to various presses; radio announcer.

AWARDS, HONORS: Certificate for Excellence in Poetry, University of Colorado, 1982; Medalla della Valpescara, Italy, 1983; Second Place, Celestino Gorostiza

National Competition for Theater for Children, Mexico, D. F., 1984; Honorable Mention, Celestino Gorostiza National Competition for Theater, 1985; Silver Medal, International Villa Alessandra Competition, Alanno, Italy, 1985; First and Second Place respectively, at the Poblana Story and Legend Competition, 1985; numerous awards at the Juegos Florales and diverse awards from Puebla, Zacatecas, and Michoacan.

WRITINGS:
Versos, prosas y cuentos. 1965.
Taller de teatro. Mexico: Ed. Edamex, 3rd ed.,1986.
Y era yo misma quien hablaba. 1980.
Poesías para la infancia. Mexico: Ed. Edamex, 1986.
"Guiti y su gran secreto." *Antología de ganadores del Primer Concurso de Teatro*. Mexico: Editores Mexicanos Unidos, 1985.
"El duende metalillo." *Antología de ganadores del Primer Concurso de Teatro*. Mexico: Editores Mexicanos Unidos, 1985.
Recuerdos de cristal. Mexico: Ed. Federación, 1986.
Juegos al servicio del aprendizaje. Mexico: Ed. Para el maestro, 1987.
Por entre el campo de flores rosadas. Mexico: Ed. Taller Libre de Artes Plásticas, 1988.
El umbral del espejo. Mexico: Ed. Tlapac, 1989.
Teatro escolar. Mexico: Ed. Edamex, 1990.

SIDELIGHTS: "I write from an internal necessity that is both beautiful and profound. I write about being human, love, and real values. Through my work in the theater, I try to send messages to young people about qualities we have lost or that we are at the point of losing; nevertheless I do not consider my works moralistic in the strict sense of the word. They are light and portrayed with vitality and joy. Every work of mine has humor and references to history and legends. They are easy to represent, without the need for spectacular scenography or costumes, but which are still very beautiful."

CRITICAL SOURCES:
Albert Chantrian. *Paix*. Belgium.
Miguel Fajardo. *Análisis*. 63.
José Jurado Morales. *Azor*, XXXV, XLI, XLIX. Barcelona, Spain.
Otello Martinelli. *Controvento*. Alanno, Italy, 1983.

VALERO BURGUETE, Carlos (1952-)

PERSONAL DATA: Born February 9, 1952, in Madrid, Spain, the son of Luis and Amelia, he is married to Gadea. *Education:* Holds degrees in biology and geology.

ADDRESS: (Home) Valdebernardo 8, 12° B, 28030 Madrid, Spain. Telephone: 7726619. (Office) Severino Aznar 6-8, 28011 Madrid, Spain. Telephone: 4632441/42.

CAREER: Professor of secondary education.

WRITINGS:
El cuerpo humano I y II. Madrid: Ed. Bruño, 1990.
La fotosíntesis. Ed. Madre Nostrum, in print.
La evolución y el origen del hombre. Ed. Madre Nostrum, in print.

VALLE TEJADA, Julia Maritza (1956-)

PERSONAL DATA: Born June 5, 1956, in Lima, Peru, the daughter of Luis Fernando Valle Degregori and Gladys Tejeda, she is married to Luis Felipe Rossel and has two children, Mauricio and Braulio. *Education:* Advanced studies in administration and business.

ADDRESS: (Home) Querecotillo A 29, La Capullana, Surco, Lima, Peru. Telephone: 482602. (Office) Juan de Arona 830, San Isidro, Peru. Telephone: 704870.

CAREER: Worked for Air France, 1975-92.

PROFESSIONAL ORGANIZATIONS: APLIJ.

WRITINGS:
Uno para cada uno. Ed. EDIPROCSA, 1992.

SIDELIGHTS: "I write because I love children, because I feel for them, and because I feel that they need more dedication from us today than ever before. I write about any theme that is adaptable to the clear language of childhood. I prefer themes that give value to human qualities."

CRITICAL SOURCES:
Nori Rojas Morote. *Boletín APLIJ.*

VALLEJO DE BOLÍVAR, Gaby (1941-)

PERSONAL DATA: Born September 24, 1941, in Cochabamba, Bolivia, the daughter of Oscar Vallejo and Carmela Canedo, she is married to Gastón Bolívar and has three children, Huáscar, Grissel, and Américo. *Education:* Licentiate in educational science and Hispanic-American literature.

ADDRESS: (Home) Casilla 5240, Cochabamba, Bolivia. Telephone: 46918. (Office) Casilla 544, Cochabamba, Bolivia. Telephone: 43137.

CAREER: Has been a teacher since 1965 and a university professor since 1982; researcher at the Instituto de Investigaciones en Humanidades, 1987-; has promoted reading and teaching in Centro Portales since 1977.

PROFESSIONAL ORGANIZATIONS: Taller de Experiencias Pedagógicas; Unión Nacional de Poetas y Escritores; president, IBBY of Bolivia.

AWARDS, HONORS: Erick Guttentag Award for the Novel, Bolivia, 1976; IBBY Honors List, 1988; Award of Merit from the city of Cochabamba, 1990; Mircea Eliade International Award, Venice, 1991.

WRITINGS:
Los vulnerables. La Paz: Ed. Amigos del Libro, 1973.
Hijo de Opa. Cochabamba: Ed. Amigos del Libro, 1977.
Juvenal Nina. Cochabamba: Ed. Poligraf, 1981.
Detrás de los sueños. Cochabamba: Ed. Puente, 1987.
En busca de los nuestros. Cochabamba: Ed. Amigos del Libro, 1987.
Del libro a la vida. Cochabamba: Ed. Poligraf, 1988.
Mi primo es mi papá. Cochabamba: Ed. Puente, 1989.
Manual del promotor de lectura. Cochabamba: Centro Portales, 1990.
La sierpe empieza en cola. Cochabamba: Ed. Amigos del Libro, 1991.

SIDELIGHTS: "I write because I want to act as a witness to my times. My novels for adults are ultimately about the lives of my people. I write for children because there are virtually no Bolivian children's books. The little that is read by Bolivian children is terribly foreign. In order to help make a significant change in the relationship between teachers, books, and students, I have written a manual for teachers. In relation to what is specifically written for children, my books try to recover the myths and legends of my people and incorporate them in narrative more dynamic, interesting, and appropriate to today's children. In other cases, I write satire about family relations, giving precedence to humor and mystery. My sources of inspiration are life itself, observation of children, my own childhood, and the past captured in legend."

CRITICAL SOURCES:
Mario Lara. Los Tiempos. 1981.
Amanda Arriarán de Zapata. Los Tiempos. February 2, 1982.
Alfonso Gamarra D. Presencia Literaria. 1990.

VALLVERDÚ, Josep (1923-)

PERSONAL DATA: Born in Lerida, Spain, in 1923.

CAREER: Professor of language and history; advisor to the journal Cavall Fort; translator.

WRITINGS:
El vendedor de peces. 1960.
Trampa bajo las aguas. 1963.
La caravana invisible. 1968.
Historia de la literatura catalana. 1978.

 Consisting of more than fifteen books, the work of Josep Vallverdú is originally written in Catalan.

VANDEN BROECK (GUERITOT), Fabricio (1954-)

PERSONAL DATA: Born October 1, 1954, in Mexico, D. F., the son of André Vanden Broeck and Jacqueline Gueritot, he is married to Nadia Pigozzi and has a son, Carlo Stefano. Education: Studied industrial design at the Universidad Iberoamericana, Mexico, 1973-77; studied basic design and graphic design at the Ecole d'Art de Lausanne, Switzerland, 1979-82.

ADDRESS: (Home) Emilio Castellar 6-203, 11560, Mexico, D.F. Telephone: 2541172. (Office) Campos Eliseos 110, 11560 Mexico, D.F. Telephone: 5316770.

CAREER: Independent graphic designer and illustrator since 1983.

AWARDS, HONORS: Honorable Mention, Antoniorrobles Competition for Illustration, IBBY of Mexico, 1983; "Encouragement Prize," Noma Award in Illustration from UNESCO, Japan, 1990.

ILLUSTRATED WORKS:
ABC Animales. Mexico: Ed. Patria, 1987.
Animales mexicanos. Mexico: CONAFE, 1989.
El caminante. Mexico: CONAFE, 1990.
Secuestrador de sueños. Mexico: CONAFE, 1991.
Pepenar palabras. Mexico: Ed. Patria, 1992.

VÁZQUEZ-VIGO, Carmen (1923-)

PERSONAL DATA: Born in Buenos Aires in 1923.

CAREER: Actress in the National Comedy Theater of Buenos Aires; in 1947 she went to Spain and worked in radio and theater in Madrid and Barcelona; advisor for the journal *Don José* and for various other magazines.

AWARDS, HONORS: National Award for Stories, 1963; Doncel Award for Stories for Young People, 1966; Chest of Silver Award, 1970.

WRITINGS:
La fuerza de la gacela. 1964.
Historia de un tomate paliducho. 1964.
Quiquiriquí. 1967.
Verónica y compañía. 1969.
Mambrú no fue a la guerra. 1970.
Animales charlatanes. 1980.
Caramelos de menta. 1981.
Guau. 1981.
Sirena y media. 1984.
Palabra de árbol. 1984.

VEGA HERRERA, César Gabriel (1936-)

PERSONAL DATA: Born February 28, 1936, in Arequipa, Peru, the son of César

Vega Vargas and Victoria Herrera, he is married to Estela Huamán and has two children, Victoria Estela and Juan Gabriel.

ADDRESS: (Office) Puno 421, Lima 01, Peru.

CAREER: Journalist since 1970 and professor of theater since 1972.

PROFESSIONAL ORGANIZATIONS: APLIJ; Asociación Nacional de Escritores y Artistas (ANEA).

AWARDS, HONORS: Fountains of Culture National Award, 1974.

WRITINGS:
La noche de los Sprunkos. Ed. El Sol, 1974.
El soldadito de molde. Ed. El Sol, 1974.

SIDELIGHTS: "I write because I feel the need to communicate with others. I love classical Spanish poetry, Greek theater, classic children's literature, and current Latin American writers. My favorite stories change with every writer that I read. Sources of inspiration: classic literature in general and popular stories. All of this combined with my personal experiences."

VELÁZQUEZ ROJAS, Manuel (1931-)

PERSONAL DATA: Born January 20, 1931, in Piura, Peru, the son of Juan Luis Velázquez and Sabina Rojas, he is married to Beatriz Castro Romero and has three children, Marcel, Tesania, and Mauricio. *Education:* Doctorate in literature from the Universidad Mayor de San Marcos.

ADDRESS: (Home) Malachowski 218, Torres de Limatambo, San Borja, Lima, Peru. Telephone: 750134. (Office) Facultad de Humanidades y Artes, Universidad Nacional de Educación, Chosica, Peru.

CAREER: Supervisor of Publications for the UNE, 1968-75; dean of the Facultad de Humanidades y Artes at the Universidad Nacional de Educación.

PROFESSIONAL ORGANIZATIONS: APLIJ; Asociación Nacional de Escritores y Artistas.

AWARDS, HONORS: Member of Honor to the Casa del Poeta, Peru.

WRITINGS:
La voz del tiempo. Lima: Ed. Perú Joven, 1960.
Isla de otoño. Lima: Ed. Perú Joven, 1966.
Antología temporal. Lima: Ed. Perú Joven, 1975.
Kratios. Lima: Ed. Perú Joven, 1988.
Literatura infantil. 1988.
Ojos de venado. 1990.

SIDELIGHTS: "The fundamental motivation for my writing is communication. I believe that people need to communicate in order to know each other. This knowledge reveals the highest spiritual values, as much in the individual as in the society. In the case of literature for children, I think children should be exposed to poetry and prose appropriate to their age and level of education, but this is obviously a flexible classification. Often literature that is not written for children is nevertheless comprehensible to and appreciated by them. This has been one of my criteria for selecting texts for inclusion in my anthology, *Literatura infantil.* Moreover, I think it is important for children to read literature from other countries."

CRITICAL SOURCES:
Alberto Escobar. *Antología de la poesía peruana.* 1966.

VIGIL-ESCALERA NOYA, Orlando (1938-)

PERSONAL DATA: Born October 25, 1938, in Víbora, Havana, Cuba, he is the son of Guillermo and Angélica. He is married to Regla de la Sierra Xenes and has three children, Víctor, Milko, and Orlando. *Education:* Studied dramatic arts at the Escuela de Artes Dramáticas de La Habana, as well as courses, workshops, and seminars at the Associate School of Theater and Art in Moscow, the Taganca Theater in Moscow, and the Berlin Ensemble.

ADDRESS: (Home) Línea 812, 3-A, Esq. a 4, Vedado, Havana, Cuba. Telephone: 325283. (Office) Calle 21 y 8, Vedado, Havana, Cuba.

CAREER: Had been a dramatist, theatrical director, and professor of acting and directing for the theater; has taught courses, workshops, and seminars in various countries; and is now at the National Central Theater for Cultural Work for the Community Ministry of Culture's director general of the theater groups Galpon and

Plaza, who perform theater for children and young people in Havana.

PROFESSIONAL ORGANIZATIONS: President of the Drama Section of the National Union of Writers and Artists of Cuba; Association of Scenic Artists.

AWARDS, HONORS: National Award for Drama, 1965; Honorable Mention, *La Edad de Oro* Awards, 1973, 1974, 1978, 1979; Marcos Behemaras Competition for the ICRT, 1979; Award at the Seventh Festival of Theater for Children and Young People, 1981.

WRITINGS:
El gato con botas. Mexico: Consejo Nacional de Cultura, 1966.
Conversación sostenida. Letras Cubanas, 1980.
El tractorcito. Letras Cubanas, 1980.
Estamos de pesca. Letras Cubanas, 1980
Cantando, jugando y contando. 1984.
Hombrecitos de la prehistoria. 1988.

SIDELIGHTS: "I write theater for children and young people above all because I am interested in those who are, as José Martí says, 'the hope of the world.' My source of inspiration is life, humanity, and human relations. I believe in life, in humans, in excellence and human growth. I believe in the future, even as it appears a utopia; and I want to continue believing in it, in this utopia, in the future."

CRITICAL SOURCES:
Bohemia.
Granma.
Juventud Rebelde.

VILAR I ROCA, Anna (1956-)

PERSONAL DATA: Born December 6, 1956, in Barcelona, Spain, the daughter of Antoni Vilar and Mercè Roca. She has two children, Roger and Adrià. *Education:* Professor of EGB.

ADDRESS: (Home) Arizala 66, 3a, 08028 Barcelona, Spain.

CAREER: Public school teacher for the Generalitat de Catalonia since 1978.

PROFESSIONAL ORGANIZATIONS: Asociación de Escritores en Lengua Catalana; PEN Club; Amigos del IBBY.

WRITINGS:
Éranse una vez siete reyes. Barcelona: Ed. La Galera, 1982.
El saber perdido. Barcelona: Ed. La Galera, 1983.
Y un día será mañana. Barcelona: Ed. La Galera, 1985.

The literary work of Anna Vilar is originally written in Catalan. The works cited here are translations into Spanish.

SIDELIGHTS: "I write for children and young people because I am in continual contact with them through my profession and because I am interested in their world. I began to write stories so that I could use them as tools in my classroom. A favorite theme is the use and/or abuse of scientific knowledge and technology for the benefit of the few at the cost of many."

WALSH, María Elena (1930-)

PERSONAL DATA: Born February 1, 1930, in Buenos Aires, Argentina, the daughter of Enrique Walsh and Lucía Monsalvo. *Education:* Studied at the Escuela Nacional de Bellas Artes.

ADDRESS: (Home) Scalabrini Ortiz 3237, 12° B, 1425 Buenos Aires, Argentina. (Office) SADAIC. Lavalle 1547, Buenos Aires, Argentina. Telephone: 401163.

CAREER: Author; composer; singer. Has created television programs for children and adults.

PROFESSIONAL ORGANIZATIONS: SADAIC; ARGENTORES; ALIJA.

AWARDS, HONORS: Municipal Award for Poetry, 1948; Grand Prize of Honor from SADAIC and from the National Foundation for the Arts; Argentina Foundation for Poetry; Doctorate Honoris Causa from the Universidad Nacional de Córdoba, 1990.

WRITINGS:
Tutú Marambá. Buenos Aires: Ed. Sudamericana, 1960.

El reino del revés. Buenos Aires: Ed. Sudamericana, 1965.

Zoo loco. Buenos Aires: Ed. Sudamericana, 1965.

Dailan Kifki. Buenos Aires: Ed. Sudamericana, 1966.

Versos tradicionales para cebollitas. Buenos Aires: Ed. Sudamericana, 1967.

Aire libre. Buenos Aires: Ed. Sudamericana, 1967.

La sirena y el capitán. Buenos Aires: Ed. Sudamericana, 1970.

Angelito. Buenos Aires: Ed. Sudamericana, 1970.

El diablo inglés. Buenos Aires: Ed. Sudamericana, 1970.

El país de la geometría. Buenos Aires: Ed. Sudamericana, 1970.

Chaucha y Palito. Buenos Aires: Ed. Sudamericana, 1977.

Bisa Vuela. Buenos Aires: Ed. Sudamericana, 1986.

La nube traicionera (version of a story by George Sand). Buenos Aires: Ed. Sudamericana, 1989.

The literary work of María Elena Walsh consists of other publications for adults, principally poetry. She has made more than fifteen records of songs and games for children.

Appendix

This appendix lists writers/illustrators alphabetically under their country of origin and/or citizenship.

Argentina

Barthe, Raquel Marta
Bornemann, Elsa (Isabel)
Calny, Eugenia (Fany Eugenia Kalnitzky de Brener)
Clemente, Horacio (Domingo)
Coluccio, Félix
Daroqui, Julia Carmen
De Santis, Pablo (Ulises María)
Doumerc de Barnes, Beatriz
Giménez Pastor, Marta
Granata, María
Malinow, Lydia Inés
Martínez (De Sosa), Paulina (Dorlisa)
Monkman, Olga (Gómez de)
Murillo, José
Nanni de Smania, Estela
Pastor, Rodolfo (Sigfredo)
Ramb, Ana María
Rosemffet, Gustavo Ariel
Schussheim, Victoria
Shua, Ana María
Vázquez-Vigo, Carmen
Walsh, María Elena

Austria

Neumann De Rey, Eva
Roth, Kornelia

Bolivia

Alfaro, Oscar
Bedregal, Yolanda
Calvimontes Salinas, Velia
Vallejo De Bolívar, Gaby

Brazil

Machado (Martins), Ana María

Chile

Arteche, Miguel
Balcells, Jacqueline Marty de
Balcells Katz, Alberto Ignacio
Beuchat Reichardt, Cecilia E.
Carvajal Valenzuela, Víctor Enrique
Condemarín, Mabel
Gerber (Fetense), Thomas (Rudolf)
Gevert, Lucía
Lezaeta Castillo, Gabriela
Morel, Alicia (Chaigheau)

242   **Appendix**

Paz, Marcela (Esther Hunneus Salas)
Rojas Maffioletti, Carlos
Silva Bafalluy, María Luisa
Uribe (Arce), María de la Luz

Colombia
Castrillón Zapata, Silvia
Da Coll (Röström), Ivar
Díaz, Gloria Cecilia

Costa Rica
Luján, Fernando

Cuba
Artiles Machado, Freddy
Calzadilla Núñez, Julia Lydia
Díaz Mendez, María Nieves
Fernández Valdés, Olga
Gallego Alfonso, Jacoba Emilia
Perera, Hilda
Pérez Valero, Rodolfo
Rodríguez Bonachea, Juan Vicente
Vigil-Escalera Noya, Orlando

Great Britain
Solís, Valerie Anne

Italy
Bosnia, Nella
Turin, Adela

Mexico
Arredondo, Inés
Cárdenas (García), Magolo (Magdalena
    Sofía)
Corona, Pascuala (Teresa Castelló
    Yturbide)
Del Río, Jocelyn
Fierro, Julieta
Fraire, Isabel
Jáuregui Prieto, Diego
Krafft Vera, Federico Gerardo

Méndez y Mercado, Leticia (Irene)
Monay Quirarte, David
Montes de Oca, Marco Antonio
Ortiz Monasterio Garza, Valentina
Ortiz Monasterio Prieto, Fernando
Pellicer López, Carlos
Pettersson, Aline
Ponce de León Patiño, Soledad
Robleda Moguel, (Nidia) Margarita
Santirso (Martínez), Liliana
Sastrías de Porcel, Martha
Schon, Isabel
Serrano Díaz, Francisco
Steiner de Weiss, Susan Emily
Tamayo Rosas, Loreto Ramón
Uzcanga Lavalle, Alicia María
Vanden Broeck (Gueritot), Fabricio

Morocco
Delgado Cavilla, Pedro E(ugenio)

Peru
Amat y León Guevara, Consuelo
Cerna Guardia, Juana Rosa
Colchado Lucio, Oscar
Cuadros López, Luis Alexander
De La Cruz Yataco, Eduardo Francisco
Manyari Rey De Córdova, Olga
Mathews Carmelino, Daniel Alfredo
Morante Campos, José Gonzalo
Panaifo Teixeira, Arnaldo
Pantigoso Pecero, Manuel Trinidad
Rivas Mendo, Felipe
Rodríguez Chávez, Iván
Rojas Morote, Nori (Alicia)
Sologuren Moreno, Javier
Urteaga Cabrera, Luis Antonio
Valle Tejada, Julia Maritza
Vega Herrera, César Gabriel
Velázquez Rojas, Manuel

Romania
Ionescu, Ángela

Spain

Alfonseca, Manuel
Alibés i Riera, María Dolors
Almárcegui, José María
Almena, Fernando Santiago
Alonso, Fernando
Alonso Gómez, Manuel Luis
Anglada d'Abadal, María Àngels
Aranda Vizcaíno, Vicente
Armijo Navarro-Reverter, Consuelo
Arrieta, Yolanda
Ávila Granados, Jesús
Ballaz Zabalza, Jesús
Ballesta, Juan
Balzola, Asun
Banacloche Pérez-Roldán, Julieta
Baquedano Azcona, Lucía
Bellver, Lourdes
Benet Roqué, Amelia
Blanco López, Cruz
Blánquez Pérez, Carmen
Borrell, Joaquím
Bravo-Villasante, Carmen
Cabré Fabré, Jaume
Calleja Guijarro, Tomás
Canela Garayoa, Mercè
Cañizo (Perate), José Antonio del
Capdevila (i Valls), Roser
Carbó, Joaquím
Cela, Camilo José
Climent (Carrau), Paco (Francisco)
Company (i González), Mercè
Del Amo (Y Gili), Montserrat
Del Burgo González de la Aleja, Miguela
Delgado Mercader, Josep-Francesc
Díaz, (González) Joaquín
Díaz Plaja, Aurora
Domínguez (Hernández), Carlos Guillermo
Echevarría (Molina), Pablo
Escardó I Bas, Mercè
Escrivá, Viví
Esteban Noguera, Asunción

Fabregat, Antonio-Manuel
Farías, Juan
Ferrán, Jaime
Ferrer Bermejo, José Francisco
Fuertes, Gloria
Ganges, Montserrat
García Jambrina, Luis M(iguel)
García Martín, Pedro
Gil Grimau, Rodolfo
Gisbert (Ponsole), Joan Manuel
Gómez Cerdá, Alfredo
Gómez Yebra, Antonio A.
Gregori, Josep
Guerra Cáceres, Juan
Hernández Cárdona, Francesc Xavier
Herrera García, Juan Ignacio
Janer Manila, Gabriel
Kurtz, Carmen (Carmen de Rafael Mares)
Laiglesia (González-Labarga), Juan Antonio de
Lalana, Fernando
Lanuza (I Hurtado), Empar de
Lara Peinado, Federico
Larreula (Vidal), Enric
Llamazares, Julio
Llorens Llonch, Rafael
López García, David
López Narváez, Concha (Concepción)
Martín (Farrero), Andreu
Martín Fernández De Velasco, Miguel
Martín Gaite, Carmen
Martín Iglesias, Francisco
Martín Vigil, José Luis
Martínez Gil, Fernando
Martínez (López-Hermosa), Alicia
Martínez-Menchén, Antonio (Antonio Martínez Sánchez)
Masgrau, Fina
Mateos (Martín), Pilar
Matute, Ana María
Mendiola (Insausti), José María
Molina Llorente, Pilar
Monterde (Heredia), Bernardo

Mozo San Juan, Paloma
Muñoz Martín, Juan
Murciano, Carlos
Obiols (Prat), Miguel
Olaizola (Sarría), José Luis
Pacheco, Miguel Ángel
Páez, Enrique
Pérez Avello, Carmen
Pérez-Lucas (Alba), María Dolores
Peris Lozano, Carme
Piérola, Mabel
Pinto Cañón, Ramiro
Pla, Imma
Prieto Martínez, María Yolanda
Puncel (Reparaz), María
Ramon i Bofarull, Elisa
Ramos de la Torre, Luis
Rayó Ferrer, Eusebia
Rayó Ferrer, Miguel
Ribas Puig-Agut, Teresa
Rico, Lolo (Dolores Rico Oliver)
Rius, María
Rodríguez Almodóvar, Antonio
Romero Serrano, Marina
Rubio (Puertas), Rodrigo
San Miguel, Juan M.
Sanz Martín, Ignacio

Serrano, Javier
Sierra i Fabra, Jordi
Solá Llopis, María Lluisa
Soler Garijo, Aranzazu
Solís Ruiz, José Luis
Taranilla de la Varga, Carlos Javier
Teixidor (Viladecás), Emili
Terzi Huguet, Marinella
Torrents (Puig), Jacint
Torres Oliver, Francisco
Valero Burguete, Carlos
Vallverdú, Josep
Vilar I Roca, Anna

United States
Belpré, Pura
Bustamante de Roggero, Cecilia
Lomas Garza, Carmen
Soto, Gary

Uruguay
Alcántara, Luis Ricardo
Bertolino Sirito, Roberto Noel
Marcuse, Aída E(imer de)
Posadas (Mañé), Carmen de

Venezuela
Gutiérrez (Oviedo), Douglas (Miguel)

Index

About the Editor

ISABEL SCHON is Founding Director of the Center for the Study of Books in Spanish for Children and Adolescents at California State University, San Marcos.